THE JEWISH FESTIVAL COOKBOOK

THE JEWISH
FESTIVAL ♈
COOKBOOK

By Fannie Engle and Gertrude Blair

Dover Publications, Inc., *New York*

Published in Canada by General Publishing Company, Ltd., 30 Lesmill Road, Don Mills, Toronto, Ontario.

Published in the United Kingdom by Constable and Company, Ltd., 10 Orange Street, London WC2H 7EG.

This Dover edition, first published in 1988, is a slightly abridged republication of *The Jewish Festival Cookbook According to the Dietary Laws,* first published by David McKay Company, Inc., New York in 1954. The outdated "Eighteen-Year Calendar of Jewish Festivals and Fasts" has been omitted.

Manufactured in the United States of America

Dover Publications, Inc., 31 East 2nd Street, Mineola, N.Y. 11501

Library of Congress Cataloging-in-Publication Data

Engle, Fannie.
    The Jewish festival cookbook.

    This Dover edition is a slightly abridged republication of the work published by David McKay Co., Inc., New York in 1954.

    1. Cookery, Jewish. I. Blair, Gertrude. II. Title.
TX724.E568 1988   641.5′676   87-27440
ISBN 0-486-25573-5 (pbk.)

Preface

How this book began:

It began one day when my mother was making Chanukah *latkes*. I had to stand on tiptoe to see the *latkes* frying in the pan. What magic to see the batter turn to round, golden-brown pancakes! Could I do it? Could I turn them? I begged my mother and she let me. The wonderment of it still lives.

It began at another time when I had to write a story as a child. I wrote about how I loved the Sabbath and our holidays and how sad I was when they were over.

The book began when I went to college and studied home economics. Now is the time, I thought, to set down my mother's recipes and my aunt's and some of our neighbors'. My five sisters all wanted copies so that they could really prepare the dishes as Mother made them.

The book became a reality when Gertrude Blair said, "Fannie, why don't you do a Jewish Festival Cookbook? You know, of course, how much the traditional dishes are in demand around the holidays." And I said, "Why don't we do it together?"

FANNIE ENGLE

What we have tried to do:

In this book we have assembled traditional dishes for the important festival seasons of the year. We have included also a brief word on the history and significance of each festival so that the colorful customs and traditions that have grown up over the years can be seen as a meaningful part of each holiday.

Although the book includes recipes from many parts of

the world, showing the international character of Jewish dishes, it is not written as a history of Jewish cooking. It is designed to place emphasis on the particular dishes that have a background in the rich customs, legends, and symbols connected with Jewish life. Throughout the book these dishes are placed in their holiday pattern. It is truly a guide in preparing and serving the symbolic and traditional special foods and meals eaten during festival times.

We have intentionally taken the Orthodox Jewish observance as our standard, but it is hoped that this book will also be used by Reform and Conservative groups, by non-Jews, by schools, by cooks everywhere.

We are deeply grateful to the many who have helped us in writing this book. We would like to express our particular gratitude to Rabbi Seymour Siegel for his scholarly criticism of the completed manuscript; to Rabbi Philip Goodman, Executive Secretary, Jewish Book Council of America, Samuel S. Solender, Executive Director of the Y.M. and Y.W.H.A. of Washington Heights and Inwood, New York City, and Sanford Solender, Director Jewish Center Division, National Jewish Welfare Board, who have given so generously in counsel to the ensuing pages.

FANNIE ENGLE AND GERTRUDE BLAIR

Contents

THE JEWISH FESTIVAL COOKBOOK

ALL THROUGH
THE YEAR

The Sabbath

Begins at sundown each Friday and lasts until sundown on Saturday.

It is the Sabbath eve. There is a holiday air about the house, and every inch of it is scrubbed, clean and orderly. The cares of the work-a-day world have been folded neatly away out of sight. This is the climax of all the preparation that has been going on for two days, beginning with marketing on Thursday morning. Everyone has had some part in this preparation, even in homes where there is household assistance, for there is a *mitzvah* (a deed of religious merit) in work for the Sabbath day. It is written in the Talmud that, to do honor to the Sabbath, sages of ancient times would reserve for themselves certain homely tasks, such as chopping wood and salting the fish.

Even the children are expected to assist with Sabbath preparations. They can help with the cleaning of the house, the polishing of table silver and candlesticks, the setting of the table.

The mother has spread the dinner cloth, the finest the family affords. Two loaves of *challah* (Sabbath twists) have been placed at the head of the table. These are covered with a special white embroidered cloth. This practice derives from the ancient custom whereby twelve freshly baked *challah* (loaves of shewbread), representing the twelve tribes of Israel, were placed on the altar of the Temple in Jerusalem in honor of the Sabbath. The two loaves are a reminder, too, of the double portion of manna gathered for the Sabbath by the Israelites in the wilderness. The special cover over the loaves is symbolic of "the manna which lay as if covered with dew."

The beautiful Sabbath candlesticks, each with a fresh white candle, have been placed in the center of the table. There are always at least two candles, although in some homes there may be one for each member of the family. A goblet to be filled with wine for *Kiddush* is placed near the *challah*. There is peace and quiet in the home.

As the sun goes down, the mother lights each candle, while the children watch silently. She stands quietly for a moment with hands spread toward the flames, then places them for a moment over her eyes. Silently she recites a benediction, then she looks at the candles and, in a whisper, adds a meditative prayer.

The quiet ceremony of lighting the candles is a beautiful and impressive one. For countless centuries Jewish mothers, in Jewish homes all over the world, have reverently and faithfully observed this same ceremony just before sundown each Friday evening.

"*Gut Shabbas! Gut Shabbas!*"—"Good Sabbath! Good Sabbath!" The greeting breaks the quiet of the house as mother and children greet each other after the lighting of the candles.

"*Gut Shabbas! Gut Shabbas!*" resounds through the house as the men of the family return from the synagogue.

Every man returning from synagogue is so spiritually imbued with the Sabbath that it is said two angels accompany him home. If the mother and children are prepared for the Sabbath and the house in readiness, then the good angel triumphs over the bad angel and the greeting of the good angel is heard. "May it be the same next Sabbath." Each child, son and daughter, then receives a blessing from his father. The love and dignity that surrounds the women in a Jewish household is nowhere more clearly in evidence than at this time every week, when the father chants from the Book of Proverbs this incomparable tribute:

"A woman of valour who can find?
For her price is far above rubies.
The heart of her husband doth safely trust in her;
And he hath no lack of gain."

When all are assembled about the dinner table, the father recites the *Kiddush* (the prayer of sanctification of the Sabbath) over a cup of wine. This, like the kindling of the lights, symbolizes joy and cheer. After he has lifted the cup of wine and chanted the blessing, he passes the cup around the table for all to sip. Or, more often, a little "blessing" of wine is poured for every person at the table. Then each one washes his hands.

The covered *challah* must now be blessed. The father breaks or cuts one loaf and gives to each a piece for the *hamotzi* (blessing over bread) which is then spoken by each in turn.

Now follows the first of the Sabbath meals, the most delicious of the week, and all must partake. This is in obedience to the ancient precept that after *Kiddush* a meal must be eaten to make the blessing complete.

Folk tales recall many a hurried journey homeward on a Friday afternoon. Visions of the Sabbath table spurred the homecomer to greater and greater haste and he would exclaim to himself, "Oh, beautiful *goldene yoich!*" (golden chicken soup). "Oh, carrot *tzimmes!*" (carrots cooked in golden honey). "And gefillte fish . . . what could be more perfect! *A zah geschmak!* Oh, so delicious!"

The Jewish housewife takes deep and abiding pleasure in making the Sabbath table completely different from that of other days. Her table is set with every care, with her finest china, silver, and linen. She reserves for the Sabbath the choicest of meat, fish, dessert, and wine, even though it may be necessary to scrimp for the rest of the week.

The meal itself is a gay one. The father may have brought home a guest from synagogue, who may be drawn out to talk about the Law and the prophets. Or he may tell humorous anecdotes that lovingly illustrate some facet of Jewish life. Children are gently encouraged to ask questions and inquire into the reason for various customs. *Zemiroth* (religious table songs) are sung between courses. Many of these are famous; some modern, and some ancient. This is a leisurely meal that fills the hearts of all with love and grace.

All the festive meals of the Sabbath are distinctive in that they follow long-established patterns.

Friday Night Dinner
(FIRST SABBATH MEAL)

Wine   Challah

Gefillte Fish   Beet Horse-radish   Garlic Dill Pickles

Goldene Yoich with Lukshen

Boiled or Roast Chicken   Helzel   Carrots and Peas

Prune and Potato Tzimmes

Lettuce and Tomato Salad

Strudel   Tea with Lemon

Nahit   Bob   Arbas

After dinner the evening is spent quietly. Children read or go for a walk or play quiet games. Sometimes visitors drop in and the table is again spread with Sabbath delicacies. These are served with steaming glasses of hot tea with *varenyah* (preserves) and lemon.

The morning of the Sabbath is quiet and many go early to the synagogue. On returning from the synagogue, the family assembles for the second Sabbath meal. It is prescribed that three meals shall be eaten on this day, the third just before sunset, which marks the end of the Sabbath day.

The second meal differs very greatly from the first. Food has been sealed in the oven since long before sunset on Friday. Now all look forward expectantly to the first beautiful fragrance of the *cholent*, of the *tzimmes* and often, too, of the *kugel* that may have been crowding the oven. These are the inspired dishes that generations of Jewish housewives have devised and perfected in obedience to the precept that no work, and therefore no cooking, shall be done on the Sabbath. There is such flavor, such fragrance, to these dishes that they have become world famous.

Noonday Sabbath Dinner
(SECOND SABBATH MEAL)

Wine   Challah
Cold Gefillte Fish   Beet Horse-radish   Pickles
Hot Petcha with Garlic Challah
Roast Brisket   Cholent   Stuffed Kishka
Mehren Tzimmes with Knaidel
Compote   Sponge cake   Tea with Lemon

The atmosphere of the table for the second meal of the Sabbath is as blithe and gay as that for the first. And when the meal is over, a soft glow of joy and contentment pervades the Sabbath afternoon. The father takes a little nap before going to the synagogue—and this is a custom that might be part of the ritual of the Sabbath, so generally has it always been observed. Then he may go to join a study group or to hear a lecture given by a rabbi. Families, dressed in their best, visit friends and relatives. Children visit their grandparents and are indulged with *kichlach* (cookies) and nuts.

And so the day is spent in study, prayer, and social life. It is a day of recreation and refreshment.

There is no work to occupy any one. This is the very cornerstone of the Sabbath. "And on the seventh day God finished His work which He had made; and He rested on the seventh day." It is not merely to prepare a delectable dinner, or to garnish the house for the Sabbath, that the mother has toiled for two busy days. All this has been done in observance of the precept: "Remember the Sabbath day, to keep it holy."

The Sabbath has its beginning in ancient times, when it was singled out as the most important of all festivals. The Sabbath, alone of all the festivals, was included in the Ten Commandments. There is a legend which records that God said to Moses: "I have a precious gift in my treasure house, and its name is Sabbath. I wish to present it to Israel. Go make it known to them."

Over the years delightful customs grew up in the celebration of the Sabbath. One of the most colorful began when the Amoraim, sages of the third century, took very literally the fanciful personification of their beloved day. These scholars, dressed in their Sabbath best, would ride in joyous procession to the edge of the town to greet the approach of Queen Sabbath, the Bride of Israel, with exhortations of "Come Bride! Come Bride!" The custom was then adopted in other places. In greeting Queen Sabbath melodic lines were chanted, many written by the poets of the times. One of these, written in the sixteenth century, "Come My Friend to Meet the Bride," became famous and was accepted by important leaders as part of the Sabbath ceremony.

The ceremony of greeting Queen Sabbath gradually spread to all Jewish communities. In the course of the centuries, in place of the procession to the gates of the town, a ceremony came to be held within the synagogue, where cantor and congregation turned to the door as if to greet the expected bride.

Certain observances of the Sabbath have been altered a little to meet some specific conditions of living. Where necessary, early evening meetings have been changed to more convenient hours.

Oneg Shabbath (meaning, delight in the Sabbath) was newly interpreted by Chayyim Nahman Bialik, the great Hebrew poet of modern Palestine. Some fifteen or twenty years ago he inaugurated wonderful meetings on Sabbath afternoons and these, together with his poetry, will forever keep his memory green. At these meetings, about two hours before sundown, youths and older folk gather together in lively study and discussion groups. They delve deep into Jewish history; they talk and sing and learn from the Torah. Then as the sun sets low in the heavens, they bid farewell to Queen Sabbath, in the old tradition, with psalms and melodies both old and new.

Oneg Shabbath spread from Palestine to many busy places in Europe and America. *Shalosh Seudot* and the *Havdalah,* ceremonies bidding farewell to the Sabbath, are often included in *Oneg Shabbath* gatherings.

Shalosh Seudot, the third Sabbath meal, has its own delightful ceremonies filled with meaning. Just as the sun is beginning to set, the family gathers about the table. Unlike the other two Sabbath meals, this one is tinged with sadness. The beloved Sabbath is about to depart. This meal is a simple one. Usually the housewife brings out some of her dishes that are delicious when served cold. These may be jellied or pickled fish, cold fried fish, *petcha,* or many others. When winter days are very short, *Shalosh Seudot* may consist of the dessert of the second Sabbath meal, served with hot tea.

Shalosh Seudot Meal
(AFTERNOON SABBATH MEAL)

Fried Fish, Cold	Challah	
Cucumbers Tomatoes	Celery	Pickles
Apple Kuchen	Coffee	

As sunset nears, the children of the family watch eagerly to report the "first three stars" in the heavens. These mark the close of the Sabbath day. In the twilight, the mother recites the prayer of farewell to the Sabbath: "O God of Abraham, Isaac and Jacob, guard Thy people Israel for Thy praise." Then she adds a prayer for "A good week, a full week upon us." If the men have been at the synagogue, their return is heralded with more greetings of "A good week, a full week."

The ceremony of the *Havdalah* (meaning separation) is the signal that the joy of the Sabbath is over, the weekday responsibilities begun. For this ceremony, two candles, often candles especially braided together for the purpose, are lighted. One of the children is allowed to hold the candles high, while another holds the *bessamim* (the spice box). A special part of this ceremony is the filling of the wine cup to overflowing to signify a "full week." Then a benediction is said over the spice box to signify the fragrance of life that has been tasted with the Sabbath. In the benediction thanks is given to God for the creation of the world and the first day of light; for distinction, also, "between things sacred and profane, between light and darkness . . ."

Following the departure of the Sabbath, a refreshing hot meal is served, for now cooking may be done. This repast is known as *M'lavah Malkah,* the farewell feast to Queen Sabbath. This after-the-Sabbath supper has become very popular in recent years as part of the social get-togethers in temple rooms—as part of the after-the-*Oneg Shabbath* meetings, too.

M'lavah Malkah Meal
(SATURDAY NIGHT MEAL)

Herring and Potatoes
Lox and Scrambled Eggs   Pickled Fish
Bagel   Rolls
Sliced Cucumbers with Sour Cream
Cheese Cake   Coffee   Tea

Beautiful *challah* are most important for every Sabbath table. They are made of finest wheat flour. It is true that Sabbath Twists can be purchased in most modern communities today, but not many years have elapsed since the baking of *challah* was a labor of love to which all Jewish housewives looked forward each week. There was joy in the setting of the dough on Thursday night for Friday morning baking. There was pleasure in getting up at dawn on Friday to knead the risen dough. Today many are again baking their own *challah* and delighting in the joy of working this risen dough.

Whenever the housewife bakes bread, she casts a bit of dough into the fire while whispering a prayer for her home and for peace for the world. This is an old tradition that goes back to the time when loaves were carried as tribute to the priests in the Temple in Jerusalem. Intimate devotions such as this, performed by the housewife, are significant because they give her a feeling of importance and stature in her home and in the community.

A wonderful story is told of the devout wife of a saintly Hebrew scholar who was so poor that she could not afford the good wheat and other ingredients needed for making *challah*. To hide her poverty from the neighbors, she continued to heat her oven every Friday morning until the smoke fairly rolled from the chimney. One of her neighbors, knowing of her poverty, was filled with curiosity and came to see what was going on. The poor housewife fled to another room as the neighbor came into the kitchen. Then a miracle happened! When the visitor peeked into the oven, it was filled with *challah* on the very point of burning. "Come quickly!" she called. "Your *challah* is burning!" Some protecting angel must surely have whispered to the wife, for how else could she have known to reply, "I'm coming, I'm coming. I just went out to get a pan to set the loaves on!"

Challah
(SABBATH TWIST)

2 envelopes dry yeast (or 2 cakes compressed yeast)	3 tablespoons vegetable oil
½ cup lukewarm water	1 tablespoon salt
2 cups hot water	1 tablespoon sugar
pinch of saffron (brew in a little hot water and strain)	2 eggs, beaten
	8 cups all-purpose flour
	poppy seeds

Note: The amount of yeast given here is for quick rising, generally desired in modern kitchens; if bread dough is set to rise overnight, use just half the amount of yeast. All other ingredients remain the same.

Soften the yeast in the lukewarm water. To the boiling hot water, add the saffron (brew), oil, salt, and sugar. Stir until the sugar is dissolved. Cool and when lukewarm, not before, add the softened yeast. Reserve about 2 tablespoons of the egg for brushing loaves later, and add the remainder to the liquid. Turn into a large mixing bowl; add about three cups of flour. Stir and beat to a smooth, thick batter. Set aside for 10 minutes; add flour to make dough that can be handled. Turn out on a floured board and knead until smooth and elastic. Shape into a ball and grease the whole surface well. Place in well-greased mixing bowl; cover with a clean cloth. Let rise in a warm, never hot, place to double in bulk—2 to 3 hours. Knead again until dough is fine-grained. Divide dough to make two loaves.

Cut each portion into three pieces, with a small extra piece that can be braided for the top of the loaf. Roll each of the three pieces into long strips; fasten ends together; braid into a twisted loaf. Divide and braid the small portion for a braid on top of loaf. Prepare the second loaf in the same manner. Place loaves on a greased baking sheet. Cover; let rise to double in bulk in a warm, not hot, place. Add a spoonful of cold water to the egg; then brush the surface of both loaves; sprinkle with poppy seed. Bake in a hot oven (400° F.) for about 15 minutes. Then reduce temperature to moderate (350° F.) and bake for 45 minutes. Makes 2 *challah.*

There is always a place in the Jewish household for small attentions that recreate for the children the beauty and reality of their heritage. Such are the miniature *challah* set before the young son who is the eldest male child. He, like his father, may say *Kiddush* over his bread.

Miniature Challah
(SMALL SABBATH LOAVES)

Before shaping the *challah* for the Sabbath baking, pinch off a small portion sufficient for two small coffee rolls. Braid and shape these in the same way as the family-sized loaves are shaped. Let rise to double in bulk, brush with egg and sprinkle with poppy seed as for large loaves. Bake on a greased cooky sheet in a moderately hot oven (375° F.) for 20 to 30 minutes, depending upon size.

Buelkalach are little hot rolls, baked from *challah* dough. How the children love them and look forward to them on Friday morning is seen in the story of the child who was stolen from his home by a band of robbers and hidden in a forest. He found his captivity a thrilling adventure until the cold gray dawn of Friday morning. Then, when no *buelkalach* were forthcoming, he gave vent to such piercing screams of disappointment that he was hastily returned to his parents before his whereabouts could be traced.

Buelkalach
(LITTLE ROUND ROLLS)

Shape a small portion of the *challah* dough into small round balls. Let rise to double in bulk—as with bread. Bake on a greased baking sheet in a moderate oven (375° F.) for about 20 minutes.

Over and over again it is repeated, the best is none too good for the Sabbath. In the households of many German Jews the Sabbath *challah*, which they called *barches*, was made with special richness. The Butter Barches are indeed delicious.

Butter Barches
(GERMAN CHALLAH)

Use ⅓ of the basic *challah* dough (recipe page 12). Make a deep well in the center and add: 3 tablespoons softened butter, 1 egg, ¼ cup sugar, spices as desired, raisins and nuts. Knead these in, beginning with a light folding and turning of the dough, pressing deeper as the ingredients are better distributed. When well blended, shape into a loaf; or press into a well-greased tube pan; or form into small rolls. Toppings of spices, sugar, fruits, or cheese may be added if desired. Let rise again to double in bulk in a warm, not hot, place. Bake in a quick oven (375° F.) for 20 to 35 minutes, depending upon size of cake. These will, of course, not be served at a meat meal.

Delicious Kuchen
(BASIC DOUGH FOR MANY COFFEE CAKES)

1 envelope dry yeast (or 1 package compressed yeast)	1 teaspoon salt
¼ cup lukewarm milk	¾ cup sugar
1 tablespoon sugar	1 cup butter (or vegetable fat)
1 cup scalded milk	2 eggs
	5½ cups flour

Stir the yeast into the lukewarm milk, making certain that the milk is tepid. Stir the 1 tablespoon of sugar into the yeast and set aside. In a deep mixing bowl combine the scalded milk, salt,

¾ cup of sugar and the butter. Stir until the butter is dissolved. When this mixture is lukewarm, add the yeast and then the eggs. Beat all together well. Add about half of the flour and beat to a smooth batter. Add the remaining flour to make a tender dough. Turn out on a floured board and knead lightly for about 2 minutes. Shape into a ball and place in a greased bowl. Roll the ball around so that all surfaces are covered with the fat. This will keep the dough from drying. Cover and let rise in a warm, not hot, place until double in bulk. Use for Filled Cinnamon Kuchen, Fruit- and Nut-filled Ring, Apple Kuchen, and other varieties of coffee cakes.

Filled Cinnamon Kuchen
(FILLED CINNAMON COFFEE CAKE)

⅓ to ½ of dough for Delicious Kuchen (see preceding recipe)
butter, melted

sugar, brown or white
cinnamon
raisins
nuts

Divide the dough into three parts. Spread one part in a well-greased tube pan about 9" x 3½". Brush with melted butter and sprinkle with sugar, cinnamon, raisins, and nuts, if desired. Repeat with the second and third layers. Omit raisins on the top layer because they burn too quickly when exposed to the heat. Cover and let rise in a warm, not hot, place to double in bulk. Bake in a moderate oven (350° F. to 375° F.) for 35 minutes—until well baked through and richly brown on top.

Fruit- and Nut-filled Ring

½ of dough for Delicious Kuchen (recipe page 14)
butter, melted
sugar, brown or white
cinnamon

raisins, candied cherries, slivers of dried apricots, chopped nuts (use any or all, as desired)

Roll out the dough on a floured board to about ⅓ inch in thickness. Spread with the melted butter; sprinkle with the sugar, cinnamon and fruit and nuts. Roll like a jelly roll and place in a greased 10-inch pie pan or other baking dish. Join

the ends to form a ring. With scissors, make cuts in the roll
about 1½ inches deep, but not through the roll. Turn out each
cut point to show the filling. Cover and set to rise in a warm,
not hot, place to double in bulk. Brush with melted butter,
sprinkle with chopped nuts and bake in a moderately hot oven
(350° F.) for 25 to 30 minutes—until a nice golden brown and
well baked through.

Apple Kuchen

⅓ of dough for Delicious   sugar, brown or white
    Kuchen (recipe page 14)   cinnamon
3 or 4 tart apples   butter

Spread the dough in a well-greased 9-inch pie plate or square
pan. Pare, quarter, core, and slice the apples. Press the slices of
apples into the dough so that they stand in neat rows and close
together. The dough should be well covered with apples. Sprinkle
with the sugar mixed with cinnamon, and dot with butter.
Cover and set to rise in a warm, not hot, place until the dough
spreads and rises up through the apples to about double in bulk.
Bake in a moderate oven (350° F.) for 20 to 25 minutes—until
the apples are tender and the *kuchen* is a golden brown.

The good Jewish housewife prides herself on the wonderful variety of relishes she provides for the Sabbath. There
may be sauerkraut, brined with little apples and cranberries.
Dill pickles, rich with garlic, are delicious at so many different stages of pickling. New pickles are a special delight
of the summer time, and the beauty of red-hot peppers,
scarlet and green, is something to excite the appetite.

Such relishes as Vinegar Dressed Cucumbers and Beet
Horse-radish are not staples of the relish shelf. These must be
freshly mixed for each family dinner. "Proper horse-radish is
so fresh," declared one who prides herself on her table, "that
it stings the nose and starts the tears." Woe to anyone at her
table who leaves the cover off the horse-radish jar even for
a split second after using!

Beet Horse-radish

1 cup freshly grated horse-radish	½ teaspoon salt
	pinch of sugar
1 medium-sized raw beet, finely grated	vinegar

Mix the horse-radish with the grated beet, salt, and sugar. Stir in the vinegar to make proper consistency. Bottle tightly. Makes ½ pint of relish.

Garlic Dill Pickles

4 dz. medium-sized cucumbers (about 3½ inches long)	mixed pickling spices, if desired
coarse salt	dill
cloves of garlic	

Wash the cucumbers well. Pack tightly in upright position in quart jars, adding a teaspoon salt, 4 cloves of garlic, and, if desired, ¼ teaspoon mixed pickling spices, to each jar. Pack a good-sized bunch of dill, with seed heads, in each jar. Fill jar with cold water, letting it run off slightly to carry off air bubbles. Seal tightly and let stand for about 2 weeks.

Pickled Green Tomatoes

4 dozen small green tomatoes	1 tablespoon pickling spices
1 cup salt	piece ginger root
4 cups water	1 cup vinegar
dill	6 qts. water
cloves of garlic	2 cups salt

Wash the tomatoes; let them stand overnight in a brine made with 1 cup salt and 4 cups water. Drain. Arrange in a deep earthen bowl or crock, in layers, with sprigs of dill and a clove (or 2) of garlic over each. Tie pickling spices with ginger root in cheesecloth, loosely. Add to vinegar, water, and salt; bring slowly to boiling. Pour over tomatoes, taking care that all are covered. Put weighted cover, such as a plate, directly over tomatoes to keep them under the vinegar sauce. Cover with several layers of cheesecloth. Let stand for 2 weeks; then pack in hot sterile jars.

Vinegar Dressed Cucumbers

fresh cucumbers   salt and pepper
sliced onion, sweet or green   sugar
   scallions   vinegar

Pare and slice the cucumbers quite thinly. Add the sliced
onion, salt, pepper, and a dash of sugar. Cover with vinegar.
Chill for about 10 minutes and serve.

Men have waxed poetic over far less than a wonderful
Goldene Yoich, the "golden" chicken soup of the Sabbath
table. Preparation of this soup, beginning with the careful
selection of the plump, perfect fowl, to the final serving, is
no less a rite than the making of the Sabbath *challah*.

Goldene Yoich
(GOLDEN CHICKEN BROTH)

4 to 5-lb. soup chicken   ½ cup celery, diced
boiling water to cover   parsley root or parsnip
1 tablespoon salt   sprig of dill, if desired
1 cup carrots, diced   salt and pepper
1 onion

Wash and clean the chicken. Use gizzard, heart, and feet. (To
clean feet, scald in boiling water for a minute or two; remove
the skin and cut off the nails.) Place chicken, halved or quartered, into the soup pot with gizzard, heart, and feet. Add boiling water to cover, and the salt. Bring to boiling and add the
vegetables and dill, if desired. Cover and cook gently until
chicken is tender—about 2 or 3 hours. Do not remove scum, a valu-
able protein food. To serve, remove the chicken, and some of the
fat if desired. Season with salt and white pepper, and serve with
or without the vegetables and with noodles or other soup
garnishes. Makes 6 to 8 cups.

Note: The soup chicken can be made into a variety of ap-
petizing dishes; broiled, served in a rich sauce, or baked in a
casserole (*see* page 29).

The making of homemade noodles to be served in the Goldene Yoich is still for many an important part of preparation for the Sabbath. Homemade noodle dough is rolled out in large sheets, paper thin, and then draped carefully over covered chair backs. Here they are left to dry before being rolled out and cut. The picture of these drying sheets of dough, spread all over the dining room, remains as an unforgettable memory in the minds of all who have ever helped their mothers make Homemade Noodles.

Homemade Noodles

4 cups all-purpose flour   4 eggs
1 teaspoon salt

Mix the flour and salt. Make a well in the flour and drop in the eggs. Stir gently with a fork, gradually working eggs into the flour to make a stiff dough, but one that can be handled. Knead on a lightly floured board—as nearly without flour as possible—until soft and elastic. This takes 5 minutes or longer. Divide dough into portions easy to handle, and roll out to paper thinness, again with as little flour as possible. Hang these sheets to dry slightly—only until not sticky. If it is at the proper stage of dryness, the dough will neither stick nor crack. Then carefully roll up, one sheet at a time, into tight, precise little rolls. It can then be cut into neat, fine noodles, or into graded sizes of broader ones. (It was the privileged daughter of the family who was permitted to "shake out" each little tightly wound noodle scroll and see that uniform-sized noodles were put together for storage.) Noodles that are not to be used immediately must be well dried before storage. Makes about 3 quart storage jars of noodles.

To prepare for serving drop 1 cup noodles into about 2 quarts of boiling soup or boiling salted water, and cook until tender—7 to 10 minutes. Noodles cooked in boiling water should be drained before serving.

Einlauf, little egg drops, are also a fine garnish for the golden chicken soup and require less time for preparation than noodles.

Einlauf
(EGG DROPS FOR SOUP)

1 egg, slightly beaten   3 tablespoons flour
few grains salt   3 to 4 tablespoons water

Combine the ingredients in a smooth batter. Take a small bit of batter on tip of spoon; drop into soup. Continue until all batter is used. Cover pot tightly. Boil gently for 10 minutes, by the clock, before removing the lid. Sufficient for 2 quarts of soup.

Gribenes are the crisp little curls that are left when fat and skin of goose, duck, or chicken are rendered to remove the precious oils.

Rendering of Schmaltz for Gribenes
(RENDERING FAT TO MAKE CRACKLINGS)

2 cups fat and skin of duck,   1 or 2 onions
   chicken, or goose

Cut the fat and skin into small pieces. Melt the fat over low heat in a heavy frying pan, baking pan, or saucepan on top of the stove or in the oven. Drain off fat as it accumulates. Before fat is completely rendered, add the onions, finely cut, and cook slowly until golden brown. Drain through a fine strainer, pressing gently to remove all fat. Store fat for later use. Serve *gribenes* as desired. Makes about 1 cup clear fat.

There is never a time when fingers are not reaching for the *gribenes*. They are served before the soup, with the soup, before or after dinner. Everyone loves to nibble on them. But far more important to the housewife is the *schmaltz* taken from the *gribenes*. This precious rendered fat is carefully stored for later holiday cooking.

Chopped Herring originated with the Russian Polish Jews, who dearly love it and often serve it as a main dish. It has become the traditional appetizer for the Sabbath noon meal.

Chopped Herring

2 schmaltz herring
3 hard-cooked eggs
1 thick slice bread
vinegar

1 tart apple
dash of pepper
sugar to taste

Soak the herring in cold water over night. Drain; skin and bone. Chop in a wooden chopping bowl. Add 2 of the hard-cooked eggs. Moisten the bread with vinegar; then squeeze dry and add to the herring. Add tart apple, pared, cored, and cut fine. Chop until all are well blended. Season to taste as needed with vinegar squeezed from the soaked bread, pepper, and a dash of sugar. Mound on a platter and sprinkle with the remaining chopped white of egg. Crest the mound with the yolk pressed through a sieve. Serves 6.

For Wine Chopped Herring, add ½ cup prepared "wine herring" to the above recipe and soften the bread in the wine sauce instead of in the vinegar. To serve, garnish with hard-cooked egg as above.

Chopped Liver

½ lb. beef liver or 6 chicken
    livers
1 medium-sized onion
1 teaspoon salt

⅛ teaspoon pepper
2 tablespoons chicken fat
    (about)
2 hard-cooked eggs

Prepare the liver following the directions for kashering liver given on page 183. Chop liver with the onion or put through a meat grinder. Add the salt, pepper, and chicken fat and continue chopping until the mixture is well blended and smooth. Add more chicken fat or water, if preferred, to make it the consistency desired. Mound on a platter and sprinkle with the finely chopped whites of egg. Press the yolks through a sieve and make a crest on the very top or sprinkle over the mound. Some prefer to chop part of the hard-cooked eggs into the mixture and to garnish with the remaining egg.

Variation: ¼ cup of *gribenes* may be added to the liver, making this a real Sabbath treat.

Eier and Schmaltz
(EGGS WITH POULTRY FAT)

4 hard-cooked eggs, chopped   salt and pepper
2 onions, minced   black olives
2 to 3 tablespoons poultry fat

This is not a paste. It is a delicate blend of all the ingredients except black olives. These are used as garnish after all the other ingredients have been mixed together (mix lightly to protect the texture), then piled high on a serving plate. Serves 4 to 6.

Schwartze Retach mit Schmaltz
(BLACK RADISHES WITH POULTRY FAT)

black radishes   coarse salt
chicken fat

Scrub the radishes; pare or not, as desired. Cut into ⅛-inch-thick slices. Spread each slice with the chicken fat; sprinkle with coarse salt. Serve crisply cold.

Along with the appetizers, there should always be served the little wafers called *kichlach*. Their texture is delicate and tender. They are traditionally served with chopped herring for the midday Sabbath dinner, after the reciting of the *Kiddush*.

Kichlach
(EGG WAFERS)

3 eggs   ½ teaspoon salt
2 teaspoons sugar   ½ teaspoon baking powder
¼ cup vegetable oil   sugar and cinnamon, if desired
1½ cups flour

Beat the eggs until they are puffing with air, then beat in the sugar. Follow with the oil, adding slowly and beating well. Mix and sift together the flour, salt, and baking powder; stir into the egg mixture to make a tender dough. Roll to ⅛-inch thickness on a lightly floured board. Cut into squares or diamonds. Brush with oil; sprinkle lightly with sugar and cinnamon, if desired;

prick with a fork. Bake on a well-greased cooky sheet in a moderately hot oven (375° F.) for 25 to 30 minutes—until light brown. Makes about 3 dozen.

Fish plays a very important part in the Sabbath meals. It is recorded in a sixteenth-century code drawn up by Jewish leaders that "It is desirable to eat fish at every Sabbath meal." In addition to this, fish is reserved for the Sabbath because it is such a favorite food. There is a legend, too, that the fish is a symbol of fertility.

The preparation of Gefillte Fish, the prize fish dish, requires great care and long hours in the kitchen. Nevertheless, many a housewife approaches this task with love and tenderness, so that the Sabbath table may be enhanced by the serving of this choice dish. The true Gefillte Fish is made with a variety of fresh water fish. This is due to the fact that it was first made by, and earned its reputation among, inland people for whom fresh water fish was most readily obtainable.

In olden days the housewife selected her fish alive from a tank at the market and cleaned, scaled, sliced, and filleted the fish, reserving the skin for stuffing. With small fish like perch and suckers, a small pocket of flesh was removed. Today much of this preparation is done at the market.

Gefillte Fish
(TRADITIONAL STUFFED FISH)

3 lbs. fish (white fish, pickerel, carp, yellow pike, or any other fresh water fish)
2 eggs
½ cup cold water

3 tablespoons matza meal
salt and pepper
2 medium-sized onions
3 carrots

Choose two or three varieties of fish in equal quantities to make up the required 3 lbs. Have the dealer filet the fish, but carry home the head, bones, and skin. Salt lightly and chill for several hours. Rinse. Reserve skin for stuffing fish the traditional way.

Grind the filet with finest knife of grinder or have this done at market if such service is offered. Turn into a chopping bowl. Chop with a kind of chop-and-fold-over motion, adding the eggs, one at a time, as you chop; then add water; next matza meal, about 2 teaspoons salt, and ⅛ teaspoon pepper. All ingredients will then be finely chopped and blended together lightly and smoothly. Set aside to chill for 5 to 10 minutes, then shape into balls of desired size.

To make broth for cooking the prepared fish, place the fish head and the bones (well-washed after having been salted and chilled) into the bottom of a large kettle. Slice the onions and carrots, and arrange in a thick layer over the bones. Season with salt and pepper; and cinnamon, if desired. Cover with cold water; bring to boiling and cook for about 5 minutes. Add prepared fish to boiling broth, placing neatly over the vegetables. Dot with slices of carrot. Cover. Bring again to boiling; then turn heat low and simmer gently for 1 hour. If necessary, add water from time to time to prevent pot from cooking dry. Adjust seasoning to taste with salt and pepper. Cool slightly before removing fish to platter. Serve hot or cold, garnished with the slices of carrot and the broth. If cold, the broth will be jellied. Serve with Beet Horse-radish and dill pickles. Serves 6 to 8.

A wonderful Talmudic legend has in the course of years come to be applied to Gefillte Fish. It seems there was once an Emperor who delighted in joining the family of a famous rabbi for the Sabbath dinner. One dish was his special favorite, and he finally asked that his chief cook be given the directions for making it. Somehow the cook's dish was not a success. In wrath the Emperor accused the rabbi's cook of giving wrong directions. But the rabbi explained, "Your Majesty, it is not your cook's error, nor is it the recipe that is at fault. You see, Jews have a singular spice which gives the dish the inimitable flavor you so much enjoy. The essence of this spice has come down through the ages; it is known as the Sabbath."

Today, in many places salt water fish are far easier to obtain than fresh water varieties. Many have therefore experimented with different kinds of fish in preparing Gefillte Fish, and they have done so quite successfully. It is our experience that haddock and quite a number of salt water fish are most satisfactory as ingredients. We have found too that a little oil and sugar added to any filet seems to increase the richness of the flavor. Haddock Fish Balls were inspired by the traditional Gefillte Fish.

Haddock Fish Balls

3 lbs. haddock, cod, or halibut	4 tablespoons matza meal
3 medium-sized carrots	1½ teaspoons salt
3 medium-sized onions	1 teaspoon sugar
stalk celery	1 tablespoon vegetable oil
2 eggs	¾ cup water

Salt the fish with coarse salt; let it stand in the refrigerator several hours. Rinse. Place the head, skin, and bones in a large kettle for broth, adding salt, 1 carrot, 1 onion, and the stalk celery. Cover with water; simmer for 30 minutes, then strain if desired. Grind fish, remaining onions and carrots very fine. Put this in a chopping bowl; add remaining ingredients, except broth and chop until puffy and smooth. Shape into balls. Cook in fish broth, as for Gefillte Fish. Serves 6 to 8.

Crisp coated fish, fried in oil, is a contribution of the Jews of Portugal to the Jewish table. In Portugal there was such a wealth of wonderful fish that they learned to prepare it to perfection. It was probably the German Jews, however, who were responsible for introducing it into other Jewish communities. This fish is often served cold with dill pickles, olives, and mayonnaise for the late Sabbath afternoon meal. Mayonnaise, considered distinctly modern by so many people, has its roots in a very similar sauce first prepared hundreds of years ago in the Middle East.

To fry fish properly, special attention should be paid to

"crumbing," to the temperature of the oil for frying, and to draining off excess oil after frying.

Fish Fried in Oil

3 to 4 lbs. haddock or other preferred fish	2 or 3 eggs
	1 tablespoon water
salt and pepper	vegetable oil
flour or matza meal	quartered onions

Sprinkle the fish with coarse salt and let it stand, covered, in the refrigerator overnight or for several hours. Rinse, then wipe very dry. Salt and pepper the fish. Spread the matza meal on a sheet of waxed paper. Thin the eggs with a tablespoon of water and beat slightly to mix. Use a large, heavy frying pan and put in the oil to generous ¼-inch depth; heat gently; add the onions and cook to golden brown in the fat. Keep heat medium all through the cooking, once the fat is hot. To fry, coat each piece of fish with the matza meal, then dip into beaten eggs and quickly place in the hot fat. Do not crowd the frying pan. Brown first on one side, then turn and brown on the other, allowing about 10 minutes in all. The first side will require about 6 minutes. Have absorbent paper towels or heavy brown wrapping paper ready to receive the hot fish; this will remove excess fat. This dish is served hot or cold. When served cold with a mayonnaise, it is a special Sabbath treat. Serves 6 to 8.

Jellied Fish lends itself both to a simple and a most decorative kind of serving. It is therefore frequently prepared not only for the Sabbath but also for many family holidays.

Delicious Jellied Fish

4 to 5 lbs. haddock, carp, or other preferred fish	1 carrot, sliced
	5 peppercorns
coarse salt	salt to taste
5 onions, sliced	boiling water
bay leaf	

Slice the fish into pieces about 1-inch thick. Save milt or roe, the head and tail. Sprinkle all lightly with salt and let stand in the refrigerator several hours or overnight. Rinse. Tie the head and tail in a cheesecloth bag. Place the onions in the bottom of a large kettle, then add the bag of head and tail bones. Add bay leaf, carrot, and seasonings; cover with boiling water. Cover and cook slowly for about 30 minutes. Strain broth, forcing any pulp through the strainer. Bring broth again to boiling; add fish slices and milt. Cook gently for about 20 minutes—until fish is just tender. Remove fish with slotted spoon to deep platter. Reduce the broth by further cooking to about 1 cup. Pour this over the fish. Chill until jellied. Garnish with lemon slices, black olives, and mayonnaise. Serves 6 to 8.

Marinierte Herring
(PICKLED HERRING)

6 milch herring	7 peppercorns
1 lemon, sliced	¼ cup vinegar
3 medium-sized onions, sliced	1 tablespoon sugar
2 bay leaves	1 cup sour cream

Wash the herring in several waters and soak overnight. Clean, skin and slice, reserving the milt. Place in a crock or jar layered with lemon, onions, and spices. Mash the milt with vinegar and press through a strainer. Add sugar and sour cream to make a blended sauce. Pour over the herring. Cover with a cloth and let stand in a cold place several days before using. Makes about 3 dozen pieces.

Marinierte Fish
(PICKLED FISH)

4 lbs. pickerel, haddock or other desired fish	¾ to 1 cup vinegar
6 large onions, sliced	3 tablespoons sugar
1 teaspoon salt	1 tablespoon mixed pickling spices (with bay leaves)

Cut the fish into 1-inch slices, or slices large enough so that they can be handled without breaking apart. Sprinkle lightly with coarse salt; then let stand in refrigerator overnight, or at least for several hours. Place 4 of the onions in the bottom of a large shallow pan; add salt, and boiling water to cover generously. Cook until onions are soft; rub through a strainer. Combine pulp and broth. Bring to boiling and add fish carefully.

Cook gently in this onion broth for about 20 minutes. Remove with slotted spoon to stone crock or bowl, arranging in layers with remaining sliced onions between the layers. Add vinegar, sugar, and spices to broth. Bring to boiling; then cool and pour over fish in crock. Cover. Store in a cool place for about two days before serving. Serves 8 to 10.

Sweet and Sour Salmon

2 lbs. salmon or white fish
1½ teaspoons salt
boiling water
2 cups fish broth
6 gingersnaps
4 tablespoons vinegar
4 tablespoons brown sugar

4 tablespoons raisins
2 tablespoons blanched and sliced almonds
1 tablespoon butter (or vegetable fat)
lemon juice

Sprinkle the salmon with salt; cover with boiling water. Cook in a large shallow pan; or better, tie fish in cheesecloth and cook in a deep pot. Cook gently for about 20 minutes. Remove from the water with a slotted spoon; keep hot.

To prepare sweet and sour sauce: Measure out 1½ cups of the fish broth or add water to make up the amount; add gingersnaps, crumbled, and the rest of the ingredients, except the lemon juice. Cook for about 10 minutes—until smooth; stir constantly. Season to taste with salt and pepper, lemon juice, and, if desired, additional sugar. Pour the sauce over fish. Serve hot or cold. Serves 5.

Variations: (1) Add 2 tablespoons vinegar to water in which fish is simmered, and a teaspoon of mixed pickling spices tied in a square of cheesecloth. (2) Half a cup of wine may be substituted for ½ cup of fish broth, in the preparation of the sauce.

The *schochet* is a man highly respected in every Jewish community. He has been trained in slaughtering animals according to the ritual. Through his care only the finest meat is made available for Jewish tables. This brings back wonderful memories of the tall dignified *schochet* of the neighborhood where one of us grew up with her five sisters. In recalling those days, we have laughed together many a time.

No one of us was allowed to miss her turn at carrying the Sabbath fowl from the market to the *schochet*. We were provided with a large market basket with a cover that was supposed to turn it into a secure cage, but, as it happened, first you pushed a head back under cover, then a leg. And many a perverse fowl would suddenly push through and be off down the street, squawking and with feathers flying. What a relief when at last the smiling *schochet* took the bird in his hands, asking after Mother as if nothing had happened!

Although the soup chicken cooked for the famous Goldene Yoich simmers for long hours, it is still a favorite dish for many when served as plain boiled chicken with noodles. Others prefer it seasoned and dressed to heighten the flavor and enhance its appearance, as is done in the recipes for Savory Broiled Chicken and Chicken Casserole.

Savory Broiled Chicken

chicken from soup pot
1 clove garlic
2 tablespoons flour
½ teaspoon paprika

½ teaspoon salt
¼ cup chicken fat (or vegetable fat)

Mash the garlic to a paste. Mix with the remaining ingredients. Spread over the chicken. Broil slowly until chicken is heated through and the skin a golden brown.

Casserole Soup Chicken

chicken from soup pot
2 onions, sliced
1 green pepper, minced
1 clove garlic

½ cup tomatoes, canned or fresh
1 teaspoon salt
chicken fat (or vegetable fat)
¼ teaspoon paprika

Arrange the onions and green pepper in the bottom of a casserole that will be large enough to hold the chicken. Add the garlic, rubbed to a paste, tomatoes, and salt. Mix and pour over the vegetables. Rub the surface of the chicken generously with fat and sprinkle with paprika. Place on the bed of vegetables. Bake in a moderate oven (350° F.) for about 45 minutes. As sauce forms, baste the chicken from time to time.

Turkey holds a favored place on the Jewish table both on the Sabbath and on other holidays. It is roasted in the same manner as chicken.

Roast Chicken or Turkey

4 to 6 lb. chicken or 9 to 16   vegetable fat or poultry fat
      lb. turkey   salt and pepper
stuffing

After kashering (see page 183), wash the fowl well, letting water run through the cavity; wipe dry. Rub well with salt, both inside and out, and with a little ginger, if desired. Stuff the bird with any desired stuffing (see page 33). Truss firmly, pressing thighs against body and tieing in place. Or push a long skewer through one thigh, then through the body and out through the second thigh. Fasten wings into place, either by tieing against the body or with skewers. Tie the whole body into a firm position for roasting; taking a long string begin at the neck or at the legs; cross and re-cross it around the body several times before tieing the ends of string together firmly. Brush outside of bird well with fat and sprinkle with salt and pepper. Place on a rack in uncovered roasting pan, breast side up. Roast, uncovered, in a slow oven (300° F. to 325° F.) according to the time table which follows. Basting occasionally. (If desired, bird may be covered with double layer of cheesecloth dipped in oil. This is placed over the breast and is sprinkled with a little extra oil or fat as it becomes dry during baking. It should be removed toward the end of the roasting period to assure even browning.) Remove to platter for serving and garnish as desired.

Time Table for Roasting Chicken or Turkey
(For larger birds, allow shorter roasting time per lb.)

Chicken: 30 to 40 minutes per lb., according to size
                 40 minutes per lb. for a 3-lb. bird
                 30 minutes per lb. for a 4½-lb. bird

Turkey: 18 to 30 minutes per lb., according to size
            30 minutes per lb. for a 7-lb. bird
            18 minutes per lb. for a 15-lb. bird

The directions for roasting goose and duck have changed a little in modern years, due largely to the fact that an association of duck growers has carried on some actual cooking experiments. A certain proportion of older cooks, for instance, used to advocate pricking the skin before and during roasting "to let some of the fat pour out more easily." Others thought that pricking merely marred the appearance and contributed little to drawing out the fat. This latter opinion has been upheld in modern kitchen testing. For better appearance and juicier meat, it is now advised that no pricking be done. There have been various schools of thought, too, on proper roasting temperatures. Experimental results have persuaded everyone to adopt low, steady heat both for better flavor and to avoid actual weight loss in cooking.

Roast Duck or Goose

3 to 5 lb. duck or 7 to 10 lb.   stuffing
    goose (about)

After kashering (see page 183), wash the fowl inside and out with cold water; dry. Fill with favorite stuffing, and do not pack too full. Remember the stuffing expands during roasting. Or the bird may be roasted with only a few stalks of celery, a few slices of onion. These will be discarded after roasting. To close vent, insert small poultry pins from one side to the other and lace over with light twine. Goose and duck do not need to be trussed since legs are short and wings lie close to the body. Place bird breast upon a rack in a shallow baking pan. Do not cover; add water or baste. Do not prick skin. Roast in a slow oven at (325° F.) according to the size of the bird.

Time Table for Roasting Duck or Goose
(For larger birds, allow shorter roasting time per lb.)

Duck: 35 to 40 minutes per lb., according to size
           40 minutes per lb. for a 3-lb. bird
           35 minutes per lb. for a 5-lb. bird

Goose: 25 to 30 minutes per lb., according to size
           30 minutes per lb. for a 7-lb. bird
           25 minutes per lb. for a 10-lb. bird

This fricassee of chicken has taken many a bow at such elegant functions as wedding feasts and dinner parties and as an appetizer at important functions. It is generally served in individual ramekins or casseroles and is most inviting. It is also popular as a hearty dish for the family.

Chicken Fricassee

giblets from 2 chickens (necks, wings, gizzards, hearts, and feet)
2 medium-sized onions, diced
2 to 3 tablespoons chicken fat
2 cups boiling water
1 teaspoon salt
⅛ teaspoon black pepper
½ lb. ground beef
2 tablespoons cold water
1 egg, slightly beaten
salt and pepper
1 tablespoon flour

After kashering (see page 183), wash the chicken well. To prepare the feet, scald in boiling water for 1 to 2 minutes. Remove and peel off skin. Brown the onion lightly in the chicken fat in a 3-qt. kettle; then brown the chicken parts, stirring constantly to brown evenly. Add the boiling water, salt, and pepper and cover tightly. Cook gently until just tender. Mix the ground beef with the cold water, egg, and salt and pepper. Mix lightly with a fork to keep the meat from packing tightly. Shape into small balls and add to the fricassee broth. Cook gently for 15 minutes. Thicken the broth with the flour mixed with about 2 tablespoons of cold water. Stir this into the broth, season with additional salt and pepper to taste and continue cooking gently for 5 to 7 minutes. Some prefer not to thicken the broth with flour, and let it cook down to its own savory richness. As a main dish this will serve 5 or 6, as an entree, about 8.

Stuffings for poultry are many and varied, as the following recipes indicate.

Potato Stuffing

3 medium-sized potatoes, grated
1 egg
1 teaspoon salt
pepper
1 onion, minced
2 tablespoons minced parsley
4 tablespoons matza meal
¼ cup melted chicken fat (or vegetable fat)

Mix all the ingredients together lightly. Season with additional salt and pepper to taste. Stuff the bird lightly. This is sufficient for a 4 to 5 lb. bird.

Bread Stuffing

6 cups day-old bread, in cubes or small pieces
hot water
2 medium-sized onions, minced
1 cup celery (with tops), diced
¼ cup chicken fat (or vegetable fat)
1 egg, slightly beaten
salt and pepper
poultry seasoning

Soak the bread in the hot water for a few minutes, then squeeze dry. Cook the onions and celery in fat until yellow. Add to bread; add the egg. Blend. Season to taste with salt, pepper, and poultry seasoning. Sufficient to stuff a 5 to 7 lb. bird.

Giblet Stuffing: Add chopped cooked giblets to the above recipe.

Prune or Apple Stuffing: Add 1 cup chopped fruit, such as raw apples or cooked prunes, with 1 to 2 tablespoons brown sugar to the above recipe.

Kasha Stuffing
(BUCKWHEAT GROATS STUFFING)

2 cups buckwheat groats
1 teaspoon salt
1 egg, slightly beaten
2 cups boiling water
2 tablespoons chicken fat (or vegetable fat)
2 medium-sized onions, chopped

Mix together the buckwheat groats, salt, and egg, in a heavy frying pan and stir over moderate heat until the kernels are well coated with the egg and dry. Remove from heat to control the sizzling of the water when it is added. When sizzling stops, add fat and onions; cover, return to moderate heat, and let the *kasha* steam gently for about 20 minutes. This amount is for stuffing a large bird; use half the recipe for a bird 5 lbs. or under.

Note: This may be turned into a casserole, if desired, and baked for 1 hour in a moderate oven. To keep the dish from drying out, add a few tablespoons of the meat sauce from the roast, chicken soup, or hot water.

In Hungary the Jewish housewife uses paprika with a generous hand, as do all her neighbors and fellow countrymen. These have taught Jews everywhere to delight in Chicken Paprikash for the Sabbath table. Veal, too, has been used in this recipe, and is a most acceptable substitute for the chicken.

Chicken or Veal Paprikash

1 or 2 roasting chickens, cut in serving pieces, or 3 lbs. veal
2 medium-sized onions, sliced
2 tablespoons chicken fat (or vegetable fat)
salt and pepper
½ cup boiling water
1 green pepper, minced
1 cup minced celery with leaves
2 medium-sized carrots, sliced
1 tablespoon paprika
2 tomatoes, peeled and quartered, or ½ cup canned tomatoes

Brown the meat and onions in the fat in a heavy 4-qt. saucepan; add salt, pepper, and boiling water. Cover tightly and simmer for ½ hour. Add green pepper, celery, carrots, paprika, and tomatoes. Cook until the meat is tender. Stir occasionally, adding more hot water if necessary. Serve with rice or noodles. Serves 6 or 7.

Since cooking on the Sabbath is considered work, the women solved their problem by preparing foods in advance. This led to the invention of some of the finest dishes from Jewish kitchens. One of the most appreciated is *cholent*.

This famous dish, beloved of the Sabbath table, has inspired poetry, folk tales and songs. Behind its preparation lie the cooking wisdom and skill of countless generations of Jewish housewives. Its name may be derived from the Italian *caldo,* or it may be a corruption of the French *chaud.* It has also been explained as derived from the Yiddish *shul ende,* meaning end of synagogue—and time for that wonderful fragrant dish of the second Sabbath meal. Whatever the origin of its name, *cholent* itself is no mystery. It is a robust meal-in-one-dish, savory with meat and vegetables. In order to bring out its richest flavor, it must be cooked in the traditional way, in a slow oven, overnight. In some cities today Jewish bakers still offer the service of their ovens, after the fire is turned out, to cook their neighbors' Sabbath *cholent.*

There are many variations of the Sabbath *cholent.* Every family, in fact, has a special recipe, often pointing back to the country from which it came. Each housewife will declare solemnly that hers is the truly authentic dish. Some are combinations of meat, potatoes, and peas, or lima beans or barley, while others use *kasha,* especially the buckwheat groats.

Cholent
(A SABBATH OVEN DISH)

2 lbs. brisket or other fat meat	marrow bone or calf's foot in
1 cup onions, thinly sliced	pieces
2 tablespoons chicken fat	4 medium-sized potatoes
2 teaspoons salt	1 cup dry limas, soaked
pepper	boiling water

Fry the onion in fat until golden. Salt and pepper the meat, and brown it in the fat. Turn meat, fat, and onions into a 4-qt. casserole or baking dish with a tightly fitting cover. Arrange the bones, potatoes, and the soaked lima beans around the meat. Add boiling water to cover, using also the water in which limas were soaked. Add additional seasoning of salt and pepper (and any spice that might be desired). Traditionally it is baked overnight, tightly covered, in a very slow oven. It may also be cooked gently on the top of the stove for 3 to 4 hours, or until the meat is tender. Serves 6.

Favorite additions to the *cholent* are little calves' feet or a large savory dumpling. The *knaidel* or dumpling is placed in the center of the baking dish just before it is tightly covered and ready for baking.

Knaidel
(DUMPLING FOR CHOLENT OR TZIMMES)

½ cup beef or chicken fat, unrendered
1 cup flour
1 teaspoon baking powder
¼ teaspoon salt

pepper, black
1 tablespoon minced parsley
1 tablespoon minced onion
3 tablespoons water (about)

Chop the fat quite fine. Sift together the dry ingredients; mix with fat. Add the parsley and onion. Stir in the water a little at a time to make a delicate ball of dough. Place in center of *cholent* or *tzimmes* just before baking.

Stuffed *derma*, known also as *kishke*, is often served as a special Sabbath treat. It has become so popular that in cosmopolitan cities of America slices of *kishke*, frankfurters, and *knishes* can be seen grilling in many restaurants.

Stuffed Derma or Kishke
(STUFFED BEEF CASINGS)

2 lbs. beef casings
1 cup flour
½ teaspoon salt
pepper

1 onion, finely minced
¼ to ⅓ cup chicken fat (or vegetable fat)

Wash and clean the beef casings even if they seem clean. Kasher (see page 182). Cut into 8- to 10-inch lengths. Sew or tie one end of each securely. Mix the ingredients of the stuffing together and fill each section lightly—about ⅔ full to allow for expansion. Now sew or tie the other end. Plunge into boiling water; scrape clean. Place in a shallow baking dish and bake in a slow oven (325° F.) until cooked through and well browned. Baste with fat. If desired, roast with poultry, or cook in a carrot or other *tzimmes.*

Kasha has come to mean a savory baked dish of buckwheat groats, but from time immemorial the real meaning was plain boiled mush or cereal that might be made from wheat, barley, lima beans, or buckwheat groats.

Kasha and Mushrooms
(BUCKWHEAT GROATS AND MUSHROOMS)

1 cup buckwheat groats	2 cups boiling water
1 egg	6 to 8 dried mushrooms, soaked
½ teaspoon salt	and washed thoroughly
2 tablespoons chicken fat	
(or vegetable fat)	

Place buckwheat in a large frying pan. Add the unbeaten egg and mix well. Place over low heat and stir constantly until each grain is coated. Place in a 3-qt. casserole; add the salt, fat, and over this pour the boiling water. Stir in the cleaned mushrooms cut in pieces. Cover and bake for 1 to 2 hours in a moderate oven (350° F.). Or if desired, this dish may be cooked on top of the stove for 30 to 45 minutes. Add water or meat stock as necessary. Serves 4 or 5.

Two favorite foods combine to make Kasha Varnishkas.

Kasha Varnishkas
(NOODLE AND KASHA)

To prepare, use 2 cups of cooked noodles of the bow-knot type, or use squares cut from broad noodles. Mix lightly with the *kasha,* prepared as in the preceding recipe, omitting the mushrooms. Stir together the cooked and drained noodles and the *kasha.* Season with about 2 tablespoons of chicken fat, and salt and pepper to taste. Then cook gently on top of the stove until heated through, or bake in a greased 2½-qt. casserole until piping hot. Serve with the meat course. Serves 6.

Sweet and sour dishes of every variety are favorites for the Sabbath. Such are these Sweet and Sour Meat Balls.

Sweet and Sour Meat Balls

1 lb. ground beef
½ cup water
¼ cup matza meal or 2 slices bread
1 teaspoon salt
pepper
1 onion, minced
1 egg, slightly beaten

flour
chicken fat (or vegetable fat)
1½ cups boiling water
3 tablespoons sugar
juice of 1 lemon or sour salt, to taste
3 tablespoons raisins (about)

Mix together meat, water, meal or bread, salt, pepper, onion, and egg. (If bread is used, soak in water, press dry and crumble fine before adding to the meat.) Shape into small balls; roll lightly in flour. Brown in hot fat in a large, heavy frying pan. Simmer the remaining ingredients together over low heat for about 5 minutes. Add the meat balls to the hot sauce. Cover tightly and cook over low heat, or in a slow oven (300° F.), for 40 minutes. (To vary seasoning of sauce, add a bay leaf and lemon, thinly sliced.) Serves 4.

Sauerbraten is a very, very special dish. The mere mention of it sends everyone to the table in a flurry of pleasant anticipation.

Sauerbraten
(SPICED BEEF, POTTED OR ROASTED)

4 lbs. brisket or chuck
4 bay leaves
6 cloves
1 large onion, sliced
1 teaspoon salt
2 cups vinegar
2 cups water

¼ cup chicken fat (or vegetable fat)
¼ cup brown sugar
¼ cup raisins, if desired
2 tablespoons *einbren,* browned flour (*see* next recipe)
4 to 6 gingersnaps, crumbled

Use meat whole or cut into serving-sized pieces. Simmer together spices, onion, salt, vinegar, and water for about 5 minutes; then pour over the meat. Store in a crock in a cool place overnight to ripen and tenderize. (In former days, tougher—unfinished—meat required several days for this ripening.) Drain sauce from meat; save. Brown meat slowly in fat, in a deep, heavy pot, to develop rich flavor. Heat sauce, add brown sugar, and raisins if they are to be used. Pour over meat. Cover tightly and simmer on top of stove, or in slow oven (300° F.) until meat can be broken with a fork. This takes at least 2 to 3 hours. Replace onion with a fresh one, thinly sliced. There should be about 2 cups of gravy; add water if liquid has evaporated. When ready to serve, remove meat to serving dish. Skim extra fat from top of broth; and to thicken, mix *einbren* with a little cold water to make a smooth paste, and stir into the liquid; add ginger snaps. Stir over heat until gravy is rich and creamy. Pour over meat and serve. Serves 8 to 12.

The simple directions for *einbren* follow. Many housewives like to prepare a quantity at a time, to have it ready for constant use.

Einbren
(BROWNED FLOUR FOR GRAVIES)

Spread a thin layer of flour in a shallow baking pan or heavy frying pan. If browned in the oven, stir from time to time to prevent burning. If browned over direct heat, stir continuously until all is browned. Store in jar for use at any time. Browned flour does not have the thickening power of white flour; slightly more is needed for thickening gravies and sauces.

Brisket of beef, boiled, roasted, or potted, is a rich savory dish. So frequently is it served that it is almost a staple on Jewish tables.

Brisket mit Beblach
(BRISKET WITH BEANS)

2 lbs. brisket	ginger, if desired
2 cups dried beans, navy or limas	bay leaf
	1 large onion, cubed
salt and pepper	

Wash the beans; soak overnight in water to cover. Salt to taste the next morning; bring to boiling. Turn heat low; simmer for 20 minutes, or until skin of beans will crack when cooled by blowing upon them. Brown meat in a little hot fat; add salt and pepper, and sprinkle with a little ginger, if desired. Place in a deep baking dish with beans, liquid, bay leaf and onion. Cover tightly; bake in a moderate oven (350° F.). Limas will take only 2 to 3 hours; navy beans require a full 6 hours to be tender. Both can be baked in a slow oven overnight with wonderful results. To vary seasoning, ¼ cup brown sugar or molasses may be added with ½ teaspoon mustard. Serves 8 to 10.

Rich Brown Pot Roast of Brisket or Chuck

3 to 5 lbs. brisket or chuck
salt and pepper
2 tablespoons chicken fat (or vegetable fat)
4 or 5 onions, sliced
2 cups tomatoes, canned or fresh
2 tablespoons browned flour (*see* Einbren page 39)

Sprinkle the meat with salt and pepper, and brown slowly in the fat in a heavy roasting pot or Dutch oven. Meat may be removed while onions are browned in the same fat. Return meat to pot; pour tomatoes over it; add onions and season with additional salt and pepper. Cover roasting pot and bake in a moderate oven (350° F.) for about 3 hours, until tender; or cook gently on top of the stove for about the same length of time. If desired, thicken the gravy with browned flour mixed to a paste with cold water. To do this, remove meat, skim off surplus fat and stir in the flour paste. Cook gently and stir constantly until smooth and thick. The meat may then be sliced and returned to this gravy for a quick reheating, or it may be sliced and gravy served in a separate bowl. Potatoes and carrots may be cooked with the roast for about ¾ of an hour before the meat is done. Serves 6 to 12.

Boiled Beef with Chrein
(BOILED BEEF WITH HORSE-RADISH)

3 lbs. brisket
boiling water
2 teaspoons salt
1 bay leaf
1 medium-sized onion, sliced
1 medium-sized carrot, sliced

Cover the brisket with boiling water; add the rest of the ingredients; cover and simmer gently for 3 hours—until tender.

Let stand in the broth for about 15 minutes. Slice and serve with Beet Horse-radish (*see* page 17). To serve cold, let the tender meat remain in the broth until cold. Use the broth for soup or stock. Serves 6.

Brisket with Prunes and Sweet Potatoes

2 lbs. brisket
1 lb. prunes
4 large sweet potatoes

3 tablespoons sugar
juice of 1 lemon

Simmer the brisket with prunes in water to cover for about an hour. Scrub and pare sweet potatoes. Quarter into a 3-qt. baking dish. Add the steaming meat and prunes, along with their liquid. Sprinkle the sugar over the top and add the lemon juice. Cover tightly and bake in a moderate oven (350° F.) for about 2 hours, although longer baking will add to the richness of the flavor. Serves 6 to 8.

A meat loaf in any language is a juicy, well-flavored dish made from tough cuts of meat ground fine. The Jewish housewife devised a Sabbath loaf that is as good the second day as when fresh out of the oven.

Sabbath Meat Loaf

1½ lbs. ground beef
1 teaspoon salt
pepper
1 egg, slightly beaten
1 onion, minced
½ cup bread crumbs or 2 thick
    slices bread

2 tablespoons water or tomato
    juice
2 or 3 hard-cooked eggs
slices of tomato
onion rings
2 tablespoons chicken fat (or
    vegetable fat)

Mix together beef, seasonings, egg, onion, crumbs. If bread is used, soak in water; press dry and shake into crumbs. Mix and add the liquid. Handle lightly. Pack half the mixture into a well-greased loaf pan, smoothing the surface. Press hard-cooked eggs down the center, the length of the loaf. Cover with the remaining half of the mixture. Garnish top with sliced tomatoes and/or onion rings. Dot with fat. Bake in a moderate oven (350° F.) for 1½ hours. The loaf can be shaped and baked on a shallow pan, if preferred. Serve hot or cold. Serves 6 or 7.

Sabbath Veal Chops bring to mind to one of us the veal chops that her mother used to make. What was her secret? Without a recipe, her six daughters wondered. Was it in the quality of the finest young veal—or the matza meal and egg dip, or the way the chops were fried in chicken fat and then baked slowly? They were determined to find out. This recipe approximates the elusive delightful dish they remember.

Sabbath Veal Chops

6 chops, cut from very young veal	2 eggs
	chicken fat (or vegetable fat)
salt and pepper	1 onion, quartered
matza meal	

Season the chops with salt and pepper, then dip in matza meal, covering them evenly. Beat eggs to a good frothiness. Heat enough fat in a heavy frying pan to almost reach the surface of the chops. Fry the quartered onion in the fat until it is a light golden color; remove from fat and set aside. Dip the crumbed chops one by one into the beaten eggs and then place quickly in the fat that is hot, but not smoking. Fry first on one side and then on the other. When brown on both sides, remove chops to a shallow baking dish, top with the fried onion, and bake gently, uncovered, in a moderate oven (350° F.) for about 20 minutes. These are delicious even when reheated. Serves 6.

The next recipe, for Stuffed Breast of Veal, comes from the kitchen of the same famous cook. She uses garlic and ginger, an oriental touch of seasoning that adds much to the savory goodness of the dish.

Stuffed Breast of Veal (or Lamb)

4 to 5 lbs. breast of veal (or lamb)	ginger or paprika
	stuffing (recipe page 33)
garlic	chicken fat
salt and pepper	

Have the butcher cut a pocket in the meat. Rub outer surface and inside cavity of the meat with garlic, or, if fond of garlic, make little slits in the meat and insert tiny pieces of it. Sprinkle with salt and pepper and a very little powdered ginger or paprika or both. Stuff with your favorite stuffing; then sew up the pocket. Spread fat over the top surface. Roast on rack in uncovered roaster in a moderate oven (350° F.), allowing 30 minutes to the lb. Serves 8 to 10.

Gebrutenah Miltz
(ROASTED SPLEEN)

1 beef *miltz* (spleen)	2 tablespoons chicken fat (or
stuffing (*see* page 33)	vegetable fat)
salt and pepper	2 medium-sized onions, sliced
1 clove garlic, mashed	1 cup boiling water

After kashering *miltz* (*see* page 183), make a pocket along the side and scrape out about a cupful of the meat. Mix with desired stuffing and fill lightly to allow room for expansion during cooking. Sew up the opening. Sprinkle with salt and pepper. Place in a hot, greased roasting pan; spread with garlic paste and dot with fat. Place the onions around the meat and pour boiling water into the pan. Roast in a moderate oven (350° F.) for about 2 hours or until crisp and brown. Baste occasionally, adding more water if liquid evaporates too rapidly.

Petcha (calf's foot jelly) runs a close second to *cholent* as the Sabbath favorite. It may be served hot at the Sabbath noonday meal, but it is always chilled when served as a jellied dish for *Shalosh Seudot*, for which it was originally invented.

Petcha or Sulze
(CALF'S FOOT JELLY)

calves' feet, 1 or 2	2 tablespoons vinegar
2 medium-sized onions,	6 cups boiling water
quartered	*challah*
2 cloves garlic	garlic
1 teaspoon salt	2 hard-cooked eggs
pepper	1 lemon, thinly sliced

Have butcher saw calves' feet into about 2-inch pieces. Clean them thoroughly. Pour boiling water over the pieces; drain and scrape. After kashering (*see* page 183), place in a 4-qt. kettle with onions, garlic, salt, pepper, vinegar, and boiling water. Cook until meat and gristle begin to separate from the bones; this will take about 3 hours. Strain and save the liquid. Remove gristle and meat from the bones; cut into small, neat pieces.

To serve as a hot soup: Bring broth and meat to boiling. Rub chunks of *challah* (toasted or dried in the oven) with garlic. Serve broth with meat and gristle and garlic toast in individual soup plates. Chopped hard-cooked egg may be sprinkled over each, with a garnish of thinly sliced lemon, if desired.

To serve as a cold jellied dish: Arrange pieces of the meat and gristle in a deep platter or mold. Cover with a thin layer of the broth and allow to chill until set. Add the remaining pieces of meat and the remainder of broth that is by this time cool and beginning to thicken slightly. Add slices of egg and thin slices of lemon for garnish. Chill until hardened. Serve from platter or turn out to serve. Serves 8 to 10.

The *tzimmes* is a time-honored dish, and such a favorite that its name has crept into the folk language. "To make a *tzimmes*" over someone has come to mean lavishing him with attention, worthily or unworthily, as the case may be. There are as many *tzimmes* as one can imagine. There is a carrot *tzimmes*, a prune *tzimmes*, one of potato and prunes, and many a variety made with dried fruits. Often, to the delight of the family, a *knaidel* is hidden in the heart of a *tzimmes*, which, to whet the Sabbath appetite, must be richly golden in color, fragrant with honey and fruits.

Prune and Potato Tzimmes

1 lb. brisket or other fat meat
2 teaspoons salt
1 tablespoon chicken fat (or vegetable fat)
1 medium-sized onion, sliced
5 potatoes, sweet or white

½ lb. prunes, sour
2 tablespoons flour
½ teaspoon cinnamon
dash of nutmeg
⅓ to ½ cup honey or brown sugar

Sprinkle meat with salt and brown in fat with onion. Add water to cover and cook for about 1 hour. In a greased 3-qt. baking dish, place meat in the center and surround with potatoes, cut in thick slices, and prunes washed thoroughly. Add the water in which the meat was cooking and more water if necessary to cover contents. Make an *einbren* by browning the flour lightly in a frying pan; stir constantly to prevent scorching. Remove from fire; stir in about ½ cup meat broth. Add cinnamon, nutmeg, honey or sugar and stir until smooth. Pour this sauce into one side of the pot and shake gently to distribute the thickness. Cover and bake in a moderate oven (350° F.) for 2 hours—until meat is tender. Bake without cover for the last 30 minutes to have a golden brown top. Serves 6.

Variation: This *tzimmes* may be made without meat if desired, and instead of baking, may be cooked on top of the stove. Dried apricots or peaches are delicious in a *tzimmes* and may be used instead of the prunes.

Almost every Jewish family has its favorite *tzimmes,* and this preference is usually indicative of the country from which the family came. Those delighting in carrot *tzimmes* probably came from Russia or Poland. A taste for one of dried fruits or lima beans most likely originated in the Balkans.

Rusell Fleisch
(MEAT COOKED WITH FERMENTED BEET JUICE)

This may be prepared for the Sabbath table with plain beets, cooked or canned. Prepare exactly as directed in the Passover recipe (*see* page 138), except that lemon juice or sour salt (citric acid) is used to make it tart, to taste.

A *kugel* is a pudding—but this is too simple to describe its time-honored place among Sabbath dishes. Just mention the Lukshen Kugel and all sorts of sweet memories are conjured up by many.

Lukshen Kugel
(NOODLE PUDDING)

broad noodles, ½ lb. or 2½ cups, broken	2 tablespoons chicken fat (or vegetable fat)
2 or 3 eggs, separated	2 tablespoons sugar
	½ teaspoon salt

Cook the noodles in boiling salted water until tender. Drain, but not too dry; moist noodles make a more tender pudding. Beat the egg yolks with the fat, sugar, and salt. Fold into the hot noodles. Beat egg whites until stiff, but not dry, and fold in also. Pour into a greased 8½″ square pan. Bake in a moderate oven (350° F.) for about 30 minutes. Raise heat slightly, if necessary, to brown top. For a sweeter *kugel*, fold in ¼ cup of raisins. Serves 4 or 5.

Lukshen Fruit Kugel
(NOODLE-FRUIT PUDDING)

½ lb. noodles, broken
2 eggs, separated
2 tablespoons chicken fat
    (or vegetable fat)
2 tablespoons sugar
½ teaspoon salt

½ cup chopped raisins
½ cup chopped apples
¼ cup broken nut meats
¼ teaspoon cinnamon
⅛ teaspoon nutmeg

Cook noodles as in the preceding recipe. Beat the egg yolks with fat, sugar, and salt. Fold into the hot noodles. Fold in the fruit mixed with the spices. Then fold in the stiffly beaten whites. Pour into a well-greased casserole and bake in a moderate oven (350° F.) for 45 minutes, or until nicely browned. Serves 6.

Fruit compotes (stewed fruits) are invariably prepared for the Sabbath midday meal and served with the meat dish. Each country in which Jews make their homes has added variety in the types of compotes made. Here is one typically French.

Compote of Pears in Wine Sauce

6 medium-sized green winter
    pears
water to cover
1 teaspoon grated lemon rind
1 tablespoon lemon juice

a few slivers of ginger root or
    crystallized ginger
¾ to 1 cup sugar
1 cup Concord wine

Wash and pare the fruit and add just enough water to cover. Cook until tender but not too soft. Add remaining ingredients and simmer for about 10 minutes. Chill and serve in the sauce. If pears are large, cut in halves and core before cooking. Serves 6.

In some Eastern countries the main portion of the Friday night Sabbath meal consists of fresh fruit served in a great many different ways. This has undoubtedly come about because fruit is so plentiful in that part of the world. It is now customary for the Jewish housewife to serve, among other things, a large bowl of assorted fruit while family and friends sit around socializing on a Friday night.

Pies for the Sabbath are of every possible kind and modern cooking has added many new recipes. Even the famous *strudel* occasionally finds a rival in the easier-to-make modern American pie. According to an old legend, making pies for the Sabbath is in commemoration of the manna which lay "as if in a box having dew on top and dew on the bottom."

Muerbe Teig is a traditional pie pastry and is used for fruit and all other pies and *torten*. It is rich and tender and requires light handling.

Muerbe Teig
(PIE PASTRY)

⅓ cup butter (or vegetable fat)
1 cup flour
¼ teaspoon salt

1 tablespoon sugar
1 egg yolk
water or milk

Add the butter to the flour which has been mixed with salt and sugar. Cut the butter in with knives or pastry blender until the mixture is as coarse as corn meal. Stir in the egg yolk. Add water or milk by drops, adding just enough to hold the mixture together. Pat evenly into a 10-inch pie pan. Chill in the refrigerator. Fill with any desired fruit or other filling and bake according to the temperature required by the filling.

To many, no Sabbath or holiday would seem complete unless a sponge cake were on hand to serve with wine when guests drop in. Besides, the family would be gravely disap-

pointed if there were no sponge cake to go with tall glasses
of hot tea and lemon to complete the midday Sabbath meal.

Golden Sponge Cake

4 large eggs, separated	1 teaspoon lemon extract
1 cup sugar	1 cup cake flour
juice and pulp of a good-sized orange, or scant ½ cup juice	¼ teaspoon salt 1 teaspoon baking powder

Separate the eggs. Beat whites to a froth in large bowl; add ½
cup of the sugar, gradually; set aside. Beat yolks well; add the
remaining ½ cup of sugar gradually and continue to beat until
very light and very fluffy. The yolks must be well beaten to avoid
a soggy bottom. Add yolks to whites; then add the orange juice
and lemon extract and beat for 7 minutes. Gently fold in the
flour, which has been sifted three times, with the salt and
baking powder. Bake in an ungreased 9″ x 3″ spring form in a
slow oven (325° F.) for 1 hour. Invert to cool before removing.
To serve, sprinkle with confectioners' sugar, or frost if desired.
Cuts 10 to 12 pieces.

For many years Jews used to while away a Sabbath and
a holiday afternoon drinking tall glasses of hot tea with
varenyah, the fine fruit preserves prepared by every housewife during the season when fruits were plentiful. The temperature made no difference in the vast quantities of hot tea
that were consumed. The children were allowed to partake
of this "tea sweet," as they called it. For them it was really
hot water barely colored with tea, but the deep layer of
varenyah that could be dipped out from the bottom of the
glass with a spoon was balm to the soul!

This serving of preserves with tea was a comforting sign of
security among those who could afford it. Poorer folk were
more apt to reserve their precious fruit preserves for some
time of illness among friends or in the family. They would
store the *varenyah* away with these words: "*Allevia zol men*

dos nit darfen"—"We hope and trust there will be no occasion to use these."

Hot tea with *varenyah* is now often served after dinner on the Sabbath eve with dishes of salted *arbas* (peas), *nahit* (chick peas), and *bob* (fava beans) set out on a lace-covered table. These salty, peppery tidbits that can be prepared so quickly are favorites on many holidays throughout the year. They are particularly popular during the Purim festival.

Tea after the Traditional Manner

A strong essence of tea is made by pouring boiling water over leaves in a small earthenware pot. To serve, small amounts of this essence are poured into tall tea glasses, which are then filled with boiling water from the samovar. Lemon and sugar are passed around. Rarely does sugar go into the glass. It is held in the mouth and the tea drawn through the sugar as it is drunk.

THE HOLIDAYS

THE HIGH HOLY DAYS:

Rosh Hashanah, Yom Kippur, and the Days Between

The 1st through the 10th of Tishri—usually in late September or early October.

The High Holy Days are the ten most solemn days of the Jewish year. Rosh Hashanah, known also as the Day of Judgment, is celebrated for the first two days, which are also the first two days of the New Year. Yom Kippur is the last of the High Holy Days. These days, as well as the days between, are known as *Yamim Noraim,* the Days of Awe, and they are marked by profoundly religious observance.

It is believed that during these days all persons must render their accounts to the Lord, who will judge and inscribe their names accordingly in the Book of Life, and decide their fate for the coming year. Unlike most other days of special observance, these are not concerned with the bounty of nature or with great historical events. The Ten Days of Penitence are deeply personal, and the New Year that is beginning is greeted not with revelry and gaiety, but with solemn prayer and quiet joy.

The slow approach of the solemn days is first announced a month in advance. Beginning at that time, the *shofar* is

51

blown in the synagogue each day to bring the people to an
awareness of the need for prayer in preparation for the High
Holy Days.

The *shofar*, made from a ram's horn, is a natural wind in-
strument, one of the oldest in the world. In ancient times it
had many uses outside of the synagogue, such as calling
people to assembly, warning of crises, announcing important events. The *shofar* plays so important a part on Rosh
Hashanah that the holiday has become known as Yom
Teru'ah, the Day of Blowing.

The stirring blast of the ram's horn is heard during the
morning and afternoon services on the Holy Days, and when
it comes it seems to fill everyone with a sense of the Divine
Presence in their midst. All through the ceremonies this
blowing of the *shofar* continues in short blasts, long blasts,
tapping staccato blasts, as prescribed by the ritual. Prayers
of the worshippers rise in answer to it.

At the end of the service the people turn to each other
and wish each other a happy New Year. *"L'shanah tova
tikatevu"*—"May you be inscribed for a good New Year"—
resounds throughout the synagogue. In fact throughout the
season, in the synagogue, at home, and everywhere, the air
is full of good wishes expressed in this greeting.

A ceremony that takes place on the afternoon of the first
day of Rosh Hashanah is known as *Tashlich*, "the casting."
It is a service of purification held near any body of water
where fish may be found, "because man is likened to a fish,
who may be caught in the net of trouble if he fails to watch
his conduct." After *Tashlich* at the water's edge, each shakes
a corner of his garment. This is symbolic of the ability of each
to cast himself free of sin if he wills to do so, and to correct
his ways. This service of purification is still observed in many
places.

Rosh Hashanah begins at home when the mother lights the candles just before sundown and recites the prayers that good may come to all. She has prepared the table for the dinner to be served on returning from the synagogue. The cup for *Kiddush* (the prayer of the sanctification of the holiday) is in its place with the wine decanter beside it, and there are two loaves of *challah*, Sabbath bread, made very special for Rosh Hashanah with ladders or birds baked on top. These decorations are symbolic of the hope that prayers may ascend on high. There is also a bowl of honey on the table, symbolic of the wish for "sweetness in the New Year." After *Kiddush* is recited, the family dip into the bowl of honey with bread and slices of apple. On the second night there is, in addition, a blessing over some of the first fruits of the harvest that have not yet been tasted this season.

Many are the duties of the housewife during the Days of Awe. There are few limitations or directions for the food to be served at this time, but in planning the meals, she will be mindful of the blessing given by Ezra and Nehemiah to "the good things and sweet wine" served for these days. And she will remember, too, that sour or bitter foods have no place on the joyous table.

In former years certain other traditions concerning foods were also observed. In ancient times, for reasons now unknown, nuts were not eaten during these days. It was customary too, in an earlier day, to serve a sheep's head or the head of a fish to the master of the household. Serving the head expressed the hope on the part of his family that for the coming year he would be a leader among men, and it symbolized also his place as head of the family.

The meals for the High Holy Days are made up from traditional and symbolic dishes.

Rosh Hashanah Dinner

Wine   Apples Dipped in Honey   Challah
Gefillte Fish   Sliced Tomatoes and Cucumbers
Goldene Yoich with Farfel or Mondlen
Roast Turkey, Duck, or Chicken   Helzel
Mehren Tzimmes   String Beans
Apricot Compote   Honey Cake   Sponge Cake
Teiglach   Apples and Grapes

Rosh Hashanah Midday Meal

Apples Dipped in Honey   Chopped Liver   Challah
Roast Brisket   Browned Potatoes
Carrots Glazed in Honey   Fresh Peas
Celery   Cucumbers
Apple Strudel   Tea

The days between Rosh Hashanah and Yom Kippur are days of thoughtful penitence. There is the Sabbath between, which is known as the Sabbath of Repentance. It is the occasion of special prayers, and sermons on the significance of the season and the day, with selected readings from the Prophets.

Yom Kippur, the Day of Atonement, is the great fast day of the year. The fervent prayers and preparations that have gone before, the reckoning of personal accounts made ready for the Lord—all has been leading up to the great climax of this most high and holy day. The time has now come when, through a long and devout day of fasting, the judgment of the Lord will be received in the recesses of the heart. All are prepared for this through fasting as this puts one into a frame of mind that makes prayers and confessions more deeply felt. Children over thirteen are required to fast just as their parents do. However, the sick are urged to refrain from doing so.

Before Yom Kippur each must make his peace with his fellow man. There is the beautiful custom, that still persists, whereby enemies come together, sometimes with the help of a peacemaker, to settle their disputes and make amends for wrongs they have committed against one another. Each member of the family, including the children, strives to make peace with his friends and enemies and settle his personal as well as his monetary debts.

The meal before the fast is eaten long before sundown on the eve of Yom Kippur. The women of the household have prepared a holiday meal. For it is commanded that there be eating and drinking on this day before the fast so that each may take unto himself the "power of food" in order to serve God with greater zeal. Dishes served at this meal must be bland, without spices, herbs, or salt, so that they will not induce thirst during the fasting hours. At table, quiet and peace surround the family. It is written that one should indulge in no controversy before the high and holy day. Rather, each should prepare himself with calmness for this most solemn day of the year.

Dinner before the Fast
Goldene Yoich with Kreplach
Plain Boiled Chicken   Mehren Tzimmes
Green Salad with Bland Dressing
Apple Sauce   Tea

After the meal a memorial candle is lighted in memory of the departed. Then the family leaves for the synagogue.

The evening service of Yom Kippur opens with the beautiful *Kol Nidre*. The haunting loveliness of this melody has made it a musical classic. Its origin is obscure, but its words of pleading to annul forgotten vows were known as early as the ninth century and set to melodious cadence some time in the twelfth (some say in the sixteenth) century. The music has become of such importance that the night service of Yom Kippur is often known as the Night of *Kol Nidre*.

Prayers in the synagogue during the day that follows include the Long Confession. This is a special prayer in which the Jew, mindful of the old injunction that "All Jews are responsible for one another," prays not only for himself but for all Jews everywhere. With the final sounding of the *shofar* the solemn day of fasting is over, and throughout the synagogue is heard the joyous greeting: *"G'mar chatima tova"*— "May the final inscription be good."

All now return home to dinner, to a meal as simple or as elaborate as the family desires, and they while away the time before dinner is ready drinking coffee and nibbling on apples dipped in honey, and on *honey leckach* or coffee cake. This is a typical menu for the dinner.

Dinner to Break the Fast

Chopped Herring
Chicken Soup   Mondlen
Roast Duck or Chicken   Stuffing   Green Limas
Carrot, Sweet Potato and Apple Tzimmes
Fruit Compote   Sponge Cake
Teiglach   Fresh Fruit   Tea with Lemon

Honey is a symbol of sweetness, and throughout the season it appears again and again as a wish for "sweetness in the New Year." That is why slices of apples and bread are dipped in honey before meals. All honey dishes are traditional for these holidays, but Mehren Tzimmes is perhaps the top favorite.

Mehren Tzimmes with Knaidel
(CARROT PUDDING WITH DUMPLING)

1 lb. brisket or other fat beef
boiling water
2 teaspoons salt
3 sweet potatoes
6 *mehren* (carrots)
1 medium-sized onion

3 tablespoons honey
2 tablespoons flour
dash of ginger
pepper
knaidel (see recipe p. 36)

Cover the meat with boiling water; add salt; simmer for about one hour. Remove the meat to a 3-qt. casserole, saving liquid of course. Scrub and pare the sweet potatoes; then quarter and arrange about the meat. Add the carrots, scrubbed and scraped and cut into thick slices; and the onion, sliced. Add meat broth sufficient to cover contents of casserole; stir in honey. Cover and bake in a moderately hot oven (375° F.) until meat is tender—about 1 hour. Mix flour, ginger, and pepper with a little cool broth, to make a thin paste. Stir this into the liquid of the casserole dish until well mixed. Return to oven while mixing a *knaidel.* Clear a place in the center of the casserole dish to insert this *knaidel* (which is a large ball of dough). Then cover again and bake at reduced heat for an additional hour. Uncover and if necessary add a little extra broth. Continue baking until browned on top. Serves 6.

For Rosh Hashanah and Yom Kippur the *challah* are shaped into well-rounded loaves, symbolic of the hope for a well-rounded year to come. Some of these loaves are topped with a dove, some with strips of dough suggesting the rungs of a ladder. These decorations symbolize the hope that prayers may ascend on high.

Challah Decorations

To make the ladder for the top of the loaves, dough is twisted into two long strips that are well greased to prevent their sinking back into the loaf. These form two "uprights" on the top of the loaf, and crosswise pieces made from strips of dough form the ladder steps. When the loaf is baked, the ladder stands out quite distinctly.

To make the wings, top the round loaf with a small ball of dough to represent the bird and two smaller pieces to represent the wings. So that the bird and wings will keep their shape, brush these pieces with a little oil before attaching to the loaf.

Goldene Yoich, the rich chicken soup of the Sabbath table, prepared as well for all holidays, is served with the garnish of small round soup nuts. As with the roundness of the Sabbath loaves for Rosh Hashanah, their little round shapes are symbolic, too, of the wholeness and perfection so desired for the New Year. The word *mondlen,* meaning almonds, is an affectionate tag for these little "nuts of dough."

Mondlen
(SOUP NUTS)

2 eggs, slightly beaten	1 cup flour (about)
½ tablespoon vegetable oil	½ teaspoon baking powder
½ teaspoon salt	

Combine the eggs with the oil; add dry ingredients mixed together, stirring to make a soft dough just firm enough to handle. Divide into four parts; then, with floured hands, roll each into long strips about ¼ inch thick. Cut strips into small pieces with a floured knife. Bake in a well-greased shallow pan in a quick oven (375° F.) for 12 to 15 minutes, shaking occasionally to brown evenly. *Mondlen* may also be fried to a golden brown in deep hot fat if desired. Makes about 175.

It is traditional to eat well before the fast day of Yom Kippur. Among the delicacies that have been invented for this day are the famous *kreplach,* traditionally eaten also on Purim and Hoshanah Rabbah. These are tender little meat-filled pockets of noodle dough, served in the Goldene Yoich.

Kreplach
(NOODLE TURNOVERS FILLED WITH MEAT)

1 egg, slightly beaten	2 tablespoons chicken fat (or
¼ teaspoon salt	vegetable fat)
1 cup sifted flour (about)	1 egg, if desired
1 cup cooked beef, chopped	½ teaspoon salt
2 tablespoons onion, minced	

Make a noodle dough of the egg, salt and flour, mixing together in the order named, to make a stiff dough that can be handled with fair ease. Knead on a lightly floured board until smooth and elastic. Roll out to paper thinness; cut into 2- to 3-inch squares.

Mix together the remaining ingredients and use as filling.

Place a spoonful of filling on half of each square of dough, folding remaining half over top, point to point, to make triangles. Press edges together neatly and securely with a fork dipped in flour. Drop into boiling salted water, cover tightly and cook for 20 minutes. Serve in the soup for the holidays. For other occasions *kreplach* are often fried in hot fat after boiling and served as a side dish with meat. Makes 2 dozen. (For Cheese Kreplach, *see* page 173.)

In addition to *kreplach* and *mondlen, farfel* are also prepared for a garnish to accompany the Goldene Yoich. These are tiny noodle balls, symbolic of fertile grain that may bring forth a rich harvest in the New Year.

Farfel
(NOODLE BALLS THE SIZE OF BARLEY GRAINS)

1 egg   1 cup flour
¼ teaspoon salt

Mix the egg with salt and add the flour to make a stiff dough. Dry for about an hour. Place in a chopping bowl and chop into bits like tiny balls. Or grate the dough on a fine grater. Spread on a board to dry thoroughly. Store in jars. Makes about 1½ cups *farfel*. To cook, add to boiling salted water, or drop into boiling soup. Cover and cook for about 30 minutes. *Farfel* takes longer to cook than most noodles.

Honey, symbolic of the hope for a sweet New Year, is used generously in making quantities of cookies before the holidays.

Viennese Honey Cookies

3 eggs   4 cups flour
1¼ cups sugar   1 teaspoon cinnamon
¾ cup honey   ¼ teaspoon baking soda

Beat the eggs until very light. Add the sugar gradually, continuing to beat as you add. A rotary beater is best for this. Beat in the honey gradually. Add dry ingredients sifted together; mix well. Drop from teaspoon onto cooky sheet that has been lined with heavy wrapping paper but not greased. Bake in a slow oven (300° F.) for about 15 minutes. Do not brown. Remove to cooling rack while still warm. Makes 8 dozen.

Teiglach is a delightful honey confection and kitchens at this season are fragrant with the making of this gingery sweet.

Teiglach
(HONEY CONFECTION)

2 eggs, slightly beaten
2 tablespoons vegetable oil
1½ to 2 cups flour
½ teaspoon salt
½ teaspoon baking powder

1 cup honey
½ cup sugar
½ teaspoon ground ginger
1 cup nut meats, coarsely broken

Make a dough by mixing the eggs with the oil; then with flour, salt, and baking powder, adding sufficient flour to make a soft, but not sticky, dough that can be handled. Knead until smooth. Roll and twist dough into a rope formation about ⅓ inch thick. Cut into small pieces about ⅓ inch in length. These pieces can either be baked in honey or boiled in honey, as the housewife prefers.

To bake teiglach in honey: Bring the honey, sugar, and ginger to a gentle boil, stirring constantly to prevent burning. When sugar is melted, pour syrup into a shallow baking pan; arrange the pieces of dough in this. Bake in a moderate oven (350° F.) until dough is well puffed and just beginning to brown. Do not open oven door for 20 minutes, for, like dumplings, *teiglach* must cook "covered" or they will fall. When dough begins to brown (after the 20 minutes of cooking), add nuts. Stir frequently with a wooden spoon to separate pieces. Cook until golden brown and until the *teiglach* sound hollow when stirred with a spoon. At this point have ready a board wet with cold water. Pour contents of the baking pan on this; with wet hands mold the *teiglach* into a cake about 8 inches square and 2 inches deep. Cut into 2-inch strips; then cut each strip diagonally at 2-inch intervals.

To boil teiglach in honey: Bake little pieces of dough in a well-greased shallow pan in a quick oven (375° F.) for about 10 minutes—until light brown. Shake the pan occasionally to brown evenly and to keep balls separated. Bring the honey, sugar, and ginger to boiling; boil gently for five minutes. Add the pieces of dough and nuts. Stir gently over low heat, using a wooden spoon, until mixture is a deep golden brown. Pour out on board wet with cold water; and shape as for the baked confection.

Makes 3 to 4 dozen. Stores indefinitely.

Traditional Honey Leckach

(HONEY CAKE)

1¾ cups dark honey	dash of salt
1 cup coffee, double strength	1 teaspoon baking soda
4 eggs	2 teaspoons baking powder
2 tablespoons vegetable oil	1 teaspoon allspice
1 cup sugar	1 teaspoon cinnamon
3½ cups flour	

Bring the honey gently to boiling; cool, then add the coffee. Beat the eggs until light and lemon colored, then add the oil gradually, beating well to blend; beat in the sugar gradually. Sift together the dry ingredients; then add them to the egg mixture alternately with the honey and coffee, about a third of each at a time. Mix well. Pour smooth batter into a greased 9½″ x 5½″ x 3″ loaf pan. Bake in a moderate oven (300° F. to 325° F.) for about 1 hour. Invert to cool in pan. Remove and store. This cake keeps well.

In the olden days New Year's greetings and gifts were always confections and cakes. These were generally made at home with great care. More recently the customs of exchanging New Year's cards and of sending flowers have been adopted. However, the sending of confections and cake is such a delightful custom that American Jewish housewives are reviving it. Honey *leckach*, honey cookies, and fruit cakes are among the favorite gifts exchanged at this time. Fruit Cakes are especially appropriate at this season because they can be inscribed with greetings. And then, too, they can be made weeks, even months, before the holiday season.

To decorate both fruit cakes and honey *leckach* loaves, prepare a frosting by mixing confectioners' sugar with water or fruit

juice to make a mixture that can be spread. Then with a toothpick dip into the frosting and inscribe the cake with: *"L'shana
tova tikatevu"*—"May you be inscribed for a good year."

L'shana Tova Fruit Cake
(NEW YEAR'S FRUIT CAKE)

3 cups flour
½ teaspoon baking soda
½ teaspoon salt
1 teaspoon cinnamon
¼ teaspoon cloves
1 cup vegetable fat
1 cup brown sugar
4 eggs

½ cup each, candied cherries, citron, orange and lemon peel, all finely sliced
1 cup seedless raisins
1 cup currants, washed and dried
½ cup almonds, blanched and shredded
¼ cup plum or currant jelly
½ cup honey

Sift together the flour, baking soda, salt, and spices. Cream the
fat; add sugar gradually, beating until very light and fluffy. Add
the eggs, one at a time; beat well. Add the fruit, and nuts which
have been mixed with a little flour; mix well. Add the jelly and
honey; mix well. Add flour mixture about a third at a time,
mixing well after each addition. Bake in well-greased, paper-
lined cake pans or pound coffee tins, filling each about ⅔ full of
batter. To determine baking time, weigh the filled pan. Bake in
a slow oven (250° F.), allowing an hour for the first pound of
batter, plus ¼ of an hour for "drying out"; add ¾ of an hour for
each additional pound of batter in baking pan. Makes 5 pounds
of cake.

Sukkoth

A seven-day festival (or, with Shemini Atzereth and Simchath Torah, a nine-day festival) beginning on the 15th of Tishri—usually in late September or early October.

The Festival of Sukkoth, known also as the Festival of the Booths or the Festival of the Tabernacles, is a time for living in the *sukkah,* a booth specially built outside the house, in the garden, or even on a roof top. It is the ambition of every family to have a *sukkah* of its own. Since this is not always possible, those who do have one share it with their neighbors and friends.

The *sukkah* is a charming little booth, once it is decorated, for the latticed frame is lightly covered with green boughs and vines, hung with autumn leaves and colorful fruits and vegetables. The family and friends gather in it each day for the first seven days of the festival, to feast and chat, to sing and pray.

In such a setting as this is celebrated the Festival of the Ingathering, the thanksgiving festival of the Jews. This is still another name for the Festival of Sukkoth, which is now, as in olden days, a celebration of the bounty of the harvest. For it is written: "When ye have gathered in the fruits of the land, ye shall keep the feast of the Lord seven days." This early festival of thanksgiving was succeeded by similar holi-

days in later centuries, among them the American Thanksgiving Day.

In the days when the Temple in Jerusalem was the scene of many important festivals, this Feast of the Ingathering was one of the three great pilgrim festivals of the year. Sukkoth came at the season of the year when all harvest work had been completed. Grapes had been gathered and the wine was then a-making. Olives had been pressed for oil, and fruits were drying for the winter ahead. Everyone was free to celebrate. All were filled with a spirit of thanksgiving for the richness of the harvest, and felt the need to turn to God. Greater numbers journeyed to the Holy City at this time than at any other time of the year.

For this festival Jerusalem was garlanded with fruits and flowers, green with palm leaves, olive branches and fragrant willow. Everywhere, too, in courtyards, gardens, vacant lots, booths had been built that all might feast and celebrate in the open, under the stars.

The magnificent ceremony held at the Temple in Jerusalem on the first night of Sukkoth is described in the Talmud. For this occasion the outer court was brilliantly lighted with four gold lamps placed high on pedestals. Each bore one hundred and twenty "lugs" of oil, and the "illumination, like a sea of fire, lit up every corner of the Holy City." Within the courts of the Temple, men paraded with torches, singing hymns and dancing, and the festivities continued until dawn. This night was followed by a week of celebrations such as this.

From these ancient customs derive the ceremonies and symbols of Sukkoth as it is observed today. The building of booths by each family or by groups of families helps to recapture the spirit of those early harvest celebrations in Jerusalem. It also serves to recall days when the Palestinian farmers lived in hillside huts as they guarded their flocks and

cultivated their crops, and days, too, when the Jews wandered in the desert, living in temporary shelters. It brings to mind again also the teachings of Jewish leaders who warn of the frailty of material structures as against the abiding shelter of the strength of God.

The building of the *sukkah* often begins, as has long been the custom, on the night after the close of Yom Kippur. The father of the family hammers the first uprights in place, and then the rest join in the work, as the latticed shelter begins to take shape. Trips are made to the countryside to gather pine branches for roof and sides, as well as corn stalks and fruit and sturdy vegetables. The youth of the family like to take over the decorating, festooning roof and sides with growing things they have gathered—with grapes, purple, red, and green; with apples, golden pears, green and red peppers, gourds, pumpkins, even feathery heads of cane as well as corn.

The rules for decorating the *sukkah* are few but important. The roof must be only lightly covered with greens so that the light of the stars and moon can filter through. A table and benches must be provided, for even if the *sukkah* should be very small, too small to permit the family to be seated for meals, there must still be a place for the mother to light the festival candles just before sundown, and for the chanting of the *Kiddush* (the prayer of sanctification of the holiday) over the wine.

It is not only families who build a *sukkah*. Communities too take a hand in building theirs, which are then used by all the members. Some of the most beautiful are built by synagogues and can be seen in modern cities all over the world. Sometimes Hebrew schools make a project of building a *sukkah*. In addition to all this, many a family who does not have its own outdoors will make an interesting family project of building a miniature *sukkah*. This will of course delight the children who participate, and the housewife who will use it as a decoration for the center of the Sukkoth dinner table.

Of all the ceremonies that take place, perhaps the most impressive is one that is of very ancient origin. It is the blessing that is recited over the *lulov* and *ethrog*. The *lulov* is a kind of bouquet made with branches of willow, strands of green myrtle, and the slender leaves of palm, bound together; the *ethrog* is the fragrant yellow fruit of the citron. These are the four plants mentioned in the Bible: "And ye shall take you on the first day the fruit of goodly trees, branches of palm-trees, and boughs of thick trees, and willows of the brook, and ye shall rejoice before the Lord your God seven days." The *lulov* and the *ethrog* are symbols of the fruitfulness of the earth. Each morning during the festival of Sukkoth each member of the family and friends in turn holds these two symbols in his hands to recite the benediction over each.

It is a great aspiration of many to own a *lulov* and *ethrog*. Those who can afford them share with their neighbors and friends. Others may engage the *shamash*, the sexton of the synagogue, to bring them from the synagogue each morning to their homes for the recital of the benediction.

In the modern synagogue there are processions during the festival of Sukkoth that recall those earlier ones in the Temple in Jerusalem. During the seven days of the holiday the processions within the synagogue are led by the cantor. He is followed by the rabbi and the congregation, chanting hosannahs to traditional melodies. As in former times, each person in the procession carries a *lulov* and *ethrog*.

The Reform Jews have introduced a harvest ceremony in which the children are given their special colorful role to play. They take part in the procession in the synagogue in groups, each carrying a certain fruit or vegetable. Often the groups represent the Seven Fruits of ancient Palestine.

As on all holidays, within the home the mother ushers in

the festival with the lighting of the candles. The candles are lighted on the first two nights in the *sukkah,* where the family gathers about the table after the men of the household return from synagogue. The father recites *Kiddush* over the wine and then grace over the bread, before the family partakes of the Thanksgiving Sukkoth Dinner.

Thanksgiving Sukkoth Dinner

Tiny Holishkes or Wine Chopped Herring   Kichel
Goldene Yoich with Noodles
Roast Turkey   Stuffing   Helzel   Peas and Onions
Carrot, Apple, Sweet Potato Tzimmes
New Dill Pickles   Beet Relish   Cranberry Compote
Green Salad Bowl
Strudel   Tea with Lemon   Wine
Nuts   Candy   Fresh Fruits

Sukkoth is really a thanksgiving holiday, and we find that in the United States the dinner is a combination of American Thanksgiving Day dishes and Jewish holiday dishes. This shows again the age-old pattern in which the Jews adopt many of the finest dishes of the lands in which they make their homes.

Hoshanah Rabbah, the seventh day of the holiday week, is associated with the "beating of the willows." On this day the procession in the synagogue winds around the Torah Scrolls, not once, as in the previous six days, but seven times; and the chanting of the prayers is deeply earnest.

After the procession each worshipper takes a sheaf of seven willow twigs, known as the *Hoshanah,* and these are beaten vigorously against the floor to remove all leaves. There are many interpretations of this ceremony. It is frequently repeated that it symbolizes the renewal of life: in the falling of the leaves there is promise of the new young growth in the spring.

At home, after the service, there is a wonderful meal awaiting the family. The *pièce de résistance* of the evening is *kreplach*, little pockets of noodle dough stuffed with most savory fillings. For reasons unknown, they are traditional for Purim and Yom Kippur as well as for Hoshanah Rabbah, and they are always received with enthusiasm.

The eighth day of Sukkoth, Shemini Atzereth, is a day of assembly and prayer, and some of the special prayers on this day are those for rain. All over the world Jews still observe the old custom of including a prayer for rain for Israel. Several years ago Jewish farmers in Poland assembled on Shemini Atzereth. Their prayer had a two-fold purpose: rain for Israel and rain that mud might bog down the approaching armies of Hitler.

The ninth day of Sukkoth is Simchath Torah, the day of rejoicing in the Torah (the Five Books of the Law of Moses, the Pentateuch). During the year it is read in its entirety in the synagogue. All through the year the reading progresses steadily to this day, when it is completed and begun again. This joyous accomplishment is celebrated all day and night.

At the synagogue refreshments are served during the long morning service. There is wine and *kichel* and chopped herring for the grown-ups, cakes and nuts and fruits for the children. Processions on this day are a gala affair. Young girls and matrons come forward to kiss the Scrolls. Children taking part in the procession bear flags with apples and beets impaled on top, each one hollowed out to hold a lighted candle. Some children are carried on the shoulders of their fathers. It is a long day and an exhilarating one.

Simchath Torah brings the Sukkoth holiday to a happy close. There is visiting from house to house, where one may be sure to find the choicest refreshments the house affords. The great finale of the feast comes at night, after the close of the holiday. Then is served the finest dinner of the nine-day period.

Simchath Torah Dinner

Gribenes   Chopped Eggplant
Chopped Eggs and Onions   Zemmel
Gefillte Fish Balls   Horse-radish   Dill Pickles
Goldene Yoich with Mondlen and Kasha
Roast Goose   Stuffing   Helzel   Roast Potatoes
Rutabaga Tzimmes   Apple Sauce   Beets   Cranberries
Baclava   Chestnut Preserves   Nuts   Fruit Balls   Fruit
Sponge Cake   Wine   Tea with Lemon

When the *challah* is baked for Sukkoth, it bears symbols
atop each loaf as for Rosh Hashanah and Yom Kippur. The
favorite is the ladder, signifying the hope that prayers and
supplications of the family may ascend swiftly on high. During the Festival of Sukkoth, as on Rosh Hashanah, the *challah*
is dipped in honey to celebrate the New Year that is still
young and sweet.

Quite in keeping with the harvest time are stuffed vine
leaves, tracing their origin to the vineyards of the hillsides
of Palestine, and stuffed cabbage leaves, the modern adapta-
tion of this dish. Seasoned meat, wrapped in sturdy grape
leaves, is cooked slowly to a winey flavor. In olden days the
housewife would cook it slowly in hot ashes. Jews in every
country make and serve stuffed leaves, although the name
for this type of dish varies from place to place. There are
galuptze from Russia, *holishkes* from Eastern Europe, *sarmali*
from Roumania, and *dolmas* from Armenia.

Holishkes

(VINE OR CABBAGE LEAVES, STUFFED WITH MEAT)

12 large leaves of cabbage or
  grape
1 lb. freshly ground beef
1 medium-sized onion, minced
1 teaspoon salt
pepper
½ cup cooked rice

1 egg, slightly beaten
1 cup tomato juice
2 tablespoons vinegar
3 tablespoons vegetable oil
¼ cup brown sugar
1 bay leaf

Wash the leaves; steam in a colander over boiling water for
5 to 10 minutes—until they are pliant enough to roll. Remove
from heat. Mix the meat, onion, salt, pepper, rice, and egg. Trim
hard center of leaf, if necessary; then place a spoonful of the
meat filling on the center of the leaf. Fold sides up over the filling, tucking in the edges (as for *blintzes*, see page 172), or fasten
with toothpick. Repeat until all leaves are filled. Place in a
greased 2-qt. baking dish. Mix and pour over top, tomato juice,
vinegar and oil, with salt to taste. Sprinkle the brown sugar over
top, and add bay leaf. Bake covered in a moderate oven (350°
F.) for 45 minutes, removing cover a little before the end of baking to brown top. Additional liquid may be added during baking,
if needed. Serves 4 to 6.

In an earlier day a specialty for holidays, especially for
Sukkoth, was Gebrutenah Euter, so delicate and so much appreciated that it was always served with a glass of the finest
wine to complement its flavor.

Gebrutenah Euter
(ROASTED BEEF UDDER)

1 beef *euter* (udder)   3 tablespoons poultry fat
salt and pepper   (or vegetable fat)
4 or 5 onions, thinly sliced

Kasher udder (*see* p. 183); cut into 2½-inch cubes. Spread
sliced onions over bottom of a large roasting pan; add salt and
pepper, and cover with the meat. Season with salt and pepper,
and dot with fat. Cover and roast slowly in a moderate oven
(350° F.) for about 3 hours—until tender. Stir from time to time,
so that it will cook and brown evenly. If the dish seems dry, add
a very little water, as necessary. Serves 6 to 8.

Tzimmes, beloved of the Sabbath, are sure to be enjoyed
also on many holidays. The Sukkoth *tzimmes* are made with
vegetables and fruits and so are most appropriate for a
harvest festival.

Carrot, Sweet Potato and Apple Tzimmes

3 carrots, sliced
4 sweet potatoes, sliced
3 tart apples, sliced
½ cup brown sugar

salt and pepper
3 tablespoons chicken fat (or vegetable fat)
1 cup water

Cook the carrots and sweet potatoes until tender. Drain. Pare, quarter, core, and slice the apples but not too thin. Alternate these in layers in a 2½-qt. baking dish; season each with brown sugar, salt and pepper, and fat. Add water. Cover; bake in a moderate oven (350° F.) for 30 minutes, or until apples are tender. Remove cover and continue baking until top is a golden brown. Serve hot. Serves 6.

Rutabaga Tzimmes

1 lb. brisket or other fat meat
boiling water
1 tablespoon chicken fat (or vegetable fat)
2 lbs. rutabaga (yellow turnips), cubed

2 onions, sliced
½ cup honey or brown sugar
dash of nutmeg
2 tablespoons flour
salt and pepper

Brown the meat in the fat. Add water to almost cover. Season with salt and pepper; cover tightly and cook gently for about 1 hour. Turn into a 3-qt. baking dish. Add the cubed rutabaga; spread sliced onions over top. Cover with the honey or brown sugar, and sprinkle with nutmeg (with sparing hand). Mix the flour with a little cold water to make a paste and stir into the liquid. Cover; cook on top of stove or bake until tender. Serves 5.

Cooking with wine is in keeping with the harvest time. A favorite dish prepared with wine is Baked Tongue in Wine Sauce.

Baked Tongue in Wine Sauce

1 beef tongue, smoked or pickled
boiling water
4 whole cloves
1 bay leaf
1 onion, minced

½ tablespoon potato starch or cornstarch
1 cup broth from tongue
1 tablespoon chicken fat (or vegetable fat)
½ cup red wine

Wash the tongue well. If a smoked tongue is used and found salty (taste broth after 5 minutes of cooking), pour off the water and add fresh water. If a pickled tongue is used, soak in water overnight. Drain. To cook smoked or pickled tongue, cover with water in a deep pot; add cloves, bay leaf, onion, and salt to taste if necessary. Cover and simmer for 3 to 4 hours—until tender. (When tender the little bones in the root will pull out easily and the tip of tongue will feel tender when pressed.) Cool the tongue in the broth and then reserve about 1 cup for sauce. Remove skin; trim off the root end of the tongue. Serve sliced, hot or cold. For interesting serving, cut slices diagonally across the tongue, but not all the way through. Place this whole sliced tongue in a shallow baking pan or dish. Make a sauce by mixing the cornstarch or potato starch with a little cold water. Then add to the broth. Add the fat. Cook until clear, stirring to prevent lumping. Add wine. Pour over meat. Bake in a moderate oven (350° F.) for ¾ of an hour. Serves 6.

Strudel is traditional for Sukkoth, possibly because of its lavish use of fruits and even vegetables. *Strudel* making is an art, that may have originated in Austria, but it was brought to its perfection by Hungarian and Roumanian housewives.

Experts are most disarming, not to say misleading, when they assure the novice that *strudel* is easy to make. "The secret," they say, "if there is a secret, lies in handling the dough with such care that not a single tear is made as it is stretched thinner, and thinner, and thinner."

However, those who wish to encourage the novice are likely to give this more realistic advice: "What matter if you patch a tear or two now! By the time you are married you will be so expert that your husband will never discover that you were once a novice!"

There are many in America, especially among the older generation, who still know the art. It may be summed up by the answer given to an aspiring cook when she asked how to make *strudel*. "How big is your table?" was the helpful reply.

Strudel Dough #1

(OLD-FASHIONED, PAPER-THIN DOUGH FOR FILLINGS)

2½ cups flour   ½ cup lukewarm water
¼ teaspoon salt   vegetable oil
1 egg

Sift the flour and salt into a bowl and make a well in the center for adding the egg and the lukewarm water. Mix quickly with a fork to make a dough. Place on a board and knead until smooth and elastic, and until the dough no longer sticks to board. Cover, on the board, with a hot bowl. Let stand for 30 minutes. In the meanwhile, cover a large table surface with a cloth and rub flour into its texture. Place dough in the center of the cloth and, using a rolling pin, begin to roll out to all sides. Roll as thin as possible. Brush surface with oil. Now begins the stretching: Place palms of hands down, under dough, and pull toward yourself, gently stretching small areas at a time, taking great care not to tear the fabric. Continue right around the arc of the dough, right around all sides of the table. Thicker dough over-hanging the edge of table may be cut away (to be used for *farfel* (see recipe page 59).

To fill, brush with oil and spread filling (see recipes pages 74 to 75) in rows 1½ to 2 inches apart. Sprinkle filling with oil, spices, and sugar. Fold edge of dough over one strip of the filling, then lift the cloth slowly with both hands to start a roll-ing motion of the dough to enclose the filling in many layers of the dough. Trim off ends. Cut in diagonal pieces, or cut the length of a long shallow pan. Grease pan well. Brush *strudel* with oil. Bake in a moderate oven (350° F.) for about 45 minutes —until crisp and brown—basting occasionally with oil. Remove from pan to cool; sprinkle with confectioners' sugar. Makes 3 to 4 dozen pieces.

A rolled *strudel* dough, made according to a modern recipe, is of course easier, though many think, not so choice. In this recipe no stretching is done; the dough is merely rolled to paper thinness.

Strudel Dough #2
(A MODERN ROLLED-OUT DOUGH)

2½ cups flour
½ teaspoon baking powder
¼ teaspoon salt

1 egg
4 tablespoons vegetable oil
1 cup cold water (about)

Sift together the dry ingredients, and mix in a large bowl, making a well in center, into which put the egg and the oil. Mix into a dough, using a fork, working from the center out and adding cold water as needed to make a dough that is firm enough to handle but one that does not stick to the board. Turn out on floured board and knead until smooth and elastic. This takes from 3 to 5 minutes. Cover dough on board with a hot bowl and let stand for about 30 minutes. Roll out from center to edges on a large, well-floured table surface, to paper thinness. Place filling on the dough and proceed as for Strudel Dough #1.

Filling for Apple Strudel

6 cups chopped apples
1 lemon, juice and grated rind
½ cup raisins, chopped
½ cup currants

1½ cups sugar
½ teaspoon cinnamon
½ cup nuts, chopped

Combine all the ingredients, mixing well. Use as directed in recipes for Strudel Dough #1 or #2.

To vary, dried fruits may be substituted for apples.

Mohn Strudel
(POPPY SEED STRUDEL)

See the filling recipe on page 114. Use as directed in recipes for Strudel Dough #1 or #2.

Filling for Cherry Strudel

8 cups sour cherries, pitted
½ cup cake or cracker crumbs
2 cups sugar

½ teaspoon cinnamon
dash of salt
1 cup nuts, coarsely chopped

Combine the ingredients in the order named. Use with Strudel Dough #1 or #2.

Filling for Cabbage Strudel

Plain Filling:

4 cups cabbage, chopped   1 onion, chopped
¼ cup vegetable fat

Sweet Filling: Add to Plain Filling

1 cup raisins, chopped   1 teaspoon cinnamon
1 cup sugar   ½ cup chopped nuts

Mix the ingredients well for either plain or sweet filling and use with Strudel Dough #1 or #2.

Mondelbrot

(SWEET ALMOND SLICES)

3 eggs   3 cups sifted flour
1 cup sugar   ¼ teaspoon salt
½ cup vegetable oil   4 teaspoons baking powder
½ teaspoon almond flavoring   1 cup almonds, blanched and
½ teaspoon vanilla   slivered
2 tablespoons orange juice

Beat the eggs until thick and very light. Add the sugar gradually, beating as you add. Add the oil slowly, beating well. Add the flavorings. Sift the dry ingredients together; mix with nuts. Add to egg mixture, about a third at a time, mixing well. Knead on a floured board for 10 to 12 turns. Divide the dough into several pieces and with the hand roll each piece into strips about 3 inches wide, 1 inch thick, and about 10 inches long or the length of the baking pan. Place on a shallow baking pan that has been greased and floured, and bake in a moderate oven (350° F.) for 35 to 45 minutes—to a golden brown. Remove at once to bread board; cut into ½-inch slices while still warm. Return to oven to brown delicately. Makes about 5 dozen.

Lebkuchen
(NUT AND FRUIT CAKE)

4 eggs, well beaten
2 cups brown sugar
2 cups flour
1½ teaspoons baking powder
½ teaspoon salt
½ cup nut meats, chopped

¼ cup citron, cut fine
1 teaspoon cinnamon
¼ teaspoon allspice
orange juice or water
3 tablespoons confectioners'
   sugar

Add the sugar gradually to the well-beaten eggs, continuing to beat until sugar and eggs are well blended. Sift the dry ingredients together and mix with the nuts, finely chopped citron, and spices. Add to the eggs and mix well. Add enough water or orange juice to make a dough that can be spread. Now turn into a greased shallow pan to about ½-inch thickness. Bake in a moderate oven (350° F.) for about 30 minutes—until golden brown. Mix confectioners' sugar with water to make an icing that will spread; cover top of the *lebkuchen* while still warm. Cut in strips or squares. Makes about 4 dozen.

Hazenbluzen got their very descriptive name from the children of many generations who used to beg for them "hot from the kettle," and would then have to "blow-hot—*hazen-bluzen*" in a hurry to protect their fingers from burning.

Hazenbluzen
("BLOW-HOT" WAFERS)

2 eggs, well beaten
1¼ cups flour
¼ teaspoon salt

confectioners' sugar
cinnamon

Mix the eggs, flour, and salt to a soft dough. Roll ¼ inch thick on a floured board; cut into 2-inch squares. Make a slit in the center of each square and pull a corner of the dough through the slit. Fry in deep hot fat, a few at a time. Drain on absorbent paper; dust with mixture of confectioners' sugar and cinnamon. Makes about 2 dozen.

For fancy shapes, cut dough with fancy cutters or make paper patterns and follow outlines with a sharp knife.

For flower shapes, lovely enough for any party, cut into petal shapes and put together in pairs, pressing centers together firmly and spreading the outer edges. Dry slightly before dropping into the hot fat. Fry as for the plain shapes. Tip the edges of petals with a frosting such as the one for Lebkuchen (*see* page 76).

Hoshanah Rabbah, the seventh day of the Sukkoth season, is a time for feasting on *kreplach* (*see* page 58).

There is a wonderful story that pays tribute to this delicious food. It seems that once on the night of Hoshanah Rabbah a very learned man had as his guest the son of a highly respected man whom he wished to honor. A large platter of *kreplach* was served, and the young man gave it his undivided attention. He ate one *krepel* to recall God above. The next two were to honor Moses and Aaron. Three more were consumed, for the Patriarchs. Four followed in quick succession, for the Mothers of Israel. No less than twelve were disappearing for the twelve tribes of Israel when the alarmed host called to his wife, "Leah! Leah! Come quickly! We may have to feed our guest six hundred thousand *kreplach* for the Jews who fled from Egypt!"

A favorite confection for the holidays that originated in the Middle East is the sweet, rich Baclava.

Baclava
(NUT- AND HONEY-FILLED PASTRY)

strudel dough #1 or #2 (*see* pages 73 and 74)	½ cup vegetable oil
1 cup slivered almonds	1 teaspoon cinnamon
1 cup coconut	½ teaspoon nutmeg
½ cup brown sugar, firmly packed to measure	1 cup syrup or honey

Prepare *strudel* dough. Baclava is made of 4 or 5 layers of *strudel* dough with a filling between the layers. Cut the dough to fit the pan in which it will be baked; fit one layer into the pan. Sprinkle with nuts, coconut, sugar, oil, and spices. Cover with the second layer of dough; add filling. Continue until all layers are in place, ending with dough on top. Cut through all layers with a sharp knife to mark into diamonds or squares. Trickle a thick syrup or honey over the top, slowly so that it may be absorbed. Bake in a moderately slow oven (325° F.) for 50 to 60 minutes. Makes about 2 dozen pieces.

To make syrup, simmer together to rich syrup, 1 cup sugar, 1 cup water, and grated rind of 1 lemon and 1 orange.

Chanukah

An eight-day festival beginning on the 25th of Kislev—usually in late December.

Chanukah, the Festival of Lights, comes at a most welcome time of the year. It is deep winter and everyone has begun to yearn for a celebration. It has been a long time since Simchath Torah, which was the last holiday. The home comes to life with great excitement as the holiday approaches. Children live for weeks in pleasant anticipation of the eight days of feasting and fun that lie ahead, and they look forward especially to the gifts that will be exchanged.

During the festival Jewish homes glow with the light of Chanukah candles. The Menorah, an eight-branched candlestick, is used, and the candles are lighted in a very special way. On the first night one candle is lighted, and on each succeeding night, an additional candle. Finally, on the eighth and last night of the holiday, the whole Menorah is aglow. A place is provided on it for the *shamash*, the "lighter" that is used to light the candles.

The ceremony of the lighting of the candles commemorates one of the most eventful periods of Jewish history. It goes back some two thousand years, to 165 B.C.E. At that time all that remained of the Kingdom of Judah was under the rule of Antiochus Epiphanes, King of Syria, who demanded that all his subjects worship the Greek gods and adopt the Greek way of life. This the Jews refused to do. Judas Maccabeus, a devout Jewish leader, with the help of his four brothers, led the Jews in a victorious struggle against their Syrian oppressors. Their victory made it possible for the Jews to worship again in their Temple in Jerusalem, and it eventually led to the re-establishment of the Kingdom of Judah. It was, in fact, the first great victory for religious freedom in the world.

When Jerusalem was again theirs, the first concern of the Jews was to cleanse their beloved Temple of all traces of idolatrous worship. The great Menorah was returned to its place in the court, and there was again a place for the fresh shewbread on the altar of the Temple. When the people turned to relight the Perpetual Light, they found that all but one cruse of holy oil had been defiled. This was only enough oil for one day, but when it was lighted, a miracle occurred: the oil burned for the full eight days required to replenish the supply.

To commemorate this miracle of the lights, Judas Maccabeus proclaimed an eight-day festival, to be observed yearly and to be called Chanukah, meaning dedication. It was to be an occasion for songs and psalms and great rejoicing. Over the years certain customs and ceremonies have become traditional in its observance, and all have continued to center about the Chanukah lights.

As Jews came to make their homes in many parts of the world, Chanukah celebrations have in various places taken on added local color. In the Venice of a century ago, candles burned brightly in doorways and windows on every night of the festival, and the waters of the canal were aglow with reflected light.

Today, as in the past, the highlight of the Chanukah festival is the lighting of the candles each day as the first stars appear in the sky. Evenings are given over to family games and simple pleasures in the home. After dinner the table is cleared for these games. The younger children are sure to have *dreidels,* four-winged symbolic tops that offer endless excitement as they are spun first by one, then another. Most of these tops bear the four Hebrew letters: N for *nun,* G for *gimel,* H for *hei,* and Sh for *shin.* Together, like an acrostic, they stand for "A great miracle happened there." Endless combinations are made as the top spins. *Dreidels* have become so much a part of this holiday that they are now made also of candy and sold as holiday confection gifts.

The older children like to test their intellectual skills at Chanukah time in a very old game that is known as *katowes.* This is a series of puzzles and riddles, which must be answered in numbers totaling forty-four, the total number of candles that are burned through the holiday period. Since this may be a riddle for you, to arrive at 44 count the number of candles lighted each day and add one for the *shamash* each day.

Grownups play checkers and chess, read, listen to music, have friends drop in, and pass the time pleasantly. All in all, these are mellow nights, and songs both old and new are sung during the evening. *"Ma'oz Tzur"* (Rock of Ages) is a great favorite. Started first by one in a group and then by another, it is repeated many times through the festive week.

The exchanging of gifts is greatly anticipated by the children. In many homes parents plan to give the children a gift every night during this holiday. No wonder the children look forward for months to the delightful surprises in store for them at this time.

The custom of gift giving derives from the old tradition whereby parents gave the children *Chanukah gelt* (money) as a gift for their *cheder* teacher (Hebrew school teacher). This custom still prevails although part of this money may be reserved in some homes for the children's own purchase of gifts.

Chanukah festivities are also planned today at community

centers, schools, synagogues, and temples. These include concerts and plays, parties and many other kinds of entertainment. The children in Southern Arabia plan their own parties with huge celebrations out of doors. To these each carries his own refreshments, and all sit about the Chanukah lights eating roasted corn and carrots, dried fruit and grape juice. There is much singing and dancing, and the evening ends with a rollicking procession that winds through the town, growing longer and longer as group after group joins in.

Chanukah is a season for delightful dishes, feasting and merrymaking, so much so that we find these words in the Code of Rabbinical Judaism:

> "Do not fast during Chanukah,
> Not on the day preceding
> Nor yet on the day following.
> Eat and be merry.
> Linger over your viands,
> Punctuate your meals with jest and song,
> Relate miracles."

It is an old custom to have a festival dinner on the Night of the Fifth Candle, bringing scattered members of the family together at that time. Although many families still have this dinner party on this night, some may plan to have it on another night of the holiday week that may be more convenient for all to assemble. The menu, however, never departs from Fifth Candle traditions.

Fifth Candle Dinner

Roumanian Garlic Eggplant   Gribenes on Crackers
Radishes   Celery   Dill Pickles
Mushroom Barley Soup
Roast Duck   Fruit Stuffing   String Beans
Potato Kugel or Potato Latkes
Armenian Fruit Compote   Symbol Cookies   Tea

Visitors from Israel have delighted their New York friends with parties such as they might give in their own homes during Chanukah. At one such party *bronfen* (brandy) was served with symbol cookies throughout the evening, followed by a late supper of

Potato Latkes and Pineapple Fritters
Fruit Salad with Cream Cheese Balls
Pots of Tea and Coffee

The Sabbath during the week of Chanukah is no exception to the rule that the finest dishes are reserved for the Sabbath. For this occasion roast goose is the traditional favorite—for mixed reasons. The family greets roast goose as a rare treat, and the mother sees it as providing an opportunity to begin collecting goose fat for Passover cooking.

Chanukah Sabbath Dinner
Chopped Liver   Black Radishes
Goldene Yoich with Noodles
Roast Goose   Potato Stuffing   Apple Sauce
Mehren Tzimmes
Chestnut Preserves   Sponge Cake   Tea

Traditional Chanukah dishes derive from legend and custom, not from law and ritual as do those of Passover and other religious holidays. The dairy dishes have their origin in a legend about Judith, the courageous daughter of the Maccabees. It is related that she entertained the leader of the enemy, feeding him great quantities of cheese to make him thirsty. This caused him to drink excessive amounts of wine and made his capture possible. To this day dairy dishes are eaten to commemorate her bravery.

Among the most famous of these traditional dairy dishes are cheese *latkes,* and many legends have grown up about them. It is told that in years gone by Sephardic women of Spain and Portugal would get together on the last night of the festival for a party of their own. They would enjoy music and laughter and amusing stories, and great quantities of cheese *latkes* were served throughout the evening. Instead of being prepared with the familiar spread of jam or syrup, they were sprinkled with olive oil, symbolic of the ancient miracle.

Judith's Cheese Latkes
(CHEESE PANCAKES)

3 eggs, well beaten   1 cup flour
1 cup milk   1 teaspoon baking powder
1 cup dry pot cheese ½ teaspoon salt

To the beaten eggs, add milk and cheese. Sift the dry ingredients together and stir into the eggs. Blend to smoothness. Drop by spoonfuls into hot fat in a frying pan. Cook to delicate brown on both sides. Serve with syrup or jam. Serves 4 or 5.

In some European countries where Jewish families settled, it was difficult to obtain cottage cheese in wintertime. Devoted as they might be to *latkes* made with cottage cheese, they had no choice but to find a worthy substitute for this ingredient. Their success may be judged by the present-day popularity of potato *latkes*. These are an inspired use of the potato, one of the most commonly used vegetables in those parts. Potato *latkes* now enjoy international fame. They are unquestionably the most popular of Chanukah dishes.

Potato Latkes
(POTATO PANCAKES)

6 medium-sized potatoes 3 tablespoons flour, matza
1 small onion   meal, or bread crumbs
1 teaspoon salt   ½ teaspoon baking powder
1 egg

Wash, pare, and grate raw potatoes. Strain but not too dry, and use juice for soup or sauce. If juice is retained, a little more flour will be needed for thickening. Grate and add the onion; add salt and the egg. Beat well. Mix remaining ingredients and beat into potatoes; mix well. Drop by spoonfuls into hot fat that is deep enough to almost cover the cake. Brown on both sides. Drain on absorbent paper. Serve with applesauce, if desired. Serves 4 or 5.

Every country, and often, so it would seem, every family, has its own favorite *latkes*. Our Polish butcher who comes from Schochov tells us that his mother taught him this rhyme when he was a boy.

> "If latkes you would make,
> Salt and eggs and flour take.
> Eat with jest and song and rhyme
> At the festive Chanukah time."

His mother's *ratzelach,* which are really *latkes,* are still so vivid in his mind that he cannot think of Chanukah without remembering them. Here is her recipe as he told it to us, explaining that he had noted the ingredients she used while he helped make them by beating the eggs.

Ratzelach from Poland
(PANCAKES FROM POLAND)

1 cup flour
½ teaspoon salt
1 cup milk

3 eggs, well beaten
confectioners' sugar

Sift together the flour and salt; make a well in the center and pour in the milk, stirring, from center out, to form a smooth batter. Add eggs and enclose with a folding motion. This should be a very thin batter. Melt a very little fat in a medium-sized frying pan, greasing the surface well. When hot, pour in just enough batter to cover the bottom of the pan, tilting it from side to side to spread the batter to the edges. Brown first on one side and then on the other. Stack 5 or 6 *ratzelach,* sprinkling confectioners' or crushed sugar between the layers; then cut into wedges for serving. Makes about 15 pancakes. Serves 2 or 3.

Crushed sugar has little meaning in a modern recipe, but not many years ago sugar was available only in long hard cones. Pieces were broken off with a wooden mallet, then pounded fine between towels. This is the crushed sugar, often a light brown, that used to be served over stacks of *ratzelach*.

When one considers the many variations of *latkes* made in different countries, it would seem that there are as many varieties enjoyed during the Chanukah season as there are imaginative cooks to invent them. To cheese, potato, and just plain *latkes*, Israel now adds her fruit fritters, which are fast becoming famous. The batter for them is of special delicacy, and the fruit may be any kind that is in season. These fritters are best served hot with a drift of confectioners' sugar over the top. They may be served as a main dish for breakfast, as a dessert, or as a party confection. But they are always served with tall glasses of hot tea or coffee.

Israeli Fruit Fritters

1 cup flour	2 tablespoons melted butter
2 teaspoons baking powder	(or vegetable fat)
¼ teaspoon salt	2 sliced bananas, or 3 to 4
2 tablespoons sugar	sliced apples, or 1 doz.
1 egg, beaten	thin slices fresh pineapple
⅓ to ½ cup milk	

To prepare the batter, sift together the flour, baking powder, and salt; stir in the sugar. Mix together the egg, milk, and melted butter and stir into the dry ingredients. Blend until smooth but do not overbeat. Batter should be heavy enough to coat the fruit; adjust accordingly, if necessary, with a little more milk or flour. Two cups of any well-drained cubed fruit may be stirred into the batter; then deep fry in hot fat by spoonfuls until well browned and fruit cooked through. An interesting way of preparing fruit fritters is by using round slices of cored apples or canned pineapple. These are dipped into the batter one at a time, then dropped into deep hot fat to cook through and brown all over. These will come from the frying pot like the most delicate of round doughnuts. Drain on absorbent paper. Serve hot with confectioners' sugar over top. Serves 2 or 3.

In America, blueberry *latkes* have become great favorites. These are made quite differently from the fruit fritters of Palestine.

Chanukah Blueberry Latkes

2 cups flour
½ teaspoon salt
3 teaspoons baking powder
1 tablespoon sugar
1½ tablespoons matza meal
3 eggs, well beaten
1½ cups milk (about)

4 tablespoons melted butter
2 cups blueberries (fresh, frozen, or canned)
sugar
maple sugar or maple syrup
butter

Sift together the first 3 dry ingredients; then add the sugar and matza meal. Add the milk to the eggs and stir into the flour. Stir in the melted butter. Beat until smooth. Use a large frying pan or griddle; grease surface if required by your pan, bake large *latkes*, the size of the pan, browning nicely on both sides.

To serve, heat the fruit gently, sweetening to taste. Spread the *latkes* with butter, put together in threes, with blueberries between the layers, and with maple sugar or with maple syrup over the top. Cut in wedges to serve. Serves 3 or 4. This makes an interesting dessert or party sweet with coffee.

Variation: Any other desired fruit may be substituted.

One of us remembers how in her childhood Chanukah was brought home to the children even at breakfast time with traditional buckwheat *latkes*. What a delicacy, and how good they were with plenty of butter and syrup! The taste still lingers.

Mother's Buckwheat Latkes

1 envelope dry yeast or 1 cake yeast
2 cups warm water
1 tablespoon sugar
2 cups milk, scalded
1 teaspoon salt
3¼ cups buckwheat flour

½ cup flour
¼ cup melted butter (or vegetable fat)
2 tablespoons honey
¼ teaspoon baking soda
1 egg

Soften the yeast in ¼ cup of the warm (never hot) water. Add the sugar to the milk; add the remaining water. Cool to luke-

warm—this is important. Then add the softened yeast. Mix together the dry ingredients in a large bowl; make a well in the
center and pour into it the liquid. Stir to a smooth batter. Cover
and let stand overnight, or for 4 to 5 hours, in a warm (just
slightly warm) place to rise. Beat down in the morning, adding
melted butter, honey, soda, and egg. Beat well to mix. Bake as
for any *latkes*, big or little, as preferred, either on a lightly
greased griddle or in a frying pan, browning first on one side,
then on the other. Serves about 6. (In busy modern homes, in
order to keep up the tradition of serving Buckwheat Latkes for
Chanukah, some resort to the use of prepared mixes.)

A long time ago *cheder* boys (Hebrew school boys) of the
Middle East were regaled at Chanukah time with a delectable stew called *kuskus* or *couscous*. A special delight of the
Chanukah season, it was occasionally enjoyed too at other
times of high celebration during the year. *Kuskus* is even
today a famous stew of the North African coast, but it is
less rich with raisins and honey than that earlier dish, dear
to the hearts of the boys.

Kuskus or Couscous
(ORIENTAL BAKED WHEAT STEW)

1 cup *borgoul* (coarsely milled whole wheat)	1 onion, diced
2 cups boiling water	1 lb. ground lamb meat
1 teaspoon salt	½ cup celery, diced
2 tablespoons vegetable oil (or chicken fat)	½ cup raisins
	½ cup wine
	2 tablespoons honey

Toast the whole wheat grains in a frying pan over medium
heat, stirring constantly until dried and lightly browned. Add
boiling water and salt; cover and let steam over low heat for
about ½ hour. Turn into a 3-qt. baking dish. Then heat oil in
frying pan; add onion and meat and stir over moderate heat
until browned. Add to wheat with remaining ingredients; mix
and cover. Bake in a moderate oven (350° F.) for about 45
minutes, adding liquid, if necessary, to keep dish very moist.
Serves 4 to 6.

In Holland *hutspot* is a dish so rich in flavor that it is brought out at Chanukah as a special treat. This dish had its origin in the days when Spain was extending her control over neighboring countries and had laid siege to Leyden. In a surprise counterattack the Dutch put the Spaniards to flight just at suppertime when steaming pots of stewed vegetables were simmering over their campfires. This dish, greatly enjoyed by the victors, has now become a favorite Dutch dish. Jewish housewives added a touch of garlic *wurst*, completing the recipe for *hutspot*. And "a spot of hot" it is indeed when a dash of cayenne is added. Here is a modern version.

Hutspot
(VEGETABLE DISH FROM HOLLAND)

6 each of onions, carrots, and potatoes
3 tablespoons goose fat
½ teaspoon salt

pepper, to taste
cayenne, if desired
¼ lb. garlic *wurst*

Cut the vegetables into medium-sized pieces and cook until tender in enough boiling salted water to barely cover. Drain and mash until smooth. Add the goose fat. Add salt and pepper to taste, and cayenne to desired hotness. Beat until fluffy. Fold in the *wurst* that has been cut into small pieces. Mound on a hot platter and serve immediately. Serves about 6.

Somewhat similar to *cholent*, the Sabbath specialty, are brown beans cooked with goose fat and syrup. These are favorites on the table for Chanukah in Holland.

Holland Brown Beans
(BAKED BEANS WITH GOOSE FAT AND STROOP)

1 lb. dried navy beans
1 teaspoon salt
1 teaspoon mustard
2 to 3 tablespoons stroop (molasses or syrup)

¼ cup *ganse* (goose) fat with large piece of skin
bean water

Wash and pick over the beans. Cover with cold water and soak overnight. Cook slowly next morning in the same water, until skins will burst. (To test, take a few beans in a spoon and blow to cool.) Drain, saving liquid. Mix the beans with the remaining ingredients, in bean pot or casserole, pushing the goose fat down into the center of the beans. Add bean water sufficient to rise almost to top of beans. Cover. Bake in a slow oven (300° F.), for 6 to 8 hours, removing cover near end of baking to brown top. (*Note:* Dried limas, requiring a maximum of three hours for baking, may be substituted for the navy beans. Duck or chicken fat may be substituted for goose fat.) Serves 8 to 10 generously.

Garlic is one of the traditional seasonings of Chanukah dishes. Housewives, particularly those of the Far East, accent the flavor of many of their holiday dishes with this bouquet of the kitchen, as they say, "to make the taste buds tingle." Roumanian Garlic Eggplant and Roumanian Carnatzlach truly do this.

Roumanian Garlic Eggplant or Eggplant Caviar

1 eggplant, medium
2 onions, minced
3 cloves garlic, crushed
salt and pepper

1 tomato, chopped, if desired
¼ cup vegetable oil
vinegar, to taste
black olives or pickled olives

Wash, then bake or broil the eggplant whole until tender. Turn to cook evenly; it will take about 20 minutes. Peel off the skin. Use less garlic if desired. Add all ingredients except the olives, and chop quite fine in chopping bowl. Season to taste. Serve on salad greens with olives as garnish. Serve as an appetizer, salad, or cold vegetable. Serves 4 or 5.

Roumanian Carnatzlach
(LITTLE ROUMANIAN MEAT ROLLS)

3 cloves garlic, crushed
1½ lbs. ground beef
1 onion, finely minced
2 eggs, slightly beaten
2 tablespoons water

2 teaspoons salt
⅛ teaspoon pepper
3 tablespoons flour
¼ teaspoon paprika

Crush the garlic to a paste and add to the meat. Add onion, eggs, water, salt, and pepper and blend well. Shape into individual rolls, each about 3 inches long and 1 inch wide. Mix the flour with paprika and roll the meat in this. Brown slowly in hot fat in a frying pan, turning to brown evenly on all sides, or simmer in a little soup or boiling water. Cook for about 15 to 20 minutes. These *carnatzlach* may also be broiled. If broiling is preferred, omit coating the meat rolls with flour and broil over medium heat. Serves 6.

A holiday dish may be traditional among Jewish people everywhere or only in certain places. Or it may be a cherished holiday specialty of some particular family. This is the case with *kishkelach* with oatmeal stuffing. It has become a traditional Chanukah dish in the family from which this recipe came.

Kishkelach with Oatmeal Stuffing
(BEEF CASINGS WITH OATMEAL STUFFING)

2 lbs. *kishkelach* (beef casings)
½ cup oatmeal
½ cup flour
⅓ cup chicken fat (or vegetable fat)

1 large onion, minced
1½ teaspoons salt
¼ teaspoon pepper
1 tablespoon minced parsley

For the preparation of the *kishke* for stuffing, see directions given on page 36. Mix together the ingredients of the stuffing in the order named, blending well. This will be a dry, crumbly mixture. Cut *kishke* into 8- to 10-inch pieces, or as desired. Tie or sew one end of the *kishke*, then stuff lightly, allowing for expansion during cooking. Sew or tie the other end after stuffing. Scald in boiling water, then scrape clean. Cook in gently boiling salted water or soup for about 45 minutes; or bake in a moderate oven, basting with fat, and cooking until nicely brown. Cut into serving pieces and serve with meat. Serves about 6.

Traditional Potato Teigarch

(POTATO PUDDING)

5 large potatoes
1 medium-sized onion
⅓ cup flour
1 teaspoon baking powder
1 teaspoon salt

¼ teaspoon pepper
1 egg, beaten
2 tablespoons poultry fat (or
    vegetable fat)

Wash, pare, and grate quite fine the potatoes and onion. Sift the dry ingredients together, and add with the egg and fat. Mix and pour into a greased 2-qt. baking dish, dot with additional fat, and bake in a moderately hot oven (375° F.) for 1½ hours—until top is crusty brown. Serves 6.

Although Passover is a good three months away at the time of Chanukah, it is none too soon to begin collecting poultry *schmaltz* so essential for Passover cooking. This is so important that care is taken to fatten geese and ducks for Chanukah. The birds grace the holiday table, stuffed and baked to perfection. The fat, however, is carefully removed, with some of the skin, to be rendered separately for its *schmaltz* and for its *gribenes* (cracklings of the skin). Directions for this are given on page 20.

Chanukah games, known and loved for centuries, and Chanukah symbols have had their influence on holiday cooking. Cookies are cut into *dreidels, gelt, Magen Davids,* menorahs, and elephants. There is even a Katowes Cake, so named because the ingredient content can be totaled to the magic number forty-four, the total number of candles burned in the Menorah during the Chanukah season. As a decorative touch, forty-four tiny candles may ring the cake, or the number Forty-Four may be written in frosting on the top.

Katowes Cake
(ANSWERS TO RIDDLES AND JINGLES)

16 tablespoons cake flour (1 cup)	16 tablespoons sugar (1 cup)
1 teaspoon baking powder	2 teaspoons lemon juice
3 eggs	6 tablespoons hot milk (or orange juice, for a *pareve* cake)

Sift the flour and baking powder together three times. Beat the eggs until very light, preferably with a wire whisk, for 10 minutes. Continue beating as the sugar is added gradually, about 2 to 3 tablespoons at a time, until very light and thick. Fold in the dry ingredients, about ⅓ at a time. Add hot milk all at once and fold in. Bake in an ungreased 9″ x 3″ pan or in two ungreased 9″ x 1½″ pans: if a tube pan, in a slow oven (325° F.) for about 50 minutes; if layer cake pans, in a moderate oven (350° F.) for about 25 minutes. Invert pan and let cool before removing the cake from pan. (If removed hot from pan, the cake will shrink appreciably.) Sprinkle with confectioners' sugar, or frost as desired. Serves 8.

A Glowing Menorah Cake is another way of bringing home the idea of the Feast of Lights. It truly makes a party table brilliant with its eight candles lighted at serving time.

Glowing Menorah Cake

3 cups sifted flour	3 eggs, separated
½ teaspoon salt	1½ teaspoons vanilla
4 teaspoons baking powder	1 cup milk (or orange juice for a *pareve* cake)
¾ cup vegetable fat	
1½ cups sugar	

Mix and sift together three times the flour, salt, and baking powder. Cream the fat and add sugar gradually; blend thoroughly. Add the yolks and vanilla, and beat until puffing with air. Add the flour and liquid alternately, about ⅓ at a time, starting with the flour and ending with the flour; beat until smooth after each addition. Beat whites until stiff but not dry; fold into the mixture. Turn into a 13″ x 9″ x 2″ pan which has

been greased, lined with paper, and greased again. Bake in a
moderate oven (350° F.) for 50 to 60 minutes. Bake until evenly
brown, slightly shrunk away from the pan, and until a toothpick,
cake tester, or straw stuck into the center come out clean. Then
turn out, strip off the paper, and finish cooling right side up.
When entirely cold, frost over the top with white icing. Then
with icing that has been tinted a golden yellow, outline a
menorah on the frosted cake with a pastry tube or tooth pick;
make 8 slight elevations or cups with the frosting to serve as
candle holders. Insert 8 candles in the cups and light at serving
time.

Symbol Cookies

½ cup butter (or vegetable
　　fat)
1 cup sugar
1 egg
2 cups sifted flour

2 teaspoons baking powder
½ teaspoon salt
2 tablespoons milk or orange
　　juice
½ teaspoon vanilla

Cream the butter well; beat in the sugar gradually. Beat in
the egg. Beat now until mixture is puffing with air. Add the
dry ingredients, sifted together, a little at a time, adding the
liquid (including the vanilla) whenever it will make the mixing
easier. Chill before rolling out; this makes dough easier to handle
without adding unnecessary flour. Roll out on lightly floured
board; cut into symbol shapes. (Many cutters can be obtained
today, but for shapes that may not be available, make paper patterns and follow outlines with a sharp knife.) To prevent spreading, bake on an ungreased cooky sheet; bake in a quick oven
(375° F.) for 8 to 12 minutes. Frost as indicated by symbols.
To emphasize the outline, draw a thin line of frosting around the
edges of the cookies with a toothpick or pastry tube. Makes about
3 dozen cookies.

Rich Chanukah Cookies

1 cup butter (or vegetable fat)
1 cup sugar
2 eggs
2 cups sifted flour

½ teaspoon salt
½ teaspoon baking powder
1 teaspoon flavoring—vanilla
　　and/or almond

Follow directions for Symbol Cookies. Roll very thin after
chilling. Bake in a quick oven (375° F.) for 8 to 10 minutes.
Makes about 4 dozen.

Fruit compote is a year-round favorite on Jewish tables, so when it is served at Chanukah time, it must have a festival garnish to distinguish it from the everyday variety. The simple addition of pine nuts and almonds from the markets of the Middle East adds a holiday touch.

Armenian Fruit Compote

½ lb. each, of dried apricots, peaches, and pears, cooked
2 oranges
⅛ teaspoon ground allspice

¼ cup honey
¼ cup sugar
dash of ginger
½ cup pine nuts or almonds

Drain the liquid from the cooked fruit. Sliver the yellow skin from the oranges and add to the liquid; add the juice of both oranges, the allspice, and honey and half the sugar. Bring gently to boiling and simmer until very rich in consistency. Pour over fruit; add several tablespoons sweet wine or brandy, if desired. Chill. Mix the ginger with the remaining 2 tablespoons of sugar, and mix with the nuts. Spread these in a shallow pan; sprinkle remaining honey over top. Toast in a slow oven (300° F.) until sugar begins to brown lightly. Cool. Sprinkle over top of individual servings of compote. Serves 8 to 10.

From Italy, Sweet and Sour Chestnuts were introduced into the cuisine for the Chanukah season. They have become popular wherever chestnuts, fresh or dried, may be obtained.

Sweet and Sour Chestnuts

½ lb. dried or 1 lb. fresh chestnuts
water
2 cups sugar
2 lemons
1 small orange

4 whole cloves
3-inch length stick cinnamon
root ginger
¼ teaspoon ground ginger
½ cup raisins
nuts, if desired

If dried chestnuts are used, wash well, cover with cold water, and soak overnight. Simmer in the same water until tender. Drain liquid into saucepan and measure, adding water to make 4 cups (1 quart). If fresh chestnuts are used, roast in oven and remove shell. Or slit shell of raw chestnuts, cover with water, and simmer for about 5 to 8 minutes; remove shell and skin.

For the sauce, start with 4 cups of the liquid that was used in cooking the chestnuts. Add sugar. Trim yellow skin from lemons and orange, cutting into thin slivers. Add to liquid. Add juice of 1 lemon. Slice 1 lemon and the orange very thin and add. Add spices, shaving little curls from the ginger root for the syrup. Bring all to boiling over moderate heat. Add chestnuts and raisins. Simmer, covered, over low heat for about an hour— until the sauce is rich and the chestnuts are done; add more water during cooking, keeping the sauce rich, but not too thick. Add nuts, if they are to be used, near the end of the cooking. Makes about 1 quart. Pour into sterile glasses and top with parafine, if desired, to store.

Sesame seeds are used in honey candies for Chanukah, just as *mohn* (poppy seeds) are traditional for Purim, and matza *farfel* for Passover. The basic candy is much the same for each holiday, and a warning should be given about the making of this honey candy, for many are the disappointments when it has to be eaten with a spoon like preserves. When the weather is damp or rainy, candies, particularly honey candies, absorb so much moisture that they will not harden. The best time to make candy is when the weather is clear and dry.

Oriental Sesame Seed Candy

2 cups sugar	dash of salt
⅔ cup honey	2 cups sesame seeds
½ teaspoon ginger	½ cup nut meats, chopped

Use a heavy frying pan or saucepan. Measure the sugar, honey, ginger, and salt into the pan, and begin to stir gently, preferably with a wooden spoon, to mix all ingredients. As the syrup begins to simmer, continue stirring, moving the sugar from the sides of the pan. When the sugar is completely dissolved, remove at once from over the heat. Sugar overcooks very quickly. Add sesame seeds and nuts; stir together quickly and pour out on a wet board, a marble slab, or even on a greased platter. Spread thin, with a wet knife. This candy cools very quickly. Cut into diamond-shaped pieces while still warm. Makes about 6 dozen pieces.

In Old Russia symbols embodying the use of light for the Festival of Chanukah were very popular, and none more so than Flaming Tea. There was quite a bit of drama in this ceremony.

Well in advance of serving the Flaming Tea, great cones of sugar were broken into pieces. These were piled high on a dish. Then tall glasses of tea, poured from a samovar, were passed around, each with a pony of brandy and a generous lump of sugar. Each person would dip his sugar into the brandy, then place it on a teaspoon held over the glass. Lights were then turned out as a lighted taper was passed among the guests to light the brandy-dipped sugar. As the glow spread from one to another, songs were sung and then all together the flaming cubes were dropped into the waiting glasses.

Chamishah Asar B'Shevat

The 15th of Shevat—usually in late January or early February.

Chamishah Asar B'Shevat, the New Year of the Trees, is a day set aside to do honor to trees. An arbor day celebration, its name refers to its date, the fifteenth day of *Shevat*. The festival originated in ancient Palestine, where at this time of the year the first signs of spring are appearing. Hillsides are covered with blooming cyclamen and red poppies. Fruit trees are in bud, and the almond tree is a delight to the eye. True to its name, *"shaked,"* meaning the quick one, it bursts into a cloud of rose-white flowers almost overnight.

The Jewish people, like all people who are close to the soil, have long been mindful of the importance of trees. As far back as the time when they were wandering in the desert, they have followed the counsel: "And when ye shall come into the land, and shall have planted all manner of trees for food..." And so throughout the years, with ceremony and great rejoicing, they planted trees.

In the Talmud, the New Year of the Trees is known as Rosh Hashanah L'ilanoth, the day when trees are judged. It is said that on this day the Lord chooses which trees will flourish through the year, which will perish, which will suffer from lightning, and which will bear fruit.

In an early observance of Chamishah Asar B'Shevat, new trees were set out each year on this day, and it became the custom to plant a sapling for each child born during the year.

Cedars were planted for boys, cypresses or pines for girls. Years later, when the children married, branches from their trees were cut to serve as posts for their *chuppah* (wedding canopy).

When Palestine was laid waste and the Jews found homes in many lands, they continued to observe the festival of the trees. In the Middle East and in Western places where climate and fruits are similar to those of Palestine, observance of the holiday follows the original pattern and trees are planted. Chamishah Asar B'Shevat is observed in Spain with the reading of a special book in the synagogue on this day. In Morocco fruit is served at the services in the synagogue, and this is followed by a festive meal at home.

In many Northern lands where it is still winter on this day and tree planting not possible, the holiday is observed nevertheless. Festivities center around such Palestinian fruits as dates, *bokser*, figs, raisins and almonds. These are eaten in the synagogue after the prayers of the day; they are also carried to school by the boys, to be enjoyed while they listen to stories of Palestine that recall the trees and fruitfulness of that land in the days of their forefathers.

Today, when Jews are rebuilding Israel, Chamishah Asar B'Shevat has taken on new significance. More and more, trees are needed to prevent soil erosion, to help retain the moisture in the soil, to beautify the countryside. In Israel today tree planting ceremonies are followed by dancing and feasting.

The Children's Festival of Trees in modern Tel Aviv sets a pattern for celebrations all over the world. Early on the day of this festival the ancient Judean hills resound with the call of the bugle as the school children assemble for the march to the tree-planting area. Ceremonies open with the Proclamation of the Day, read in unison by a small group of youths, clad in priestly garb. The assembled thousands respond in verse and song. Then follows a beautiful program of dancing and singing. The climax of the occasion is the presentation of saplings to each group of three or four children. These have been assigned to definite planting spots. Spades, hoes, and watering cans then go into action to the accompaniment of the band and chorus. Soon each sturdy sapling is in place. Then the band strikes up and the children sing and dance around the little trees. The ceremony closes with the singing of the national anthem.

In the Western world of today, Chamishah Asar B'Shevat is referred to as "Israel Day." Tree planting ceremonies are held in many places when weather permits. Plays, speeches, and ceremonies recall stories of ancient Palestine, its history, tradition, and agricultural life, and the ideals of Israel today.

Refreshments for parties are varied, although the feasting on fruits and nuts and *bokser* is quite general. *Bokser,* the delight of children always, because of its honey-date flavor, is the fruit of the carob tree, which dates from Biblical times. This tree is peculiar to the Mediterranean region and is said to have sustained many of the heroes of ancient times when they hid in the hills eluding enemy pursuit.

In the Far East, especially in India, some beautiful ancient rituals and customs have been preserved in celebrations in the home on Chamishah Asar B'Shevat. Around a festival table, heaped with fruits, there is enacted a solemn service of benediction over each separate variety. Every man present pronounces a benediction over each kind of fruit. It is said that as many as seventy varieties are known to have been collected for this occasion. The night ends in a banquet of fruits served to all.

In other parts of the world there may not be the elaborate variety of fruit that is found in the Orient, yet fruits, nuts, wine, and honey are used abundantly in the dishes that are served. Israel's most typical foods are served on this day, as can be seen from this menu.

Dinner for Chamishah Asar B'Shevat

Chopped Herring   Rye Bread
Wine Soup
Stuffed Patlijan with Meat   Rice
Okra with Tomatoes
Green Salad with Ripe Olives and Olive Oil Dressing
Baclava   Wine   Tea   Dates   Figs
Bokser   Assorted Fruits with Pomegranates
Salted Almonds

Wine Soup

1 cup orange juice
1½ cups cold water
3 tablespoons honey
⅛ teaspoon salt
1 tablespoon cornstarch

1 cup wine, red or white
2 tablespoons lemon juice
sour cream or egg white stiffly
beaten
nutmeg

Heat together gently, just to boiling, the orange juice, 1¼ cups of the water, honey, and salt. Mix the cornstarch with the remaining ¼ cup water and stir into the liquid. Continue cooking over low heat, stirring constantly until smooth, clear, and creamy. Chill, if desired to serve cold. Just before serving, add wine and lemon juice. Serve hot or cold with crest of sour cream or stiffly beaten egg white, and with a dash of nutmeg. Serves 4.

Stuffed Patlijan with Meat
(EGGPLANT STUFFED WITH MEAT)

1 large eggplant
¼ cup chopped onion
1 cup chopped cooked meat
½ teaspoon salt
pepper

1 egg, slightly beaten
1 tablespoon chopped parsley
½ cup bread crumbs
2 tablespoons chicken fat (or
vegetable fat)

Cook the eggplant whole in gently boiling water for about 15 minutes—until slightly tender. Cut in half lengthwise; scoop out the center, leaving ½-inch thick shell. Cut scooped-out center into small pieces; add the remaining ingredients, using only half the crumbs and fat. Mix well and pile into the eggplant shells. Mound high; cover with remaining crumbs mixed with the remaining fat. Add more crumbs if necessary and cover the mixture. Place in a baking pan or dish with water sufficient to cover bottom of baker. Bake in a moderate oven (350° F.) for 35 to 40 minutes—until well heated through and browned over the top. Serves 4 or 5.

Stuffed Dates or Figs

The fruit may be stuffed with nut meats, candied ginger, or fruit ball mixture (see page 121). Remove pits from dates. Two dates may be pressed together to form one large date. Stuff the dates or figs so that the filling is slightly exposed. Coat with sugar, not confectioners' sugar, by shaking several at a time in a paper bag with the sugar.

Salted Nuts

Almonds or filberts must first be blanched. To do this, cover the shelled nuts with boiling water and let them stand for a few moments; then plunge them into cold water, drain, and rub the skins off immediately. Let the nuts dry thoroughly on paper toweling. Work with only ½ cup of nuts at a time or they will become soggy from standing in the water too long.

To fry: Place nuts in a frying basket or strainer and fry in deep fat that is hot enough to brown a cube of bread in 50 seconds. Fry only long enough to tan the nuts lightly, as overcooking makes them harden after they are removed from the fat. Drain on paper toweling and sprinkle with salt.

To bake: Mix the nuts in a bowl with oil, allowing 2 teaspoons of oil to 1 cup of nuts. Cover the bottom of a shallow baking pan with the nuts; sprinkle with salt and roast in a moderate oven (350° F.) for 10 to 12 minutes—to a delicate brown—stirring occasionally to brown evenly. Drain on paper toweling. Cook only one kind at a time, as some nuts brown faster than others.

Shish Kcbab
(BROILED LAMB ON SKEWERS)

2 to 3 lbs. of lamb suitable   1 to 2 cloves of garlic, crushed
    for broiling   1 medium-sized onion,
salt and pepper   chopped
juice of 1 lemon   tomato wedges
½ cup wine   small onions, parboiled
½ cup water   green peppers, in squares

Cut the meat in about 1½-inch cubes. Place in a crock or bowl,
sprinkle with salt and pepper, and add lemon juice, wine, water,
garlic, and onion. Mix well through the meat. Let stand for about
4 hours or overnight. Drain well; thread on skewers, alternating
the cubes of meat with all or a choice of the vegetables. Brush
well with oil and broil before an open fire for 5 to 8 minutes,
turning the skewers to brown the meat and vegetables evenly.
Or without skewers, broil as you would other meats. Serve immediately, sizzling hot. Serves about 4 to 6.

Danish Butter Cookies

1 cup butter (or vegetable   ½ teaspoon baking soda
    fat)   ¼ teaspoon salt
1 cup sugar   1 teaspoon vanilla
1 egg   nuts, raisins, or cherries
2¼ cups flour

Cream the butter; add the sugar gradually; beat in the egg.
Add dry ingredients, sifted together; add vanilla. Mix well into a
dough that can be handled. Shape into small, marble-sized balls.
Place on an ungreased cooky sheet, about an inch apart. Press
a nut, some raisins, or a slice of a candied (or maraschino)
cherry into the top of each. Bake in a moderate oven (350° F.)
for 10 to 15 minutes. Cool before removing from pan. Makes
about 5 dozen.

Date Torte

2 eggs, well beaten   1 teaspoon baking powder
½ cup sugar   2 cups sliced dates
¼ teaspoon salt   1 cup chopped nuts
1½ cups crumbs (bread or   1 teaspoon vanilla
    graham cracker)

Add the sugar gradually to well-beaten eggs; add salt. Mix the crumbs with the baking powder, dates, and nuts. Add to the eggs with vanilla, mixing lightly. Bake in a 9-inch square (or round) baking pan or dish, in a moderate oven (350° F.) for 40 to 45 minutes. Serve hot or cold, plain or with cream. Serves 8 to 12.

Fruit and Wine Punch

2 cups sugar	1 qt. ginger ale
1 cup water	wine, as desired
1 cup strong tea	mint leaves
1½ cups lemon juice	ice
2 cups orange juice	

Heat the sugar in water to dissolve. Add the remaining liquids. Chill. "Bruise" some of the mint leaves, if desired, then strew over the ice placed in a punch bowl. Pour in the prepared punch. Add water, plain or charged, to taste. Makes about 1 gallon or 32 small cups of punch.

Purim

The 14th of Adar—usually in March.

The Festival of Purim, lasting just one day, is pure light-hearted jollity from start to finish. It is a day given over to revelry, pranks, masquerades, and play acting. There are parties everywhere, and the exchanging of food gifts is one of the delights of this holiday. Work goes on uninterrupted except for fun and foolishness, and an occasional taste of wine and Purim delicacies.

Purim is not a deeply religious festival. Even in the synagogue it is not a solemn day, for light-hearted celebration begins at the time of the reading of the Megillah, the Scroll of Esther. This book of the Bible tells the story on which Purim is based.

It is an ancient tale set in the fabulous splendor of court life in Old Persia. A great many Jews were living in Persia during this time, and they suffered persecution beyond endurance. The story relates how Esther, a beautiful Jewish maiden, saved her people.

The mighty Ahasuerus was on the throne and ruled over a vast kingdom. A powerful king, yet he was easily swayed by those about him, and he came particularly under the influence of Haman, his favorite minister. Haman was ambitious and crafty; he sought ways to increase his power and succeeded to the point where an order was given that all bow before him. Mordecai, who sat in the courts of the king and had secured many privileges for his people, refused to do this.

He was a Jew, and would bow only to God. This so enraged Haman that he determined to destroy, not only Mordecai, but all the Jews in the country. Craftily he denounced
the Jews as disloyal to their king and he so aroused the anger
of the ruler that he, in turn, decreed the death of all the
Hebrews in his land.

But things did not go so smoothly for Haman. He was not
aware that Esther, Ahasuerus' queen, was a Jewess and a
cousin of Mordecai. As soon as Mordecai learned of the de-
cree, he sought out Queen Esther and bade her save her
people. Together they decided that she should appeal to the
king at a banquet she would prepare in his honor, to which
Haman would be invited. It was a most hazardous under-
taking, and the queen fortified her spirit with prayer and
fasting before entering upon her task.

In the felicitous setting of the banquet, Esther revealed
her kinship with her people and pleaded for their lives, as
well as her own. The king, enraged by what he now saw to be
the villainous plotting of his prime minister, ordered the
death of Haman. This occurred on the very date that had
been selected for the destruction of the Jewish people. After
their deliverance, Mordecai wrote to the Jews of Persia telling them to remember this day always, making it a time "of
feasting and gladness, and of sending portions one to another,
and gifts to the poor."

At that time it was customary to choose the date for any
important event by the casting of lots, known by the Persian
word *purim*. It was in this way that Haman had selected
the day for the carrying out of his plot against the Jews.
When this day came to be celebrated as a day of thanksgiving, it came to be known as Purim, or the Festival of Lots,
as it is still called today.

Purim, symbolic of deliverance, has become newly significant with each generation where persecution has struck.

Haman has become the prototype of all despots who have assailed the Jewish people, only to be destroyed themselves, even as Hitler in modern times.

Many communities, and even many families, have declared special little Purims of their own to commemorate their escape from some particularly menacing experience. The sixteenth-century Plum-Jam Purim of the Brandeis family is an example of a family Purim.

It is recorded that David Brandeis, a shopkeeper of Jung-Bunzlau in Bohemia, was imprisoned for selling a plum jam said to have caused the illness of a whole family and the death of the father. Some good friends, convinced of his innocence, were able to prove that the physician attending the father had been in the power of a state officer who hated the Jews and had forced him to testify falsely. It was established that the illness of the family had no connection with the plum jam and that the death of the father was due to natural causes. From that time on, the family celebrated annually on the date of his release from prison.

The Festival of Purim starts on the eve of the holiday with the reading of the Megillah in the synagogue. The family goes together to hear the story of Queen Esther. It is especially important at this time for the women to hear the story of Esther, and each takes pride anew in her courage and heroism. During the reading the children wait eagerly for the first mention of the name of Haman, as this is the signal for a storm of derision that arises at each repetition of his name. Youths of the congregation have come with clattering *greggers* and other noisemakers, and are ready to deal with the villain. In oriental synagogues there is a delightful old custom whereby even the more staid members come prepared to stomp Haman to oblivion, for each has scrawled the name of Haman on the soles of his shoes.

All over the world, there is this folk quality about the celebration of Purim. After the reading in the synagogue, merriment really begins. In some countries, an old custom still persists, whereby *Purim spielers,* actors dressed in comic costumes, give performances on the streets, and visit from house to house. They portray the story of Esther and other Bible stories, often in hilarious skits. Children blacken their faces and dress up in grotesque clothes, playing all manner of pranks. Above all they love to go from house to house singing:

> *"Heint is Purim, morgen is oise.*
> *Git mir a groshen, und varft mir arois."*

> "Today is Purim, tomorrow it's o'er.
> Give me a penny and show me the door."

Everyone is delighted to see them and they are showered with gifts of pennies, fruits, and confections, prepared for their coming.

In France and Italy during the Middle Ages the masquerades of the Purim holiday developed into elaborate carnivals. Great parades with floats, burlesques, and tableaux wound through the streets. The whole day and night was filled with continuous entertainment. This carnival spirit spread to many places and continues to this day.

One of the most colorful and dramatic of modern celebrations takes place in Tel Aviv. It is called *Adloyada,* meaning "until one does not know." This is a reference to an injunction of the Talmud which prescribes that one be merry to the point where one does not know whether Mordecai is to be blessed and Haman cursed, or vice versa.

Purim celebrations in Tel Aviv include carnival parades in the old tradition. Elaborate floats and tableaux depict the story of Esther, Daniel in the lion's den, Noah with his roaring animals, Solomon with his many wives, Jonah and the whale, and many others. It is all great fun. Watching crowds along the parade route take part too in many little impromptu shows staged here and there on the sidewalks. Adding color to the whole celebration, people from Shanghai and New York, from Berlin and Moscow, from Beirut and Cracow, now making their homes in Tel Aviv, bring with them the customs and costumes of many places as they mingle with the people.

Colorful, too, are the indoor community celebrations held all over the world in observance of Purim. This is a day for plays, for indoor carnivals, for *seudahs*, and every other kind of delightful entertainment.

A unique custom that has been observed since very ancient times is a special kind of gift-giving, called *shalach monas*. These gifts are generally delicacies prepared in home kitchens, although a household gift, such as a bright table cloth or a lovely decanter, may be included among the presents planned for a friend or relative. On the night of Purim, after synagogue, many last minute touches are added to these gifts which are to be given "from our house to your house." Early the next morning messengers begin to deliver these prized *shalach monas* plates, carefully covered with white napkins.

". . . . none says thank you on Purim, particularly not the poor, as it is commanded to give charity on Purim and the poor are doing a favor to their well-to-do brethren by accepting gifts." This is not to be interpreted, however, as exempting the poor from giving gifts. On the contrary, it is also written that all must share with others; no one has so little that he cannot give his neighbor some small token on this day.

Gifts other than specially prepared foods are often exchanged at the *seudah* on the night of the holiday. These parties are celebrated around festive tables laden with food. Traditionally the food is in such variety that an Italian, writ-

ing during Roman times, named twenty-four different dishes
that he could remember having seen on a *seudah* table.

No mere menu could ever be more than a suggestion of
what may rightfully appear at a *seudah*.

Purim Seudah Table

Chopped Herring   Gefillte Fish Balls   Mohn Kichlach
Dill Pickles   Horse-radish   Black Olives
Zemmel   Fruit Salad
Hamantaschen
Mohn Strudel   Mohnlach
Teiglach   Prune Fruit Balls
Wine   Tea   Coffee

In accordance with a very ancient tradition, a number of
culinary concoctions have been named for the villain of the
day, and these have somehow come to personify him. It
might well be added that they are nonetheless delectable!
The housewife deals with the villain Haman when she
bakes *hamantaschen* in her piping hot oven. The rest of the
family have their turn later, when these are consumed in
triumph!

Traditional Hamantaschen
(STUFFED THREE-CORNERED CAKES)

1 envelope dry yeast (or 1
  cake compressed yeast)
¼ cup lukewarm milk
½ cup sugar
½ cup butter (or vegetable
  fat)

½ teaspoon salt
1 cup scalded milk
2 eggs, slightly beaten
4 cups flour
1 egg yolk

Dissolve the yeast in the ¼ cup of lukewarm milk, making
certain that the milk is not too warm. Stir in 1 tablespoon of
sugar and set aside. In a deep mixing bowl, combine the butter,
remaining sugar, salt and scalded milk, and stir until all are
blended. When lukewarm, stir in the yeast. Add the eggs and
about 2 cups of the flour, and beat to a smooth batter. Add re-

maining flour to make a tender dough. Turn out on a floured board and knead for about 2 minutes. Grease a large mixing bowl; grease whole surface of the large ball of dough and place dough in bowl. Cover. Let rise in a warm, not hot, place, to double its bulk. (Takes from 2 to 4 hours.) Again knead on a floured board for about a minute. Roll out ⅛ of an inch thick. Cut into 3- to 4-inch circles.

Place filling on each. Recipes for Mohn Filling and Lekva Filling follow. To shape true *hamantaschen,* pinch edges of circle together over filling, leaving about ⅓ open, forming a cornucopia. Then fold over the flap and pinch these edges firmly together. Arrange well apart on a greased cooky sheet. Cover with a cloth and let rise again in a warm place to double in bulk. Brush tops with the egg yolk, thinned with a little water (to make it easier to apply). Bake in a moderate oven (350° F.) for 15 to 20 minutes. Makes 2 to 2½ dozen.

Modern Hamantaschen

2½ cups flour
3 teaspoons baking powder
1 teaspoon salt
¼ cup sugar

1 egg, beaten
¾ cup milk or water
⅓ cup butter (or vegetable fat)

Sift together the flour, baking powder, and salt. Stir in the sugar. Add liquid to the egg and pour into center of flour. Melt butter; cool; pour into center of flour. Stir together to make a dough that is soft but not sticky. Knead five or six times on a floured board. Roll out to ¼-inch thickness. Cut, add filling, and shape as directed in recipe for Traditional Hamantaschen. Makes 15 to 18.

Hamantaschen
(FROM A COOKY DOUGH)

A rich cooky dough may also be used for *hamantaschen.* Follow the recipe for Queen Esther Cookies on page 120. Cut, fill, and shape as directed in recipe for Traditional Hamantaschen.

Poppy seed came into traditional use as filling for *hamantaschen* largely because the German word for these is *mohn,* sounding very much like Ha—*man. Lekva* (prune or plum) filling has been popular since the time of the plum-jam episode in the Brandeis family.

Mohn Filling for Hamantaschen
(POPPY SEED FILLING)

2 cups poppy seed, finely ground
1 egg

⅓ cup honey or sugar
1 tablespoon lemon juice
¼ cup chopped nuts

Poppy seed may be purchased finely ground or they may be ground at home. If prepared at home, wash the seeds well first and grind with the finest blade; or place the seeds in a cloth and pound with a mallet. Mix with remaining ingredients, and if mixture seems thin, add cake or bread crumbs for proper consistency. This is sufficient filling for 2 to 2½ dozen *hamantaschen*.

Lekva Filling for Hamantaschen
(PRUNE FILLING)

2 cups cooked prunes, seeded and chopped
grated rind of 1 lemon

1 tablespoon lemon juice
⅓ to ½ cup sugar
½ cup chopped nuts

Mix all ingredients; flavor to taste. Will fill 2 to 2½ dozen *hamantaschen*.

A *challah* twist for the Purim *seudah* table is described by one enthusiast as "so large it reaches from one end of the table to the other." With this idea in mind, it is easy to see that the ordinary recipe for *challah* as baked for the Sabbath must be doubled or tripled, and so it is.

Keylitch
(VERY LARGE CHALLAH TWIST)

double or triple the recipe for *challah* (page 12)

1 egg
1 tablespoon water
raisins

Follow the recipe for Sabbath *challah*, and braid into one tremendous loaf. Mix egg with water and brush surface of loaf. Pattern top with raisins, pushing them down into the dough to anchor into place; then brush again with the egg. To protect the top, and especially the raisins, during baking, cover lightly with a clean sheet of wrapping paper after loaf begins to brown.

Vienna Braids
(MINIATURE KEYLITCH)

These are miniature Sabbath *challah* about 3 inches long. Sprinkle with poppy seed after brushing with egg.

Zemmel are savory little rolls, often topped with onion or poppy seed, traditionally served for breakfast on Purim.

Zemmel
(LITTLE ROLLS)

ingredients for *challah* (page 12)	coarse salt
	minced onion
egg mixed with a little water	

From a setting of *challah* dough, pinch off little pieces and shape into small round rolls. Brush tops with egg; sprinkle with coarse salt and minced onion if desired. Press each lightly in the center, working into a cupped center. This tends to protect the topping and gives the rolls a characteristic shape. Let rise on a greased cooky sheet to double their bulk. Bake in a moderate oven (350° F.) for 15 to 20 minutes.

Varation: mohn may be used instead of onion.

Piroshkes are great favorites for every *seudah*, on this holiday or otherwise. A Turkish friend tells this story on himself. One day when he was a child a fishbone caught in his throat. He was so fond of *piroshkes* that his mother promised him as many as he could eat if he kept quiet while the bone was being removed. The next day he really had a feast, and he is still trying to count how many *piroshkes* he consumed!

Pirogen or Piroshkes
(PASTRY STUFFED WITH MEAT)

1½ cups flour
½ teaspoon baking powder
½ teaspoon salt
½ cup chicken fat (or vegetable fat)
¼ cup water (about)
1 small onion, finely minced

1 tablespoon chicken fat (or vegetable fat)
1 lb. cooked lungs, finely chopped
1½ cups chopped cooked meat
½ teaspoon salt
¼ teaspoon pepper
1 egg

To make the pastry, sift the dry ingredients together, then cut in the shortening until it is in little flakes through the flour. Stir in sufficient water to make a tender dough that can be rolled. Roll out on a lightly floured board until quite thin; cut into 2½-inch squares.

To make the filling, brown the onion in the fat. Add remaining ingredients and mix lightly together.

To fill, place a spoonful of filling on half of each square of dough; fold edges over to make a triangle, pressing edges together firmly. Bake on a cooky sheet or in a shallow baking pan in a hot oven (400° F.) for about 20 minutes. Makes 16.

Kreplach, of Yom Kippur fame (*see* recipe p. 58), are equally traditional for Purim tables. On this holiday, a great variety of fillings are used, and those made of fruits are especially popular. When *kreplach* are made with fruit fillings, they are served as dessert.

Strudel, a favorite during the season of Sukkoth, is made with a poppy seed filling for the Purim table.

Poppy Seed Filling for Strudel

½ lb. poppy seed, ground
1 cup sugar
1 cup raisins, chopped

1 lemon, grated (use rind and juice)

Mix and use as filling for *strudel* dough, as directed on page 73.

Teiglach, the honey-cooked bits of dough traditional for Rosh Hashanah, are also tremendously popular for Purim *seudah* tables, and quantities are made for the *shalach monas* platters. The recipe for these will be found on page 60.

Mohn Kichlach
(POPPY SEED COOKIES)

2 cups flour	3 eggs, well beaten
1 teaspoon baking powder	½ cup vegetable oil
¼ teaspoon salt	⅓ cup poppy seed

Sift the dry ingredients into a mixing bowl; make a hollow in the center and pour in the beaten eggs, oil, and poppy seed. Mix from the center out, in a sweeping motion, to blend the ingredients together into a smooth, thick drop batter. Drop by teaspoon, about 2 inches apart, onto a greased cooky sheet or a large, shallow baking pan. Bake in a slow oven (325° F.) for 20 minutes. Makes about 4 dozen.

Steamed puddings are the specialty of English Jews, who are sure to serve them with a cherry jam at Purim table.

English Steamed Pudding with Cherry Jam

2 cups flour	1 egg, beaten
¼ teaspoon salt	¾ to 1 cup fruit juice
1 teaspoon baking powder	½ cup cherry jam
⅓ cup solid fat of beef or chicken	

Sift the dry ingredients together; chop the fat to bits and then cut it through the flour, as for pastry. Combine the egg with fruit juice; add gradually to flour; mix well. Grease a 2-qt. mold or pudding dish; put the cherry jam in the bottom and pour in the prepared pudding batter. Cover tightly with a lid or a greased paper cover that is tied tightly in place. Mold should be only ⅔ full to allow for expansion. Place in steamer over boiling water; or on a trivet in a kettle of boiling water where the water rises to at least half the height of the mold. Cover and steam for 1½ hours, taking care that the water does not evaporate appreciably. If more water must be added, be sure it is boiling and do not jar the kettle. Cool slightly before turning out of mold. Serve upside down, of course, so that cherry jam may sauce the top. Additional jam may be added if desired. Serves 6.

There is always time for a family dinner on a holiday, no matter how many *seudahs* one may attend. Purim is no exception to this rule. Certain favorite dishes can almost be said to be traditional for such dinner menus.

Purim Family Dinner

Pickled Fish on Lettuce   Mohn Kichlach
Purim Soup   Piroshkes or Kreplach
Roast Turkey   Potato Stuffing   Green Beans
Prune and Potato Tzimmes
Hamantaschen (pareve)   Fresh Fruit
Tea with Lemon   Wine
Nahit   Bob   Mohn Kichlach   Assorted Nuts

Two Nations Soup

1 lb. fat beef	2 leeks, cut fine
2 pieces of marrow bone	*bouquet garni* (a few sprigs of
2 qts. water	parsley, thyme, and basil
2 teaspoons salt	tied together
1 cup tomatoes, fresh or	1 cup sliced carrots
canned	2 tablespoons sugar
1 cup beet liquid from cooked	2 tablespoons lemon juice
beets, fresh or canned	2 eggs

In a deep kettle place the beef, bones, water, salt, tomatoes, and beet liquid. Simmer for about 1 hour. Add leeks, *bouquet garni,* and carrots. Continue cooking gently until the meat is tender. Remove meat and keep hot. Remove pot from heat and season the soup with sugar, lemon juice, and more salt to taste. Beet eggs slightly in a bowl and add gradually about 1 cup of the broth, stirring constantly. When well blended stir into the soup to thicken. Serve immediately. The meat may be cut in cubes and served with the soup, or sliced and served on a separate platter. Serves 6 to 8.

The strutting turkey, most foolish of fowl, was derisively known in those days as the cock of India. Because he was pompous and easily led, King Ahasuerus became known as the cock of Persia, and from this originated the tradition of serving turkey for Purim. The recipe for roast turkey will be found on page 30.

Knishes are sold by vendors all through the carnival hours of Purim, when crowds are wandering through the streets, singing and eating as they go. *Knishes* are seen in more elegant places, too, in fact wherever *seudah* tables are spread with good food. Among the most popular are Liver and Potato Knishes.

Liver and Potato Knishes
(POTATO CAKES STUFFED WITH LIVER)

2 cups mashed potatoes
2 eggs, beaten
2 tablespoons chicken fat (or vegetable fat)
1 teaspoon salt
dash of pepper

2 tablespoons minced onion
flour
1 cup chopped cooked liver or other chopped cooked meat (about)
1 egg yolk

Mix the potatoes with the eggs, fat, salt, pepper, and onion. When smooth, add flour to make a rather stiff dough. Shape into oblong cakes about 1½ inches thick. Make a depression in the center of each cake and fill with the chopped cooked meat. Brush with the egg yolk, diluted with a tablespoon of water. Bake on a well-greased baking sheet in a moderate oven (350° F.) for about 20 minutes—until well cooked and brown over top. Makes 10 to 12.

In old Vienna, noodles with poppy seed were a most popular dish for Purim, especially when crisp slivers of almonds, blanched and toasted, were added as a note of elegance.

Noodles with Poppy Seed

8 ozs. broad noodles

2 tablespoons poppy seed

½ cup blanched almonds, slivered

2 tablespoons chicken fat (or vegetable fat)

Break the noodles into 2-inch pieces. Cook in a large amount of boiling salted water for 8 to 10 minutes—until tender, but not mushy. Drain well. Wash poppy seed well; drain and toast with the slivered almonds in hot fat in a frying pan. Pour over noodles, dusting with salt and pepper. Toss and serve very hot. Serves 6.

In addition to *hamantaschen,* Haman's fritters, of honored tradition among English Jews, are also named for the villain of the day. Here he meets his desserts, being fried to a crisp!

Haman's Fritters

fritter batter (recipe page 86)

3 seedless oranges

3 to 6 tablespoons sugar

⅛ teaspoon ginger

1 cup honey

Skin and section the oranges. Cover them with the sugar, mixed with ginger, and allow to stand for about an hour. Drain off the juice that has collected and add it to the honey; bring this to a simmer, then pour into a pitcher to serve as sauce for the fritters. Prepare the fritter batter. Dip orange sections one by one in the batter and then fry to golden brown in deep hot fat. Drain and serve with prepared Honey Syrup. Makes 24.

Nahit (chick peas) are traditional for Purim as they commemorate the time when Queen Esther ate only vegetables in order to abide by the dietary laws. These are prepared as after-dinner tidbits to be enjoyed throughout the evening.

Nahit
(SALTED CHICK PEAS)

1 lb. dried chick peas

salt and pepper

Wash peas in several waters. Soak overnight. Do not drain off the water in which the peas were soaking. Add a teaspoon of salt and bring gently to boiling. Lower heat, cover tightly, and simmer for about 2 hours—until tender. Drain well. Shake over low heat until very dry. Add a good sprinkle of pepper, and additional salt if desired. Serve cold as niblets. Makes about 6 cupfuls.

Note: Bob, which are fava beans, are also served for Purim and are prepared in the same way as *nahit.*

Cooking for the *shalach monas* plates has always set kitchens in a whirl, and even the men of the family may be cajoled into lending a strong arm with beating and stirring. Sweets are prime favorites, always made as fancy as possible. Cookies, in particular, lend themselves to clever shaping and decoration. Figures from the story of Queen Esther always figure prominently in cooky making and include Queen Esther herself, Mordecai, Vashti (the queen before Esther), Zeresh (Haman's wife), Haman, and many others. Jewish housewives of Poland developed this type of cooky making to a fine art.

Pfeffernuesse, peppery, spicy little cooky balls, have attained an international reputation, and among the Jews they are reserved as a special treat for Purim.

Pfeffernuesse
(SPICY COOKY BALLS)

6 cups sifted flour
2 teaspoons baking powder
½ teaspoon baking soda
1 teaspoon salt
¼ teaspoon black pepper
1 teaspoon ground cloves, nutmeg, cinnamon, mixed
1 teaspoon anise seeds
1 tablespoon crushed cardamon seeds, if desired
1½ cups butter (or vegetable fat)

1 cup sugar
1 egg
¼ cup finely chopped citron
¼ lb. blanched almonds, finely chopped
¼ lb. candied orange peel, finely chopped
1 cup molasses
¼ cup corn syrup
1 cup brandy
juice and grated rind of 1 lemon

Sift together the dry ingredients as listed through ground spices. Add the anise seeds and cardamon seeds. Set aside until needed. Cream the butter with the sugar until puffing with air; add the egg and beat until very light. Add the citron, almonds and orange peel. Add about one-third of the sifted dry ingredients and mix well. Mix and add the molasses, corn syrup, and brandy. Beat together well. Add the remaining dry ingredients gradually, with juice and grated rind of lemon whenever it will help to make mixing easier. When well mixed, set aside for an hour. Shape into small balls about 1 inch in diameter. Bake on an ungreased baking sheet in a moderate oven (350° F.) for 15 to 20 minutes. Dust with confectioners' sugar while still warm. Makes about 9 dozen.

Note: If the dough seems quite soft after mixing, a very small amount of flour may be added; or better still, chill for an hour before shaping into balls. Many like to let the balls stand overnight after shaping, and before baking.

Queen Esther Cookies

½ cup butter (or vegetable fat)	2 tablespoons orange juice
	2 cups sifted flour
1 teaspoon grated orange rind	2 teaspoons baking powder
1 cup sugar	¼ teaspoon salt
1 egg	frosting

Cream the butter with grated orange rind; add the sugar gradually, beating until fluffy. Add egg and orange juice and beat well. Add the dry ingredients sifted together, to make a soft dough that can be handled. Chill before rolling out. Roll out on lightly floured board to ⅛-inch thickness. Cut into fancy shapes. Bake on an ungreased cooky sheet in a hot oven (400° F.) for 10 to 12 minutes.

Plain and fancy cookies are more attractive when the names of Purim characters are written on top. This is done with a toothpick dipped into the frosting; a contrasting color may be used to add a gay note, if desired.

Harmless Hamans are the joy of the children of the family, especially if they are allowed to help make these little gingerbread knaves. When the cookies are baked, every adventurous young fighter bites off the head of a Haman, rendering him harmless for the enjoyment of the rest of the cooky.

Harmless Hamans
(GINGERBREAD MEN)

3½ cups flour	½ cup sugar, white or brown
1 teaspoon baking soda	1 egg
½ teaspoon salt	½ cup molasses
1 teaspoon cinnamon	¼ cup lukewarm water
1½ teaspoons ginger	raisins, currants, or colored
½ cup butter (or vegetable fat)	candies

Mix and sift together the dry ingredients. Cream the butter and add the sugar gradually, creaming well. Add egg and beat well. Measure molasses in a greased cup and add, mixing well. Add flour mixture to egg mixture, alternately with the water, a little at a time, having first and last additions the flour mixture. Add more flour if absolutely necessary to make a dough which can be handled, but avoid this if possible as too much flour makes a tough cooky. Chill. Roll out to ¼- to ⅛-inch thickness on a floured board and cut out figures of gingerbread men. Use currants, raisins, or colored candies to mark eyes, nose, and mouth. Bake on a greased cooky sheet in a moderately hot oven (375° F.) for about 10 minutes. Makes about 16 good-sized Hamans.

Many wonderful honey cakes are made for *shalach monas* plates. A favorite for Yom Kippur is often borrowed for this occasion (*see* p. 60).

Children can be helpful with the mixing and shaping of such simple sweets as Little Fruit Balls, and they enjoy contributing some of their own handiwork to the preparation of *shalach monas* plates.

Little Fruit Balls

4 or 5 cups dried fruit (use any combination of raisins, dates, figs, apricots or pitted prunes)	fruit juice
	confectioners' or granulated sugar
1 cup coconut or nut meats	semi-sweet chocolate

Clean and look over the fruits. Put through a food chopper the fruit and coconut or nuts. Moisten with the fruit juice, using about 1 or 2 tablespoons of juice. Mix well. Shape into balls and roll in sugar or pat 1-inch thick on a sugared pan or board, sprinkle with sugar and let stand for about a day; cut into squares and roll in sugar. Another interesting variation is to chocolate-coat the fruit balls. To do this, melt the chocolate over hot water, then dip each ball separately and drain on waxed paper. Makes two pounds of fruit balls.

The most traditional of candies for Purim is *mohnlach,* a slightly chewy candy filled with poppy seed, and so delicious! See page 159 for special caution about cooking with honey.

Mohnlach
(LITTLE POPPY SEED CANDIES)

1 cup *mohn* (poppy seed)	1 teaspoon ground ginger
⅔ cup honey	½ cup chopped nuts
2 cups sugar	

Wash *mohn* in several waters; drain and dry between paper towels. Put into a heavy saucepan or large frying pan the honey, sugar, and ginger and stir constantly over very low heat until all sugar is dissolved. Remove at once from over heat, for sugar and honey scorch easily. Stir in nuts and *mohn.* Pour out on a board wet with cold water. Then spread the candy with a knife, and when slightly cool, mark off into squares and diamonds. Cool until firm, then cut into pieces. Makes about 2 dozen pieces.

Marzipan is ever the delight of the artist in the kitchen as it molds so easily into different forms. A friend whose childhood was spent in Poland has told us about the beautiful marzipan figures her mother used to make. In addition to leaves, flowers, pears, apples, fruits, and vegetables of every kind, she made animals, both comic and solemn, and lovely dolls—all to delight the hearts of children who had few, and often no, toys.

Marzipan

½ lb. almond paste or 1 lb.   1⅓ cups confectioners' sugar
   blanched almonds   vegetable coloring
2 egg whites

If blanched almonds are used, grind them to a paste. Beat the egg whites until foamy; stir in the sugar gradually to make a thick fondantlike mixture. Add almond paste before mixture becomes too thick to handle easily. Knead with hands until smooth and creamy, adding the sugar or a little fruit juice, as needed, to adjust consistency. Ripen the candy by storing for at least 24 hours, although some set it aside for a week before shaping into interesting forms. Divide into several portions after ripening. Color each as desired with vegetable coloring. Shape as desired. Makes from 1½ to 2 lbs.

Turkish Paste is a prized confection that has appeared on many *shalach monas* plates. It is easy to make and a great delight.

Turkish Paste

5 tablespoons kosher gelatin   ½ cup orange juice
½ cup cold water   3 tablespoons lemon juice
¼ cup hot water   green coloring and mint flavor-
1 cup sugar   ing, or red coloring and
1 cup honey   almond flavoring
¼ teaspoon salt   1 cup finely chopped nuts

Soften the gelatin in cold water for about 5 minutes. Bring the hot water, sugar, and honey to the boiling point. Add the salt and gelatin, and stir until gelatin is dissolved; then simmer gently for 20 minutes. Remove from fire and when cool, add the orange and lemon juice, coloring and flavoring. Stir in the nuts. Let the mixture stand until it begins to thicken. Stir well, then pour into a square pan that has been dipped in water. Paste should be about an inch thick. Let stand overnight in a cool place. Cut the paste into cubes, using a sharp knife that has been dipped in boiling water. Roll in powdered sugar. Makes 4 to 5 dozen pieces.

Passover

The 14th through the 21st of Nisan—usually in April.

Pesach, the Passover, is the Festival of Freedom. It commemorates in prayer, song, and feasting the flight of the Children of Israel from Egypt, which is described in the Biblical Book of Exodus. It recalls a time 3,000 years ago when as slaves they had built great cities for the Pharaohs. Led by Moses, they were delivered from bondage on the night of the Pesach. Passover takes its name from this time of Egyptian enslavement when the angel of the Lord passed over the homes of the Israelites and spared their first-born males.

This story is the heart of the Passover, the wellspring from which flow its symbols and ceremonies, rites and rituals. It is the basis for religious chants and melodic strains heard at Passover time, and it explains the special foods which, according to precept, may be eaten through the eight days of the holiday.

Passover is a time of homecoming. It is so beloved and so deeply rooted in the hearts and minds of all that everyone feels a deep yearning to come home for Pesach, to sit around the Seder table and to participate in all the rich ceremonies of the week. All wish to break the unleavened bread and to partake of the sacramental wine with the family, as well as to share in the heritage of the past.

In ancient times Pesach was a beautiful pilgrim festival

during which great caravans crowded the roads to Jerusalem. Pilgrimages were made to the holy city also at Shavuoth and Sukkoth, the other two pilgrim festivals of the year, and Jewish history is rich with tales of these colorful journeys.

In Jerusalem magnificent ceremonies were held within the Temple when the Passover sacrifices were made. Outside the Temple the streets were scenes of oriental splendor. This was particularly true of the great market place which extended the length of the city. It was a riot of color. Booths, stalls, and tables were weighted down with the riches of the soil, brought from every corner of the kingdom and from many places in the Far East. There were spices and condiments, the most exquisite wines, the freshest fish from nearby waters, syrup from the most fragrant grapes. The choicest of viands were set forth to make this a great and splendid festival.

Following the sacrifices in the Temple, the Paschal Feast was a glorious celebration observed in the homes and community places in Jerusalem. Through the span of Jewish history, many observances have become symbols and the rituals have become today even more deeply steeped in the story of the Exodus.

Only unleavened bread may be eaten during the eight days of the festival. This is in obedience to the words spoken by the Lord to Moses: "Seven days ye shall eat unleavened bread." This Biblical injunction, carefully observed over the years, recalls the day when the Children of Israel fled to freedom in such haste that they carried with them only unleavened dough to be baked under desert suns.

Since Jewish law prescribes that only unleavened bread may be eaten during Passover, it is necessary for the housewife to perform innumerable household tasks in preparation for and during the festival season. The excitement of preparation begins weeks, even months, before the holiday. There is wine to be made; *rusell*, the special Passover vinegar, must be started; perhaps a *med* (mead) is to be brewed. All this requires plenty of time.

The house must be bright and fresh for Passover. It will be scrubbed and cleaned from top to bottom, and may require some painting or new wall paper. In olden times every possible surface was whitewashed. This is the time, too, for special indulgences. If the father needs a new armchair, the family may decide to get it for Passover.

Passover is the time when the family likes to have a bright spring wardrobe. There is much excitement outfitting the children. The mother must, of course, have her new spring bonnet, even though the father may get along with only a bright new tie.

The provident housewife plans her food orders well in advance. The avalanche of foods that begins to arrive is something startling. There are crates of eggs, matzoth in five-pound packages, and great quantities of especially prepared packaged foods, all *Kasher L'Pesaach* (kosher for Passover).

Since the whole family will have come together from far and near, some relatives perhaps even coming from across the ocean, these quantities of food will disappear like magic during the eight days of festivities. Part of these provisions are ordered with the needy in mind, as many gifts of Passover supplies go out to the kitchens of the poor, so that all may feast at this time.

Ritual laws are also responsible for many of the food purchases. No foods in everyday use in the kitchen may be used during Passover. Even the most simple staple, such as an opened package of salt, must be replaced by a package that is *Kasher L'Pesaach.*

Of all the foods coming into the kitchen for Passover, none are more carefully prepared than the matzoth, the unleavened bread. These are thin flat wafers, cut in rounds or squares, made of a mixture of special flour and water. Their preparation was formerly a community project. Now they are manufactured commercially on a very extensive scale, under the strictest supervision of rabbis.

There are two degrees of ritual kashering (preparing according to Jewish law) for matzoth. The matzoth, and matza products (matza meal and matza cake meal) for general festival use are prepared in one way. The matzoth for the elders of the congregation, *matza shel mitsvah* (the matza of precept), are produced according to even more carefully guarded rituals, which regulate every step in the preparation, from the selection of the wheat in the field to the finished matzoth. This *matza shel mitsvah* is so precious, made in such small quantities, that few besides the elders can obtain it. Those who do, obtain it in quantities so small as to provide only a piece "the size of an olive" for each one at the Seder.

A day or two before Pesach the time has come for bringing out the special dishes not used at any other time of the year. There are two sets of dishes, one for *milchige* foods (dairy foods), the other for *fleischige* foods (meat foods). These are brought from the special cupboards in which they have been stored since the previous Passover. There is a special joy in handling them again, as there is in once more meeting old friends. Then, too, there are sure to be among these dishes some special ones dear to the hearts of all the family, and these are washed and dried with most loving care.

Many housewives have to supplement their Passover dishes with silver, dishes, and utensils used the year around. In order to make these kosher for Passover, a special process called kashering must be followed. The old-fashioned method was to scald them in a metal tub into which great hot coals from the stove were lifted and boiling water poured over them, hissing and sputtering. The intense heat cleansed them of all *chometz*. In kashering today, some pieces have to be dipped, others scalded. . . For the correct ritual, consult your rabbi.

When all is ready through the house, there is a special and wonderful little ceremony to assure that no *chometz*, no crumb of bread (leaven), remains. This is called the ancient ceremony of "searching for the leaven, searching for the *chometz*." It begins when the father returns from synagogue on the night before Passover. The whole family accompanies him on his search as he goes from room to room, armed with a wooden spoon in one hand and a few goose feathers in the other. The mother, following with a lighted candle, is most helpful in pointing out the few crumbs of bread she has helpfully planted to make the ceremony real. These are gathered into a cloth, bound with a string, to be burned the next day. What child could ever forget the significance of no leaven throughout the Passover week?

Everyone rises with the dawn on the day when Passover will begin at sunset. There are many last-minute things to be done, particularly for the Seder dinner. The Seder, which means literally "Order of Service," is the most impressive, most profoundly moving ceremony of the eight days of Passover. In this ceremony all relive the magnificent story of the Exodus. Every member of the family takes an active part in the prayers, chants, recitations, and songs through which the story unfolds.

The Seder table is beautiful to behold. The candlesticks are often cherished heirlooms; table linen is of the finest; fruits and flowers are most choice. Along with the Passover dishes and silver, goblets are placed at each setting, and in a place of honor there is a special goblet for Elijah the Prophet. There is also the special Passover plate upon which are placed the ceremonial Seder foods. The chair for the head of the household, who will lead the Seder service, is provided luxuriously with cushions, symbolic of the spirit of freedom and comfort found in a Jewish home on this night of nights.

According to old-established custom, it is the leader of the Seder who places the symbolic foods upon the table. These form part of the Seder ceremony and are as follows:

Three whole perfect matzoth, each covered with a napkin or doily and placed one upon the other. These represent the Bread of Affliction, and also the unity of the three religious groups of the Jews: Kohanites, Levites, and Israelites.

A roasted lamb bone, placed in the upper right hand corner of the Passover plate, is a symbol of the Paschal lamb.

A roasted egg, placed on the opposite left hand corner of the plate, is a symbol of the ancient festival offering.

Moror (bitter herb, usually horse-radish root), placed in the center of the plate, recalls the bitterness of slavery.

Charoseth, placed in the lower right hand corner of the plate, is a combination of grated apple, nuts, and wine, symbol of the clay and bricks used by the Israelites to build the "treasured cities of Pharaoh."

Parsley, watercress, endive (sweet herbs), placed in the lower left hand corner of the plate, speak of spring and growth.

Salt water, placed variously around the table in bowls and pitchers, symbolizes tears shed by captive peoples.

Glasses for wine, placed at each setting, with a special goblet for Elijah the Prophet, are filled and drunk with ceremonial meaning at four different times in the Seder.

Haggadah. This is the book of the Seder, the written order of established ceremony. One copy is placed on the table for each person, or one for every two.

The Haggadah, ritual of the Seder, began as the story of the Exodus told to the family over Passover tables. The

very word *haggadah* means "to tell." Through the years the
telling has assumed form and shape and order.

The Seder belongs particularly to the children of the
family. It is a beautifully organized service of intense interest
to everyone, but the whole intent of the ceremony is, and
has always been, to obey the precept, "... tell thy son." It
is an impressive and delightful way to teach Jewish children
the history of their people. Many little diversions are introduced during the evening to please the children, to arouse
their curiosity and to enliven their interest. The Seder lasts
far into the night, so little children are prepared for the
evening with an afternoon nap. Attractive songs and chants,
riddles and jingles keep the children, except the very young,
alert to the end.

The Ceremony of the Seder

(1) The chanting of the *Kiddush* by the leader of the
Seder (who is usually the head of the household), while he
holds the first cup of Passover wine in his right hand. The
first cup of wine is then drunk by all.

(2) The washing of hands.

(3) A sprig of parsley or watercress, given to each by the
leader, is dipped into salt water and eaten.

(4) The middle matza is broken into two uneven pieces
by the leader. The smaller part is returned to its place between the other two on the plate. The larger part is so
handled as to attract the attention of the children. It may
be placed, carelessly, between the pillows of the leader's seat,
or less conspicuously hidden, depending upon the general
age of the children. This larger piece is known as the
afikoman (dessert), and it is the privilege of the children
to try to secure possession of it at some time during the
evening. The lucky child holds it for a "ransom" when it is

called for near the close of the Passover meal. This, it would seem, is designed to amuse the children, and they love it.

(5) Raising of the platter follows, with these solemn words, "Behold the bread of affliction which our ancestors ate in the land of Egypt. Let all who are hungry come in and eat, let all who desire, come in and celebrate the Passover." The chanting that follows is in both Hebrew and English, and all take part in the reading, sometimes singly, sometimes in unison.

(6) *Mah nishtanah.* The four questions are now asked by the youngest child present. These have been proudly and carefully learned far in advance of this night. The child asks:

"How is this night different from all other nights? On all other nights we eat leavened or unleavened bread; but on this night only unleavened bread.

". . . on all other nights we eat sweet herbs, tonight bitter herbs, as well as the sweet.

". . . on all other nights we do not dip herbs, even once; on this night we dip them twice in salt water.

". . . on all other nights we eat and drink without reclining; but on this night we all recline."

And now begins the story of the Passover as taken from history and chanted from the Haggadah. It tells of the suffering in Egypt, the plagues sent upon Pharaoh, the escape from bondage, and the crossing of the Red Sea. Chanting is broken frequently by eager questions. Songs and chants are taken up by the whole group throughout the recital. It is concluded with a prayer for peace for the world, and sealed with the drinking of the second cup of wine.

All then prepare for the Passover meal by the washing of hands, followed by recital of the blessing.

(7) The upper matza is now broken and divided among all; then the remaining part of the middle matza is also

broken and divided. These are salted and eaten after the benediction over the matzoth.

(8) The bitter herb is broken into pieces for each and these are dipped into the *charoseth* before eating.

(9) The Hillel Sandwich is made by each. This is done by spreading grated horse-radish between two pieces of the matzoth, in accordance with a custom of the great sage Hillel.

(10) Now follows the wonderful dinner of the Passover served by the women of the household.

Seder Meal

Egg Soup
Gefillte Fish   Rusell Horse-radish
Goldene Yoich   Knaidlach or Halkes
Roast Chicken   Matza Stuffing   Helzel
Carrot Tzimmes   Green Salad
Compote   Sponge Cake   Macaroons
Tea with Lemon
Afikoman

(11) The hidden *afikoman* is now the object of mirthful searching. Once it is found, the lucky child may request his reward and this is duly promised. The *afikoman* is then divided between all who are present.

(12) Very young children are now put to bed, for the evening has already been a long one for them. The older children and the grownups proceed with songs and prayers.

(13) Hands are washed, each Haggadah is opened, and grace is recited. All join in the singing of psalms. This is followed by the drinking of the third cup of wine; this time the cup for Elijah is also filled.

(14) The fourth cup of wine is now filled for each, and the door is opened so that Elijah, the prophet of hope and faith, may enter to join the family. All eyes are turned toward the door and the children wait breathlessly to welcome the

great prophet. When the door is closed and all again turn to the table, the children are eagerly certain that Elijah has been among them as their guest and has sipped from his goblet of wine.

(15) Lively chants and songs now occupy the remainder of the evening. There are many, both old and new, that are beloved by all. Some of those that have been sung earlier in the evening are repeated again and again, because all delight in their melody. Among these are *"Daiainu"* (Alone 'twould have sufficed us), its rolling rhythm rising often; and *"Addir Hu* (God of Might), a beautiful chant. *"Chad Gadya"* (An Only Kid) a favorite of each succeeding generation of children. There are songs from Israel, songs from America, songs from former homelands in both Europe and Asia, and the singing goes on into the early hours of the morning. Passover is a rich and joyous experience for young and old. Happiness enfolds the family as the celebration draws to a close.

Charoseth
(FOR THE SEDER SERVICE)

½ cup finely chopped apples   1 teaspoon cinnamon
¼ cup chopped almonds or   wine
    walnuts   cinnamon bark, if desired

Apples must be *very* finely chopped; add nuts and cinnamon, with sufficient wine to make a mixture that holds together. Add cinnamon bark, if desired.

Egg Soup
(FOR THE SEDER SERVICE)

1 hard-cooked egg per person   salt water (1 to 2 teaspoons salt
                                    per qt. water)

Serve 1 egg, shelled, in a soup plate to each person. Each mashes his egg with a fork and adds salt water (from pitchers or bowls on the table), as desired. This is really the first course in the Seder meal, and though very simple, most refreshing.

In order that the housewife may be sure that her Passover kitchen is ritually fit for the holidays, it is necessary for her to observe certain rules. Matzoth replace all grain during Passover. They are made according to strict ritual procedure, with wheat flour and water, and absolutely no leavening. When finely ground, this waferlike, unleavened bread is known as matza meal. When ground extra fine, it becomes matza cake meal. Matza meal and matza cake meal are used in cooking to replace all other flour and grain. Potato starch, an exception, may be used as it is a vegetable, not a grain.

A check list of Passover restrictions:

(1) No ordinary grain of any kind may be used.

(2) Leavening such as baking powder, baking soda, and yeast may not be used.

(3) No legumes may be used (such as peas, beans, lentils, and all similar legumes).

(4) Garlic may not be used.

(5) No malt liquors may be used or served.

A check list of foods acceptable for Passover:

(1) Fresh fruits, fresh vegetables (other than legumes), fish, eggs, and kosher meats (see dietary laws, page 181).

(2) Foods specially prepared for Passover, including fats and all other foods, packaged, canned, frozen, or dried, that are stamped *Kasher L'Pesaach.*

(3) All milk and milk products bearing this same stamp are permissible.

The list of prepared packaged and bottled foods grows longer every year as alert industries increase the number of products they prepare for Pesach under strictest supervision, according to ritual requirements. The categories of foods now include wine and carbonated waters, dried fruits, nut meats, salad oils, and many others.

From the Passover foods Jewish housewives arrange a delightful variety of meals for family dinners and company fare. The following are suggestive of many dinner menus served throughout Passover.

Passover Dinner #1

Chopped Liver   Zweibella Matzoth
Celery   Radishes   Rusell Beets
Veal Chops   Passover Varenikes
Apple Matza Kugel   Green Salad Bowl
Compote   Tea with Lemon   Macaroons
Wine   Nuts

Passover Dinner #2

Chopped Egg and Onion
Hot Rusell Borscht with Boiled Potato
Rusell Fleisch   Matza Kugel   Spinach
Lettuce and Tomato Salad
Chremslach   Jam   Macaroons
Tea with Lemon
Wine   Nuts

Passover Dinner #3
(MILCHIGE DINNER)

Cheese Matzoth
Cucumbers   Scallions   Radishes
Cold Borscht   Sour Cream
Broiled Salmon   Mashed Potatoes   Glazed Carrots
Cabbage Slaw
Matza Fruit Fritters   Tea with Lemon
Wine   Pesach Walnut Cookies

Refreshment Table
(FOR HOLIDAY GUESTS)

Wine   Pesach Sponge Cake   Macaroons
Beet Eingemachts   Black Radish Eingemachts
Ingberlach   Bowl Fresh Fruit
Hot Tea in Tall Glasses with Lemon and Varenyah
Bowl of Assorted Nuts

Long before it is time to plan Passover menus, there is much food preparation to be got under way. Beet *rusell*, the Passover vinegar, must be begun well in advance of the holiday as it requires considerable time for fermentation. The women of the family hover solicitously over the crock of ruby-rich beet juice as it "makes," for the perfection of this vinegar is important to the preparation of a number of Passover dishes.

How little an ordinary recipe can tell about the real preparation of this gourmet's delight! Pleasure begins when the mother goes to market for the beets. This will be about a month before the holiday, so as to allow for three weeks of fermentation.

Pesach Rusell
(FERMENTED BEET JUICE FOR PASSOVER)

10 to 12 lbs. beets   sufficient water for a 6-qt. crock

In many homes this *rusell* making is a work of love, and one of us remembers how her mother used to make almost a ritual of it. First she would select a place to hold the precious crock. It was scrubbed to spotless cleanliness. Now for the preparation of the beets... She would wash them well, and then pare them very thin and place them, cut in quarters (or more pieces if the beets were large) into the crock. It was then filled with water to within an inch or two of the top. The lid would then be set loosely in place, perhaps even slightly atilt. To keep out dust, she would cover the crock with cheesecloth tied loosely in place.

There would follow a week of impatience, during which Mother could not forget the contents of the crock. A week to the day she would uncover it and remove all scum, dip a glass deep into the liquid and hold it between herself and the light. Her sharp eye would soften as she would note the slightly pink and cloudy liquid. This was a sign that the *rusell* was "making." She would then stir it well and cover it as before. After three more weeks of fermentation (sometimes slightly less), she would test it again. Again she would dip her glass, carefully, gently, into the now winey, fragrant vinegar. This time the juice would be a deep, rich scarlet and clear as crystal, perfect for the making of Passover Borscht and Rusell Chrein.

This recipe makes from 2 to 3 quarts of *rusell* and from 6 to 8 cups of beets.

Rusell Borscht
(BEET SOUP—HOT OR COLD)

1 qt. *rusell* liquid	salt, sugar, and lemon juice
1 cup *rusell* beets, chopped	2 eggs, beaten
1 medium-sized onion, minced	

If served hot:

1 hot boiled potato for each serving	sprinkle of hard-cooked egg, if desired
sour cream, if desired	

If served cold:

cucumbers	sour cream
scallions	sprinkle of hard-cooked egg, if desired
1 hot boiled potato for each serving, if desired	

Strain the *rusell* into the chopped *rusell* beets and onion; cook until beets are tender. Adjust seasonings to taste with salt, sugar, and lemon juice. Remove from heat. Beat eggs in a bowl and then stir in gradually 1 cup hot borscht. When well blended, stir the egg mixture into the large saucepan of borscht.

To serve hot, add a hot boiled potato to each soup plate of borscht. Garnish with sour cream, if desired.

To serve cold, chill, then garnish each serving with crisp cucumbers and scallions that have been crushed with a little salt; or stir crushed cucumbers and scallions into soup before serving, a teaspoon for each soup plate. Some like to serve also with a hot boiled potato. Top with sour cream.

If desired, sliced hard-cooked egg may be added to either hot or chilled borscht. Serves 4 or 5.

Note: If *rusell* beets and *rusell* are not available, freshly cooked or canned beets, with their juice, may be used, adding lemon juice for tartness.

Rusell Fleisch in Borscht
(MEAT COOKED IN FERMENTED BEET JUICE)

1 qt. *rusell* liquid
2 cups *rusell* beets, chopped
3 cups water
2 medium-sized onions,
    chopped
2 to 3 lbs. brisket or other fat
    meat
marrow and veal bones

2 teaspoons salt
¼ teaspoon pepper
sugar
lemon juice
1 or 2 eggs
boiled potatoes, if desired

Measure *rusell* liquid and beets into a large soup kettle with the water. Add onions, brisket, marrow and veal bones, salt, and pepper. Cook gently for 2 to 3 hours—until the meat is tender. Remove meat and keep hot. Season the broth with sugar and lemon juice to taste and remove from heat. To thicken broth, beat eggs slightly, then stir in slowly a cup of hot broth. When well blended, stir this egg mixture into the large pot of broth. To serve, slice the meat and arrange on a serving platter; then spoon some of the broth over the top as a sauce. Serve the borscht at once, while still hot, in individual soup plates, each with a hot boiled potato, if desired. Serve 6 to 8.

Rusell Cocktail
(PASSOVER BEET JUICE COCKTAIL)

Dip out sufficient *rusell* liquid from the storage crock. Bring gently to the boiling point, then strain at once. Chill. Season with grated onion and salt. Serve in juice glasses with a slice of lemon and a garnish of sour cream.

Rusell Chrein, beet horse-radish, is served by modern gourmets for as long after Passover as they can persuade their supply of *rusell* liquid to stretch. No Passover table is complete without this delicious sharp, stinging relish.

Rusell Chrein
(HORSE-RADISH WITH FERMENTED BEET JUICE)

freshly grated horse-radish
rusell, to mix

salt, to taste

Use only freshly grated horse-radish. Stir in sufficient *rusell* liquid to moisten and color the mixture a good scarlet. Season with salt (and a little sugar, if desired). Serve with Gefillte Fish and meat dishes. Use also as seasoning for salad dressings.

Passover Salad Dressing
(A MODERN USE OF RUSELL)

3 tablespoons *rusell* liquid
juice of 1 to 2 lemons
1 teaspoon salt

½ teaspoon pepper
2 teaspoons sugar
1 cup vegetable oil

Beat or stir all ingredients together just before using. Makes 1½ cups of dressing.

There is a friendly greeting, *"Mit gut appetit,"* spoken when friends meet friends who are dining. These appetizers express this same greeting, as they stimulate good eating.

Zwiebella Matzoth
(LITTLE ONION MATZOTH)

Rub the matzoth with the cut side of a sweet onion (no garlic may be used for Passover); dust lightly with salt; brush with chicken fat. Brown in a hot oven or under the broiler grill.

Schmaltz Matzoth

Brush the matzoth with poultry fat; sprinkle with salt, preferably coarse salt. Toast, if desired.

Cheese Matzoth

Break the matzoth into pieces about 3 inches in size. Put together in pairs with a filling of cream cheese or cottage cheese, seasoned to taste with a little cream and sugar. On a separate plate stir 1 egg with a tablespoon of water and a dash of salt. Dip the filled matzoth in this egg coating, one at a time, placing at once in hot fat in a frying pan. Fry to delicate brown on both sides. Serve hot as a delightful party hors d'oeuvre.

Sprinkled Matzoth

Simply pour cold water quickly over a piece of matza, shake free of moisture, dust with salt and pepper ... and eat. For some reason the cold water brings out a delightful flavor.

Passover Varenikes
(SAVORY STUFFED POTATO CAKES)

3 eggs, separated
1 cup matza meal
2 cups mashed potatoes
salt and pepper

1 cup chopped cooked meat
1 egg, slightly beaten
1 tablespoon water

To prepare potato cakes, beat the egg whites until stiff but not dry. In another bowl, combine the egg yolks with matza meal, potatoes, 1 teaspoon salt and about ⅛ teaspoon pepper. Mix well, then lightly work in the stiffly beaten egg whites. Use two-thirds of the mixture and shape into small balls, each about the size of a large egg. To fill, mix the chopped meat with salt and pepper to taste (adding a little minced onion or sweet green pepper, if desired). Make a depression in each potato ball and fill with the seasoned meat. Cover with a little of the potato mixture that has been reserved for this purpose. Coat with the slightly beaten egg that has been thinned with a little water. Fry to golden brown in hot fat. Makes 12 to 15.

Passover Stuffing
(FOR POULTRY AND MEATS)

3 cups matza *farfel* (bit pieces) or 4 matzoth broken into bits
¾ cup cold water
1 medium-sized onion, diced
3 tablespoons poultry fat (or vegetable fat)

2 eggs, slightly beaten
1 teaspoon salt
¼ teaspoon pepper
¼ teaspoon ginger
¼ cup celery, diced
2 tablespoons minced parsley

Moisten the *farfel* with cold water. Brown onion in the fat in a very large frying pan. Press water from the *farfel*, gently; do not mash. Add to the onion; add remaining ingredients and mix lightly. Stuff, with a light touch, into poultry or meats.

For *flaumen* (prune) stuffing, add ½ cup finely cut prunes, ¼ teaspoon cinnamon, and a dash of ginger. Prunes should be prepared as directed on package, soaked or not as required; then pitted and cut into pieces. Sufficient for a 5-lb. bird.

Passover Helzel
(STUFFED POULTRY NECK)

poultry neck
1 medium-sized potato, grated
¼ cup matza meal
2 tablespoons poultry fat

1 small onion, diced
½ teaspoon salt
⅛ teaspoon pepper
dash of cinnamon

Clean and scrape neck; do not cut away the fat. Sew or tie one end to keep in the stuffing. Mix remaining ingredients together lightly and stuff the neck lightly, about ⅔ full, allowing for expansion during cooking. Sew or tie open end. Dip again into boiling water and again scrape clean. Roast with bird or bake in center of a *tzimmes* or *kugel*. For a very large bird, double the recipe.

Cheese Matza Pudding

4 to 6 matzoth
4 eggs
1 cup milk
1 lb. cottage cheese

½ teaspoon salt
2 teaspoons sugar
¼ teaspoon cinnamon
2 tablespoons butter

Break the matzoth roughly into large sections. Mix the eggs with the milk; set aside ½ cup of this mixture for dipping the matzoth, and mix the remainder with the cottage cheese and seasonings. Dip the matzoth in the reserved egg and milk, and arrange in layers in a greased 3-qt. baking dish, dotting each alternately with butter and with the prepared cheese. Make the top layer of matzoth and pour any remaining milk and eggs over this. Bake in a moderate oven (350° F.) for 35 to 40 minutes. Serves 4 to 6.

Gribenes Matza Kugel
(MATZA PUDDING WITH CRACKLINGS)

5 matzoth
1 cup water (about)
3 tablespoons poultry fat
 (or vegetable fat)
3 eggs, well beaten

2 tablespoons *gribenes* (*see* page 20)
1 teaspoon salt
⅛ teaspoon pepper
2 teaspoons sugar

Soak the matzoth in the water; drain, but not too dry. Mix with 2 tablespoons of the fat. Add the eggs, *gribenes*, salt, pepper, and sugar; mix lightly. Grease a 2-qt. baking dish with remaining fat and pour in the prepared mixture. Bake in a moderate oven (350° F.) for about 45 minutes, increasing heat during the last 10 minutes to brown the top. Serve piping hot with meat. Serves 6.

Passover Blintzes
(CHEESE-FILLED PANCAKES)

4 or 5 eggs	1 lb. cottage cheese
¾ cup matza meal	3 tablespoons sugar
salt	1 to 2 tablespoons milk or
1½ cups water	sour cream

To make batter for pancakes: Beat 3 eggs slightly; then gradually beat in the matza meal, ½ teaspoon salt, and the water.

To bake pancakes: Heat a 6-inch frying pan; brush lightly with fat. Pour in sufficient batter to no more than cover surface, tissue paper thin; tip the pan to spread the batter smoothly. Brown on one side only and turn out brown side up on a clean towel. Cover with cloth. Repeat, until all batter is used, placing one cake on top of another as each is baked.

To fill: Mix cottage cheese with one or two eggs, as desired; season with ½ teaspoon salt and the sugar. Add milk or sour cream. Fill each pancake, one by one, by placing a spoonful of the cheese mixture on the brown side, then folding three sides over to cover. Roll into envelope shape and tuck in the edge to keep filling in place.

Fry or bake. To fry: when all are filled, brown in a heavy frying pan in hot fat, turning to brown all sides. To bake: Place on a well-greased shallow baking dish; then dot with butter and bake in a moderate oven (350° F.) for 25 to 30 minutes, or until a golden brown. Serve with sour cream. Serves about 6.

Goldene Yoich (recipe p. 18) is the most prized of delicate chicken soups. The glory of the Sabbath table, it appears again and again on holiday menus. It is served during Passover with the most delectable *knaidlach*.

Young housewives, please note: It is wise to develop your skill in making light feathery *knaidlach*, for there is no better way to win laurels as a cook!

Matza Knaidlach
(PASSOVER DUMPLINGS)

2 eggs, separated   ½ teaspoon salt
3 tablespoons chicken fat   ¾ cup matza meal
½ cup hot water or hot soup

Beat yolks with the chicken fat until thick and well blended. Pour over the hot water or hot soup and beat well. Fold in the matza meal mixed with the salt and then fold in the egg whites that have been beaten until stiff but not dry. Chill for about ½ hour. Wet hands with cold water and shape into small balls. Drop gently into 2 quarts of boiling soup or boiling salted water; reduce the heat, cover, and cook gently for 20 to 25 minutes. Makes about 18.

In addition to their place with Goldene Yoich, *knaidlach* have another claim to fame. They are also appreciated when served alone, as a vegetable. One family chuckles with delight over the men of their household, who are more than content to be served at table, the year round, except when there are Matza Knaidlach on the dinner menu. For these they insist, helpfully, on serving themselves in the kitchen. To this family *halkes* have but one meaning. They are huge *knaidlach*, such as only their mother could make, the delight of Brother Abe.

Enormous Halkes
(LARGE DUMPLINGS)

4 eggs, separated   1 teaspoon salt
4 tablespoons chicken fat (or   1 cup hot soup or hot water
    vegetable fat)   1 tablespoon minced parsley
1⅓ cups matza meal

Beat egg whites until stiff but not dry. Combine egg yolks, fat and salt with the matza meal. Pour the hot soup or water over the matza meal mixture and blend together. Add parsley, if desired. Fold in the stiffly beaten whites. With wet hands, shape into balls. These particular *halkes* are shaped about the size of crab apples, although they may be made as small or as large as desired. Drop gently into about 3 quarts of boiling soup or boiling salted water, and cover tightly. Cook for 20 to 30 minutes for small balls and about 35 minutes for the larger ones. Makes about 30.

Liver Knaidlach
(LIVER DUMPLINGS)

1 cup cooked liver
1 medium-sized onion
1½ cups boiling water
1½ cups matza meal
3 eggs, beaten

¼ cup poultry fat (or vegetable fat)
1 teaspoon salt
dash of pepper

Grind the liver and onion quite fine. Pour the boiling water over the matza meal and let stand until absorbed. When cool, mix with the ground liver and onion and beat together until very light and fluffy. Roll into small balls. Wet the hands to do this, as the mixture will then handle much more easily. Drop gently into 3 quarts of boiling salted water (1 teaspoon salt to 1 qt. water). Cover and cook gently for about 25 minutes. Makes about 30.

Potato Knaidlach
(POTATO DUMPLINGS)

1 cup freshly mashed potatoes
½ cup hot soup or hot water
1 teaspoon salt
dash of black pepper

3 tablespoons chicken fat (or vegetable fat)
3 eggs, well beaten
1 cup matza meal

While mashed potatoes are still warm, beat in the hot liquid to a smooth mixture. Add salt, pepper, and fat; beat until well mixed. Beat the eggs with a rotary beater until very light. Fold these into the mixture; fold in the matza meal. Chill for several hours. Roll into balls the size of marbles, wetting the hands to handle. Drop gently into 3 quarts of boiling salted water or soup. Cover; cook for about 20 minutes. Makes about 2 dozen.

Passover Egg Noodles

2 eggs
¼ teaspoon salt

1 tablespoon matza meal
2 tablespoons water

Beat the eggs slightly; add the remaining ingredients and beat together until smooth. Heat a 6-inch frying pan, grease lightly and pour in a little of the batter, just enough to cover the surface of the pan. Tip the pan from side to side for an even cake, cooking until only golden on both sides. Continue until the batter is used up. Keep the pancakes covered until all are baked. While still warm, roll each tightly and cut into strips as fine as possible. Shake out to dry. Add to boiling soup at serving time and serve at once. Makes about 1 cup of noodles.

Egg Drops

2 eggs, well beaten
¼ teaspoon salt
½ cup water

⅔ cup matza meal
dash of cinnamon

Combine the eggs with the remaining ingredients in the order named. Mix to smoothness. Drop by quarter teaspoons into boiling soup. Cover tightly and cook for three minutes. Sufficient for 2 to 3 qts. of soup.

Toasted Farfel
(TOASTED MATZA BITS)

2 egg yolks
2 tablespoons poultry fat
    (or vegetable fat)

½ teaspoon salt
1 cup matza *farfel*

Mix the egg yolks in a large bowl with the fat and salt. Add *farfel* and mix lightly to coat all particles. Spread out on a greased, shallow baking pan. Toast to light brown in a moderate oven (350° F.). Add to hot soup just before serving. Sufficient for about 6 servings.

Passover Mondlen
(ALMOND BALLS FOR SOUP)

½ cup finely ground almonds
2 eggs, separated
¼ teaspoon salt

cinnamon or nutmeg
1 teaspoon grated lemon rind

Mix the almonds with the egg yolks; add salt and flavorings. Fold in the egg whites, stiffly beaten. Drop by teaspoon into hot fat, deep enough to cover. Drain on absorbent paper. Serve in soup.

The handsome array of *latkes,* fritters, and *kugels* made with matza and matza meal and a limited choice of other ingredients is tribute again to the ingenuity of the Jewish housewife.

Fonkuchen
(A BIG PANCAKE)

2 eggs
½ cup milk
¼ teaspoon salt
dash of pepper

1 to 2 matzoth
butter (or vegetable fat) for
  frying

Beat together the eggs, milk, and seasonings. Add the matzoth, broken into small pieces. Mix lightly. Heat fat in a heavy frying pan; pour in the mixture. Cover; cook over moderate heat for 5 to 8 minutes. Turn pancake and finish cooking, uncovered, for another 2 minutes. Serve with sugar or honey. Serves 2.

The recipe for delicious potato *latkes* (page 84), popular for Chanukah, may be used during Passover provided matza meal is substituted for the thickening in the original recipe. Or use the recipes for matza meal *latkes* which follow.

Matza Potato Latkes
(MATZA POTATO PANCAKES)

2 cups mashed potatoes
3 eggs, well beaten
salt and pepper

¾ cup matza meal
¾ cup milk or water (about)

Mix the ingredients together in the order named, adding sufficient liquid to make a mixture that can be shaped into cakes. Fry in hot fat, browning on both sides. Makes 10 to 12.

Matza Meal Latkes
(MATZA MEAL PANCAKES)

3 eggs, separated
½ cup water or milk
½ teaspoon salt
1 tablespoon sugar

½ cup matza meal
butter (or vegetable fat) for frying

Beat the yolks until light; add the salt and sugar. Fold in the matza meal and the whites, stiffly beaten. Drop by tablespoon into the hot fat, that is about ¼-inch deep in a heavy frying pan. Brown on both sides. Drain on absorbent paper. Serve hot with sugar, honey, or jam. Makes 1 dozen.

Farfel Cheese Latkes
(MATZA BIT CHEESE PANCAKES)

5 cups matza *farfel* or 4 matzoth, crumbled
1 cup water
3 eggs, well beaten

1 tablespoon butter (or vegetable fat), melted
3 tablespoons cottage or cream cheese

Pour the water over the *farfel* or crumbled matzoth. Let stand until absorbed. Add the remaining ingredients. Mix well. Drop by tablespoon into hot fat in a frying pan. Brown on both sides. Drain on absorbent paper. Serve hot with jam or honey. Makes about 3 dozen.

Matza Brie
(A MATZA OMELET)

4 matzoth
boiling water
4 eggs

dash of pepper
½ teaspoon salt
sugar or honey

Break the matzoth into 2-inch pieces and place in a colander. *Brie,* or scald, by pouring boiling water over them. Drain quickly to prevent sogginess. Beat the eggs well, adding salt and pepper; then add the matzoth. Heat a large frying pan and add fat for frying. Add the egg mixture and cook over low heat to golden brown on one side, then turn carefully and brown on the other side. Serve on a hot platter as a large family-size pancake. Serve hot with sugar that has been mixed with a dash of cinnamon, or with honey. Makes 4 to 5 portions.

Passover Fruit Fritters

3 eggs, well beaten
2 tablespoons sugar
½ teaspoon salt
¼ teaspoon cinnamon
1 cup matza meal

½ cup water
2 tablespoons melted butter
(or vegetable fat)
2 cups fruit, cut in slices

To the well-beaten eggs, add sugar mixed with the salt and cinnamon. Add the matza meal, alternately with the water, about a third of each at a time, to make a delicate batter. Fold in the melted butter. Drain the fruit well; then dip a piece at a time into the batter. Drop directly into deep hot fat for frying; drain. Or fry in a frying pan with just enough hot fat to cover; brown all sides; drain. Serve with sugar. Makes about 2 dozen small fritters.

Chremslach is one of those dishes that makes one remember and talk about the wonderful foods of one's childhood. When we happened to ask an old friend what his favorite Passover dish was, without hesitation he said, Chremslach.

Chremslach
(GLORIFIED LATKES)

5 eggs
1¼ cups matza meal
5 tablespoons water
3 tablespoons chicken fat (or vegetable fat)
1 teaspoon salt

½ cup *rusell* beets (*see* recipe p. 136)
½ cup honey
⅛ teaspoon ginger
¼ cup chopped nuts
2 tablespoons wine or *med.*

To make the dough: Beat the eggs slightly; add the matza meal, water, fat, and salt. Blend well and chill until filling is ready. To make the filling: Chop the *rusell* beets; turn into a saucepan; add honey, ginger, and nuts; simmer together until thickened. Mix with wine or *med;* cool. To shape: Make oblong patties of the dough, about ¼ inch thick. Spread half of these patties with the filling and cover with the remaining half. Seal in the filling with dough, shaping it like an egg. To bake: Place on a greased shallow pan; brush with fat. Bake in a moderately hot oven (375° F.) for about 30 minutes. Turn to brown evenly, and if necessary, brush again with fat. Serve with jam or jelly. Makes 12 to 14.

Other traditional fillings:

Flaumen (prune) and nut. Combine 1 cup cooked, pitted prunes with ¼ cup each of chopped nuts, chopped raisins, and sugar. Add 2 tablespoons lemon juice and blend together.

Meat and liver. Combine 1 cup each of chopped cooked meat and chopped cooked liver. Season with 2 tablespoons minced onion, and 2 tablespoons chicken fat (or vegetable fat). Add salt and pepper to taste.

Chremslach
(OF A SPECIAL DELICACY)

1 cup matza meal	¼ teaspoon salt
1 tablespoon chopped almonds	1 cup soup stock, boiling
1 teaspoon sugar	4 eggs, separated

Mix the matza meal with almonds, sugar, and salt. Stir in the boiling hot soup. Add the egg yolks, well beaten. Beat the egg whites until stiff but not dry, and fold into the mixture. Drop by tablespoon into deep hot fat and fry to delicate brown. Drain. Sprinkle with confectioners' sugar. Serve with Wine Sauce (*see* recipe page 162) or with honey. Makes about 16.

There is something delightfully homey about a good *kugel,* and every family has its favorite. Add them together, and the variety is infinite.

Apple Matza Kugel
(MATZA APPLE PUDDING)

3 matzoth	¼ cup almonds, chopped
4 tablespoons poultry fat	grated rind of 1 lemon
(or vegetable fat)	½ teaspoon salt
5 eggs, separated	1 large tart apple, grated
1 cup matza meal	

Dip matzoth in cold water, merely to moisten, then press dry. Melt half the fat in a frying pan and pan-fry the matzoth over low heat until quite dry. Beat egg yolks until thick and lemon-colored; add matza meal and then the fried matzoth. Mix lightly

but well. Add almonds, lemon rind, salt, and grated apple. Beat
egg whites until stiff but not dry; fold into mixture. Pour into a
greased 2-qt. baking dish; dot with remaining fat. Bake in a
moderate oven (350° F.) for 35 to 40 minutes, or until fluffy
light and delicately browned. Serve with Wine Sauce (*see* recipe
page 162). Serves 6 or 7.

Farfel Sharlot
(FARFEL AND FRUIT CHARLOTTE)

2 cups matza *farfel* (matza bits)	2 tablespoons poultry fat (or vegetable fat)
1 cup cold water	1 cup sliced bananas or apples
2 eggs, beaten	½ cup chopped nuts (almonds or walnuts)
½ teaspoon salt	
¼ cup sugar	dash of cinnamon

Moisten the *farfel* with cold water and drain immediately.
Combine with the beaten eggs, salt, sugar, fat, fruit, nuts, and
spice. Mix well; pour into a greased 2½-qt. baking dish. Bake
in a moderate oven (350° F.) for about 35 minutes—until brown
over the top. Serve plain, or with jam, or with Wine Sauce (*see*
recipe page 162).

Favorite Carrot Sharlot
(CARROT CHARLOTTE)

6 large eggs	1½ cups grated carrots
¼ teaspoon salt	½ cup blanched almonds, finely ground
1 cup sugar	
⅓ cup matza meal	2 tablespoons wine

Separate the eggs. Beat the egg whites with the salt, until stiff
but not dry. Beat the egg yolks until thick and lemon colored;
add the sugar gradually, continuing to beat as you add. Fold in
the matza meal, grated carrots, almonds, and wine (in the order
named). Fold in the beaten egg whites. Pour into a greased
2½-qt. baking dish. Bake in a moderate oven (350° F.) for 50
to 60 minutes. Serve with Wine Sauce (*see* recipe page 162).
Serves 6 to 8.

Pesach Flaumen Kugel mit Knaidlach
(PRUNE PUDDING WITH DUMPLINGS)

3 eggs, separated
½ teaspoon salt
¾ cup matza meal
3 tablespoons chicken fat
  (or vegetable fat)

raisins
almonds
1 lb. prunes, stewed and
  pitted

Add the salt to the egg whites and beat until light and fluffy, stiff but not dry. Beat the egg yolks until thick and lemon colored; stir in the matza meal and fat. Mix well. Fold in the beaten egg whites. Wet hands and shape *knaidlach* into little balls the size of walnuts. Press a raisin and an almond into the center of each. Arrange dumplings in a 2½-qt. baking dish and pour prunes, with juice, gently over top. The *knaidlach* should be well covered with the juice. Prunes may be flavored with sugar and lemon juice, if desired. Bake in a moderate oven (350° F.) for about 35 minutes. Serves 4 to 6.

Variation: cherries or any other stewed fruit may be substituted for the prunes.

Passover Beolas
(SPONGE FRITTERS)

5 eggs
⅔ cup matza meal
¼ teaspoon salt

1 cup sugar
½ cup water
¼ teaspoon cinnamon

Beat eggs with a rotary beater until thick and lemon colored. Fold in the matza meal mixed with the salt. The batter will resemble a sponge cake batter. Drop by teaspoon into deep hot fat and fry to golden brown. Drain. Serve with a syrup that is made by simmering the last three ingredients together for five minutes. Or serve with honey. Makes about 4 dozen.

Passover Fruit-filled Puffs

⅓ cup butter (or vegetable
  fat)
⅛ teaspoon salt

1 cup cold water
1 cup matza meal
4 eggs

Measure the butter, salt, and water into a saucepan and bring to boiling. Add the matza meal all at once (this is important);

then turn heat low and stir together until a ball of dough is formed and completely clears the sides of the pan. Remove from over heat and begin to add the eggs, unbeaten, one at a time, beating vigorously after each addition. Drop by teaspoon in small mounds on a greased cooky sheet. Bake in a very hot oven (450° F.) for 25 minutes; then reduce heat to medium low (325° F.) and bake an additional 40 minutes—until puffs are well baked through. Remove to cooling rack or clean towel. Center of puff will be hollow. Cut slit in the side of each to fill with jam, *eingemachts* (*see* recipes pages 157 and 158), or any preferred sweetened fruit drained of all juice. Makes about 2 dozen.

Bagelach Puffs
(LITTLE BAGEL-SHAPED PUFFS)

Prepare a batter as for Passover Fruit-filled Puffs. Drop by teaspoon onto a greased cooky sheet and shape into small circles with well-defined centers. Bake as for Passover Fruit-filled Puffs. After baking, frost with confectioners' sugar, mixed with sufficient water to make a paste that will spread.

There has always been much visiting back and forth among friends during the Passover season. It is a charming custom for guests to pay compliments to the hostess on her delectable sponge cake and to the host on his fine choice of wines.

Pesach Sponge Cake

6 eggs, separated
½ cup matza cake meal, less 1
   tablespoon
½ cup potato starch

dash of salt
1⅓ cups sugar
⅓ cup hot water
juice of 1 lemon

Use the eggs at room temperature (this way they beat to better volume and make a lighter, larger cake). Sift potato starch with matza meal three times..Beat the egg whites with salt until they foam; then add about one-third of the sugar gradually as you continue to beat; beat until very light and quite stiff. Beat the egg yolks until light in color and quite thick, then begin to add the remaining sugar gradually, continuing to beat as you add. Beat in the hot water and lemon juice; then beat for 3 minutes by the clock. Fold in gradually the sifted matza cake meal and potato starch. Then fold in the stiffly beaten egg whites, blending well. Pour batter into a 9" x 3" spring form. Bake in a slow oven (325° F.) for about 1 hour—until cake is baked through. Invert on cake rack to cool. Do not remove cake from pan until completely cool.

Fruited Sponge Layers

Bake Pesach Sponge Cake (previous recipe) in layer cake pans, in a moderate oven (350° F.) for 20 to 25 minutes. Invert on cake rack; cool in pan. Put layers together with sweetened fruit or jam. Dust top with confectioners' sugar; or serve with whipped cream. Makes three 9-inch layers.

Sponge Cup Cakes

Grease bottoms only, of cup cake pans. Fill each ⅔ full with the Pesach Sponge Cake batter (recipe p. 152). Bake in a moderate oven (350° F.) for 20 to 25 minutes, depending upon the size of cups. Invert on cake rack to cool before removing from pans. Frost. Serve plain or with fruit sauce. Makes about 18 small cakes.

Wine, Spice, and Nut Sponge

8 eggs, separated
1½ cups sugar
⅓ cup Passover wine
⅓ cup orange juice
1¼ cups matza cake meal

¼ teaspoon salt
½ teaspoon cinnamon
⅓ cup almonds, ground very fine

Beat egg yolks until thick and lemon colored. Add sugar gradually, beating until mixture is light but very thick. Add wine and orange juice. Beat for 3 minutes. Sift together three times the matza cake meal, salt, and cinnamon. Add the finely ground almonds and mix lightly. Fold the dry ingredients lightly into the beaten egg yolks. Beat the egg whites until stiff but not dry; fold into the cake batter, blending well. Pour into a 10" x 3" spring form. Bake in a slow oven (325° F.) for about 1 hour. Invert pan on cake rack to cool. Remove from pan when cool.

Traditional Twelve-Egg Sponge Cake

12 eggs, separated	¼ cup orange juice
2 cups sugar	1 cup matza cake meal
juice and grated rind of 1	1 cup potato starch
lemon	¼ teaspoon salt

Beat the egg yolks until thick and lemon colored, then add the sugar gradually, beating as you add. Continue to beat until the mixture is thick and puffing with air. Add the lemon juice and rind, and orange juice. Mix together and sift three times the cake meal, potato starch, and salt; fold in lightly. Beat the egg whites until they stand in peaks, but stop beating before they look dry and shiny. (This is important.) Fold into the cake batter. Line bottom of a rectangular cake pan (about 8" x 14") with paper; pour in the batter. Bake in a slow oven (325° F.) for 1 hour, or until baked through. Invert on cake rack to cool, before removing from pan.

Almond Macaroons

4 egg whites	4 tablespoons matza cake meal
¼ teaspoon salt	3 cups confectioners' sugar
½ cup finely ground almonds	grated rind of 1 orange

Add the salt to the egg whites; beat until stiff but not dry. Mix the remaining ingredients together; then sprinkle them, a spoonful at a time, over the stiffly beaten whites, folding in gently until well mixed. Drop by teaspoon, at least an inch apart, onto a cooky sheet covered with a sheet of heavy brown wrapping paper. Bake in a slow oven (300° F.) for about 15 minutes; then increase heat to moderate (350° F.) and bake for an additional 10 to 15 minutes—until macaroons are lightly browned over the top and dried out through the center. Makes about 30.

Delicate Nut Cookies

3 eggs	3 cups finely ground walnuts
3 cups confectioners' sugar	¾ cup matza cake meal
½ teaspoon salt	

Beat the eggs until very light. Sift in the sugar gradually; beat well. Add salt, nuts, matza cake meal. Mix well. Drop by teaspoon onto a greased cooky sheet, allowing room for spreading. Bake in a slow oven (325° F.) for about 20 minutes. Makes about 5 dozen.

Coconut Cookies

5 eggs, beaten
1½ cups sugar
1 cup matza meal
¼ teaspoon salt

2 cups shredded coconut, fresh
2 lemons, juice and grated rind

To the well-beaten eggs, gradually sift in the sugar and beat until light. Add the remaining ingredients in the order named. Beat well to mix. Sprinkle a cooky sheet with a little extra matza meal; drop cookies on this by teaspoon. Bake in a slow oven (325° F.) for 30 minutes, increasing heat to moderate (350° F.) for the last ten minutes. Makes about 2 dozen.

Pesach Walnut-Raisin Cookies

6 eggs, well beaten
1 cup sugar
1 cup matza cake meal
½ teaspoon salt

⅛ teaspoon ginger
1 cup walnuts, coarsely chopped

Beat sugar gradually into the well-beaten eggs, until very light and thick. Sift together matza cake meal, salt, and ginger. Sprinkle by spoonfuls over surface of the eggs and fold in lightly. Fold in the chopped nuts. Drop by teaspoon onto a greased cooky sheet. Bake in a hot oven (400° F.) for 15 minutes. Makes 4 dozen.

Today Passover pies are among the favorite desserts of the holidays. The crusts for these pies are made with matzoth or matza meal, and they are filled with a variety of fruit or cheese fillings. Thickenings must be limited to eggs, potato starch, or matza meal, or matza cake meal.

Matza Pie Crust

2 matzoth
cold water
2 eggs, beaten
¼ cup vegetable fat

¼ teaspoon salt
2 tablespoons sugar
¼ to ⅓ cup matza meal

Soak the matzoth in cold water to cover; press thoroughly dry. To the matzoth, add the eggs; then the fat, softened; and salt, sugar, and matza meal sufficient to hold the mixture together. Blend well. Press into a 9- or 10-inch pie plate, shaping well into the bottom and sides. Bake in a moderate oven (350° F.) for about 10 minutes, or until lightly browned. If bubbles appear during baking, prick these with a fork. Fill shell as desired.

Matza Meal Pie Crust

¼ cup vegetable fat   1 cup matza meal
2 tablespoons sugar   2 teaspoons water (about)
¼ teaspoon salt

Cream fat; add sugar and salt and mix well. Gradually work in the matza meal. Add water, drop by drop, sufficient only to hold mixture together. Press into a 9- or 10-inch pie plate, shaping well into the bottom and sides. Bake in a moderate oven (350° F.) for about 10 minutes, or until lightly browned. Fill shell as desired.

Passover Lemon Meringue Pie

4 eggs, separated   2 teaspoons grated lemon rind
1¼ cups sugar   6 tablespoons lemon juice
1 tablespoon potato starch   1 9-inch matza pie shell, baked
dash of salt   (see preceding recipes)
2 tablespoons water

Mix the slightly beaten egg yolks with ½ cup of the sugar, the potato starch, salt, water, lemon rind, and lemon juice. Cook over boiling water, stirring constantly, until the mixture is thick and smooth. Then remove from heat. Prepare a meringue by beating the egg whites with the remaining ½ cup sugar. Beat the sugar in gradually, beating well after each addition. Fold about ½ of this meringue into the yolk mixture and turn into the baked matza pie shell. Cover with remaining meringue, piling it on lightly, but covering all the edges. Bake in a slow oven (325° F.) for about 15 minutes—until delicately brown. If preferred, all of the meringue can be folded into the yolk mixture, and baked as above. Either way, the pie is very delicious and a holiday treat.

Pesach Cheese Pie

3 eggs, separated
¾ cup sugar
1 lb. cottage or pot cheese
2 tablespoons potato starch

½ pt. sour cream
grated rind of 1 lemon
1 tablespoon lemon juice

Beat the egg yolks until thick and lemon colored. Add the sugar gradually, beating as you add; beat until the mixture is very light and fluffy. Press the cheese through a strainer and mix with the potato starch. Add to this the sour cream and grated lemon rind and juice; add the mixture to the egg yolks. Mix well. Beat egg whites until stiff but not dry, and fold into the cheese mixture. Pour into prepared matza crust in a 10-inch pie pan. Bake in a moderate oven (350° F.) for about 1 hour—until cheese is set.

Eingemachts are preserves. Those made from vegetables were ingeniously devised in days long ago when fruits were not plentiful, especially in the springtime for Passover feasting. Beets, black radishes, and carrots are most frequently chosen for preserving. The recipes given here are for traditional favorites that are still regarded as choice delicacies on modern tables.

The use of *rusell* beets in the preparation of Beet Eingemachts for the Passover season accounts for its unique flavor. The Jewish hostess usually serves Beet Eingemachts with a number of other refreshments, such as wine, fruit, and nuts, but it is always served with a special individual plate and spoon for each guest.

Beet Eingemachts
(BEET PRESERVES)

4 cups *rusell* beets
3 cups sugar
1 cup honey
2 teaspoons ground ginger
¾ cup water

1 lemon, peeled and sliced thin
1 cup nut meats, coarsely broken

Rinse the *rusell* beets well in cold water. Cut into julienne strips. In a large saucepan, combine the sugar, honey, ginger, and water. Stir gently over low heat until the sugar is dissolved. Bring to boiling; add the lemon slices and beets. Cook gently until the beets begin to have a crystalline texture—about 35 to 45 minutes. Add the nuts, mixing lightly. Increase heat if necessary to reduce syrup to a rich thickness. Fill sterilized jelly glasses and cover. Makes 9 to 10 eight-ounce glasses of preserves.

Note: Plain beets may be used in place of *rusell* beets if these are not on hand. Cook until tender; peel and cut julienne. Continue as directed in the recipe. Lemon juice may be used to help approximate the rich tartness of *rusell* beets.

Black Radish Eingemachts
(BLACK RADISH PRESERVES)

4 cups black radishes, cut in strips
3 cups sugar
1 cup honey

2 teaspoons ground ginger
½ cup cold water
1 cup sliced almonds

Wash the radishes well; pare thinly and cut into julienne strips. Parboil in water to cover for 10 minutes. Drain. Repeat and drain again. Measure the sugar, honey, ground ginger, and water into a large saucepan; cook to a syrup and then add radish "sticks." Cook gently over low heat until the radishes begin to look clear in texture. Add nuts and then allow the syrup to thicken to jam consistency. Turn into sterilized jelly glasses. Makes 9 to 10 eight-ounce glasses of preserves.

Confections of many varieties are made by the Jewish housewife. She must have candy for the children and many sweets to grace her refreshment table when company comes. So rich with ginger are the candies for which the recipe follows that they are called affectionately, Ingberlach (little gingers).

Ingberlach or Matza Farfel Candies
(LITTLE GINGER CANDIES)

2¾ cups matza *farfel* (matza bits)
2 cups sugar
½ to 1 teaspoon ground ginger

1 cup honey
¾ cup nut meats, coarsely chopped

Measure the sugar into a heavy saucepan; add the ginger and mix. Add the honey; stir very gently, then place pan over low heat and continue to stir till the sugar is melted. Continue cooking, over slightly higher heat if special care is taken to prevent burning. Cook until syrup is a golden brown; then remove from over heat at once (sugar changes very quickly to burning at this point). Add *farfel;* stir quickly and pour onto a board wet with cold water, spreading with a moistened knife. Sprinkle chopped nuts over the surface, pressing in lightly. Cool. Cut into squares and diamonds. Makes about 5 dozen pieces.

Caution: Never attempt to make this candy in damp or rainy weather, as it tends to remain sticky and unmanageable. It is wise to observe this caution whenever working with a quantity of honey, brown sugar, or molasses, as these absorb moisture from the air.

Mehren Ingberlach
(CARROT-GINGER CANDIES)

2 cups finely grated carrots	1 cup sugar
(1 lb. or about 5 carrots)	½ to 1 teaspoon ginger
2 cups honey	½ cup chopped nuts

Wash, scrape, and grind or grate the carrots. Add the honey and sugar mixed with the ginger. Bring gently to boiling in a heavy saucepan. Continue cooking over very low heat, stirring as necessary to prevent burning. Cook until thick and a glossy brown (be careful not to burn). Stir in the nuts quickly. Pour out onto a board wet with cold water, spreading with a moistened knife to about ¼-inch thickness. Mark candy in squares and diamonds while still warm. Let cool for about 3 hours to harden. Do not make this candy on a rainy day as it would tend to stay soft. Makes about 4 dozen pieces.

Wine of the purple grapes has ever been part of Jewish ceremonials. In early days rich and poor alike served wine from their own cellars. These homemade wines were often of finest quality. If grapes were too expensive or too difficult to obtain, there were always raisins, or honey and hops for the making of *med.*

It is the lushness of the grapes, the heaviness of their juice and the fragrance of their flavor that make the fine quality and bouquet of the wine. Therefore the stock from which the juice is to be pressed must be chosen carefully. In America many stake their reputations upon the juice of the Concord grape.

Wine of the Purple Grapes

25 lbs. juicy purple grapes (preferably Concord)	12 lbs. sugar 2 cups water

Wash and stem the grapes; then take 2 or 3 pounds at a time, whichever is most convenient for the equipment in use, and mash the grapes to a juicy pulp. As they are mashed, turn them into a large, open-mouthed crock. (In earlier days a wooden tub was often used.) Cover with muslin and let stand at room temperature for 10 days. During this period, stir the mixture once a day, after removing the scum that rises to the top. At the end of 10 days, strain the fruit through a piece of muslin that has been scalded before use. Take care not to squeeze the mashed grapes, but give the last of the pulp time to drip in the manner of dripping juice for making clear jelly. Return this clear juice to the crock. Heat the sugar and water together over low heat until the sugar is dissolved; cool and add to the fruit juice in the crock.

There are two ways of aging the wine:

(1) Do not cover the crock for 24 hours; then cover with muslin and let stand at room temperature for a week. Remove to a cooler, but not cold, place and let ferment for several weeks.

(2) A better method is followed by those who decant the liquid to a small wooden keg. Leave it open for 24 hours before putting the bung in place and sealing over the opening with clay or some similar substance. Some six months later this better-aged wine is drawn off.

Decant into bottles and cork for storage. Yield: about 5 gallons.

Not so many years ago, no matter how plentiful the harvest of grapes, a family that one of us remembers could be counted on to make their famous *med,* the honey wine of days of old. At Passover time they would bring this treasured gift to neighbors and friends who would in turn offer the

fruit of their labors in friendly rivalry. Many remember with
delight the exciting bite and sting of this liquid sunshine.

Med is of truly ancient origin, appearing early in the literature of many peoples. *Mead* and *megthelin* are some of the
other names by which it is known.

Med

(HONEY WINE)

1 oz. hops	2 medium-sized lemons, thinly
1 gal. liquid honey	sliced
4 gals. water	2 pieces of ginger root

Tie the hops loosely in a cheesecloth bag and set aside until
needed. Simmer together gently for about 30 minutes, the honey,
water, lemon, and ginger, skimming off the surface foam as it
rises during the cooking. Cool. Strain through a piece of muslin
that has been scalded. If desired, this can be done directly into
a wooden barrel, placing a big funnel into the bung hole and lin-
ing the funnel with the muslin strainer. Do not fill the barrel
more than ⅔ full; this will allow for rise of fermentation. Drop
the bag of hops into the liquid. Do not cork the barrel. Let
ferment at room temperature for about 3 weeks—until fermentation finally ceases. Then decant (draw off) the clear liquid into
bottles or jugs. Take great care not to disturb the sediment at the
bottom of the keg. Cork loosely and store in a cool, dark place.
Yield: about 4 gallons.

Amber Wine from Raisins

2 medium-sized lemons	small piece of ginger root
4 to 5 lbs. white raisins	2 3-inch pieces of stick
3 gals. water	cinnamon

Wash the lemons and cut them into a chopping bowl (do not
skin); add the raisins and chop together until all are quite fine.
Turn into a large crock (5-gallon or more). Boil the water and
cool; add to the fruit; add spices. Cover with muslin and let stand
at room temperature for a week; stir once a day, after removing
the scum that rises to the top during fermentation. Strain through
a muslin cloth that has been scalded. At the end of the week,

return the liquid to the crock. Leave uncovered for the better part of a day, taking care that dust is not raised near it. At the end of the day cover with the muslin cover and again let stand for a week. At the end of that time pour off into large bottles. Cork, but not too tightly, for the wine may still work a little. Store in a dark place for another two weeks before using. Yield: about 2½ gallons.

Many a sauce is made to grace a Passover dessert. Crystalline Wine Sauce is a typical one.

Crystalline Wine Sauce

½ cup sugar
1 tablespoon potato starch
⅛ teaspoon salt
½ cup boiling water

1 tablespoon vegetable oil
1 tablespoon lemon juice
1 cup wine

Mix sugar, potato starch, and salt in a saucepan; add the boiling water and stir to mix. Stir over low heat until crystal clear and quite thick. Add the oil and lemon juice. Remove from over heat and stir in the wine. Serve hot or cold over desserts. This is especially delicious over sponge cakes. Makes about 1½ cups of sauce.

Rich Wine Sauce

4 egg yolks
⅓ cup sugar

¼ teaspoon cinnamon
1 cup sweet wine

Place the yolks in a deep, but not too large, bowl that will fit over a pan of water. Beat until the yolks are richly thick; then gradually beat in the sugar mixed with the cinnamon. Place the bowl over hot, not boiling, water and beat as the wine is slowly poured in. Continue to beat until the sauce stands up high and fluffy. Serve at once over wedges of sponge cake or any pudding. Makes about 1½ cups of sauce.

Lag B'Omer

The 18th of Iyar—usually in late April or May.

Lag B'Omer comes on the thirty-third day of a period of deepest mourning. This holiday was set aside as a day of relief, a day of surcease from sorrow, and to commemorate a miracle. The long period of mourning, into which Lag B'Omer breaks, recalls the dark days of Roman oppression when the Israelites fought desperately for their Torah, their homeland, and their very existence.

Among the great Jewish leaders of those days were Rabbi Akiba, a revered teacher and scholar, and Bar Kochba, a great military genius. Together they led the people in revolt. At first there were victories, but as the Roman legions were reinforced again and again, they completely overpowered the Jewish army. Desperately the Jews fought on, and in this, their last revolt against the Romans, they suffered heavy losses and finally defeat.

The miracle that has made Lag B'Omer a day of rejoicing happened in the midst of the bitter losing struggle. The students of Rabbi Akiba had fallen victim to a plague that was decimating their ranks. They were dying by the thousands, not only on the battlefields but as a result of this terrible epidemic. Suddenly, on the thirty-third day of this tragic period, the plague ceased, and for a short space the dark clouds lifted for a grateful people.

Lag B'Omer is also the anniversary of the death of Rabbi Simeon ben Yohai, said to be the most outstanding of the

163

pupils of Rabbi Akiba. A great scholar, he had fled to the hills to continue his study of the Torah, and students would often go to see him in his place of hiding. On this day students make pilgrimages to Meron, where he was buried. And on Lag B'Omer, as he commanded, they lay aside their grief and rejoice together.

The fifty days of mourning are observed by many Jews. During this time they do not attend concerts or other public gatherings. As an outward sign of grief they do not cut their hair. Lag B'Omer becomes truly a holiday in this mourning period, and weddings and other celebrations to be held on this day are planned long in advance.

Lag B'Omer is also called Scholars' Day. To this day students plan to go on outings on this holiday, recalling the times when the scholars of old paid secret visits to the great Simeon ben Yohai when he was in hiding.

There are no traditional foods for Lag B'Omer except possibly hard-boiled eggs, carried on outings, as symbols of mourning, or maybe only because they are easy to carry!

Shavuoth

The 6th (or 6th and 7th) of Sivan—usually in late May or early June.

Shavuoth is the Festival of the Torah, and it is known also as the Feast of Weeks and the Feast of Pentecost. It is the day (or two days) set aside to honor the Torah, the sacred laws of the Hebrew people. This great work embodies the deepest yearnings of the Jewish people for truth, freedom, learning, and wisdom. In the words of the Bible, the Torah is "a tree of life."

Shavuoth marks the anniversary of the "giving of the Torah." It was at this season of the year, as related in the Bible, that God revealed himself on Mt. Sinai, and gave to Moses the Tablets of the Law, the Ten Commandments for all the people.

Shavuoth was not always a festival of such deep religious meaning. In the earliest observance of this holiday it was a beautiful harvest festival celebrated in the Temple in Jerusalem, and it was known also as the Festival of the First Fruits. Each year at the time of this festival, the barley crop had been harvested and stored, the wheat fields were ripe for cutting, and the earliest fruits had been gathered. The finest of these were brought to the Temple as an offering.

The Talmud tells how these fruits were selected. "When a man comes down to his field and sees a ripe fig, or a perfect cluster of grapes, or a beautiful pomegranate, he ties each with a red thread, saying, 'These are *bikkurim,* the first fruits for the Festival.' "

We know, too, how these fruits were brought to the Temple in Jerusalem. In the early dawn of Shavouth, long lines began forming outside of Jerusalem for the procession into the Holy City. Many gay family groups that had traveled from afar had camped overnight on the hills outside the city. Their camp fires had glowed through the dark night, while the tinkle of harps and the reedy sound of flutes had filled the air with music. They had brought with them gifts of the finest dried fruits, raisins, and olives. Others from places closer by carried the choicest fruits from a freshly gathered harvest. These were the gifts for the Altar, and they were carried to the Temple piled pyramid high in baskets of beautifully woven rush, even silver and gold. As with the first fruits of the fields, it was traditional also for each family to bring two of the choicest loaves from the family hearth. Many of these were brought on beautiful golden trays. Elders from the Temple and artisans from the city would come to greet the visitors, bidding them welcome and leading them to the Temple with music and song.

Those early processions are symbolized today in the greens and plants, branches and even trees that are used to decorate homes and synagogues for the Festival of Shavuoth. Through the years the ceremonies for the observance have changed, but they continue to be a source of great spiritual satisfaction for those who participate in them. In this festival which pays honor to the Torah, people give expression to their love of the Law. The Torah has ever been an inspiration to pursue knowledge and learning, and on the night of Shavuoth, many remain in the synagogue until the dawn, reading the sacred books.

Another of today's observances is the reading of the Book

of Ruth. The story carries great meaning for the Jewish people. Ruth's acceptance of the Hebrew faith is compared with the acceptance of the Torah by all Israel, while the harvest scenes in the story describe the beautiful pastoral life of ancient Palestine. The children, particularly, love this story, and it is read over and over again, not only in the synagogues but in homes and schools as well.

"The more Torah, the more life. The more schooling, the more wisdom," wrote one of the early sages. The very word "Torah" means "to teach," and so it is that the Festival of the Torah has long been associated with education. During the Middle Ages a young boy's first day in *cheder* (Hebrew school) was on the day of Shavuoth. And a sweet day it was, for the lad was showered with confections, symbolic of the sweetness of the Torah, whose study was just beginning for him. Today, many graduation exercises are held on Shavuoth, a most fitting day to climax a period of study.

In Reform synagogues and many of the Conservative synagogues, a new ceremony has been introduced in the observance of Shavuoth. On this day Confirmation exercises are held for boys and girls who have reached the age of thirteen, or religious maturity, and have been prepared in their religious schools. These youths are confirmed in their Jewish faith, as were their forefathers who received the Law from God on Shavuoth.

In Israel, there is a beautiful blending of old and new in the observances. Picturesque and elaborate harvest ceremonies are held in many places over the country. Particularly beautiful is the modern harvest festival held each year in Haifa. In this celebration the streets are decorated with flags and flowers; and thousands of children, all in white and adorned with leaves and flowers, march in unending procession, singing and cheering as they go. Sturdy youths from many colonies carry baskets filled with fruits and vegetables of the harvest, far greater in variety than was ever dreamed of in ancient Palestine. In a colorful pageant in a great open-air theater, these fruits and vegetables are presented to the city. Singing and dancing bring this delightful program to a close.

In Jewish homes all over the world today, there is also the family celebration of Shavuoth. As on a Sabbath eve, the men of the household go to the synagogue. At home the mother spreads the holiday table and lights the festival candles just before sunset. Two *challah* twists, covered with their embroidered cloth, are in their proper place on the table, and the goblet stands ready for the *Kiddush*.

"*Gut yom tov, gut yohr*" (Good holiday, good year) echoes through the house when the father and sons return. After benedictions, all gather around the table for the festive meal.

The Torah is said to be "as nutritious as milk and as sweet as honey," and since Shavuoth celebrates the Torah, many of the festival foods consist of *milchige* dishes (milk and milk-product dishes) and honey dishes. These also recall an early period in Jewish history. When Moses went up to Mt. Sinai, the people waited for long hours at the foot of the mountain. Finally when Moses came down to them bearing the Tablets of the Law, they hurried home rejoicing ... but so tired and spent, so hungry! There was no time to build fires for the cooking of meat. Milk and cheese, and bread and honey were set forth hastily that all might be refreshed.

The first fruits of the harvest are also found on the Shavuoth table of today. Tender greens, cool fruits of delicate newness, salads and compotes, greens both cooked and raw, are traditional delights. A typical dinner for one night of Shavuoth might be as follows.

Shavuoth Dinner

Oriental Spiced Pomegranate Juice   Wine

Appetizer Platter: Lox   Cream Cheese   Bagel
Sardines   Sliced Schmaltz Herring
Black Olives   Celery   Cucumber and Tomatoes

Schav   Onion and Poppy-seed Rolls
Baked or Broiled Fish   Spinach and Mushrooms
Milchige Lukshen Kugel
Cabbage and Pineapple Salad
Blintzes with Sour Cream   Schnecken
Honey Cookies   Coffee   Fresh Fruit

"I would cause them to drink of spiced wine, of the juice of my pomegranate"—Song of Songs.

Spiced Pomegranate Syrup

1 cup sugar
⅛ teaspoon nutmeg
⅛ teaspoon cinnamon
⅛ teaspoon ginger
2 whole cloves

1 cup water
pomegranate juice (fresh or bottled)
sliced lemon

Make a syrup by simmering together for five minutes the sugar, spices, and water. Remove the cloves. Chill. Add syrup to pomegranate juice, to sweeten as desired. When serving, add a twist of lemon to each glass of the spiced pomegranate juice.

This pomegranate syrup can also be used to sweeten tall glasses of hot tea.

All over Europe fruit soups are favorites for Shavuoth as they are in America. They can be served hot or cold, and with the addition of *knaidlach,* have become particularly popular.

Fruit Borscht with Spicy Knaidlach
(FRUIT SOUP WITH DUMPLINGS)

2 cups cooked apricots (fresh,
    canned, or dried)
water
1 tablespoon lemon juice
2 tablespoons sugar

½ teaspoon salt
1 tablespoon flour
spicy *knaidlach* (*see* next
    recipe)
sour cream

Drain the juice from the fruit and measure both, adding water to the juice to make 3 pints. Chop the fruit quite fine and return to liquid. Add the lemon juice. Mix sugar, salt, and flour with a little of the cold juice to make a paste; then stir into the larger mixture. Stir over low heat until well cooked, and rich and creamy in consistency—10 to 15 minutes. Chill or serve hot, adding extra lemon or sugar, as desired. Prepare *knaidlach* just before serving. Serve in hot or cold syrup. Garnish with sour cream. Serves 6 to 8.

Spicy Knaidlach
(SPICY DUMPLINGS)

½ cup flour
¼ teaspoon baking powder
¼ teaspoon salt
⅛ teaspoon cinnamon

⅛ teaspoon nutmeg
¼ cup water
1 egg, well beaten

Mix together the dry ingredients and stir in the water to make a smooth paste. Fold the batter into the egg which has been beaten to a light lemon color. Drop from the tip of a teaspoon, in neat dumplings, into 3 quarts of boiling salted water. Cover; boil, not too rapidly, for 5 to 7 minutes. The dumplings will rise to the surface; remove with a slotted spoon and serve immediately in the soup. Makes about 16.

Schav
(SORREL OR SOUR GRASS SOUP)

1 lb. sorrel
1½ qts. boiling water
1 teaspoon salt
1 or 2 eggs

sugar, if desired
cucumber, finely cut
2 scallions, finely cut
sour cream

Tender sorrel is preferred; if tender, use both leaves and stems. If not tender, remove the leaves and cook the stems first in boiling salted water until tender. Discard the stems; cook leaves in this same water, gently, for about 15 minutes. Strain the leaves from liquid, saving both. Chop the leaves quite fine and return to the broth. Beat the eggs slightly, mixing with a little of the hot broth to make a cream. Remove soup from over heat, then stir in the egg mixture. Blend well. Adjust seasoning, with sugar, if desired, and extra salt. Chill. Add a spoonful of cucumber and scallion to each serving of chilled soup. Crest with sour cream. Serves 6 to 8.

Garden fresh fruit and vegetables, dressed with sour cream, are great favorites for Shavuoth. This custom originated among the Jews in Eastern Europe.

Garden Green Salad with Sour Cream

1 or 2 cucumbers	pot cheese or cottage cheese
10 red and white radishes	sour cream
2 scallions	salad greens, as desired
2 tomatoes	

Wash and crisp all salad ingredients. Cut cucumbers, radishes, scallions (both green and white parts), and tomatoes into neat pieces. Serve with cheese and sour cream, and, of course, pumpernickel and sweet butter. Serves 4 or 5.

Two modern sour cream dressings to serve with Garden Green Salad have also become popular:

Sour Cream Dressing

1 cup sour cream	¼ teaspoon salt
2 to 3 tablespoons lemon or lime juice	1 teaspoon sugar, if desired
	¼ teaspoon dry mustard

Prepare just before serving. Stir the juice into the sour cream. Mix together the salt, sugar, and mustard and add to the sour cream. Beat well till blended. The mustard adds a very special touch and may be varied in amount according to taste. Makes 1 cup of dressing.

Spiced Sour Cream Dressing

1 cup sour cream   grated rind of lemon or orange
¼ teaspoon nutmeg, or less

Mix together just before serving, using more or less nutmeg, according to taste. Makes 1 cup of dressing.

Uncooked Honey Dressing

¼ teaspoon dry mustard   ⅓ cup honey
¼ teaspoon paprika   juice of ½ lemon
½ teaspoon salt   1 cup vegetable oil
3 tablespoons vinegar

Mix together the dry ingredients; then add the remaining ingredients and beat in a bowl or shake in a jar. Taste; add extra seasonings as desired. Serve cool, not chilled. Makes 1 cup of dressing.

Every country has its favorite *blintzes,* and so it is quite natural that those filled with cheese would become the favorite traditional dish for Shavuoth.

Cheese Blintzes
(CHEESE-FILLED PANCAKES)

3 eggs   1 lb. pot cheese
¾ teaspoon salt   3 to 4 tablespoons sugar
1 cup milk or water   dash of cinnamon
1 cup flour (about)   raisins, if desired

Blintz "leaves" (pancakes) must be made first. Beat 2 of the eggs slightly; add ½ teaspoon salt and the liquid; then add flour to make a smooth, *thin* batter. Heat a 6-inch frying pan; grease lightly. Pour in a thin covering (about 2 tablespoons) of batter, just enough to cover the bottom of the pan; tilt pan from side to side to distribute evenly. Cook over moderate heat until the edges curl. Turn out on a clean cloth, fried side up. Keep covered until all leaves are cooked. To fill, mix together the cheese, sugar, cinnamon, ¼ teaspoon salt, and the remaining egg. Add raisins, if desired. Place a heaping tablespoon of filling on a leaf; then fold over three sides, tucking in the fourth to make an envelope. When all leaves are filled, fry in hot butter in a heavy frying pan, turning to brown on all sides, and taking care not to scorch the butter. Or bake on a greased baking sheet in a moderate oven (350° F.) for 15 to 20 minutes, brushing well with melted butter before and during baking. Serve with sour cream. Makes 16.

Variation: Fill with cherry filling as for Cherry Varenikes (*see* recipe below).

Cheese Kreplach, with buttered crumbs and sour cream as topping, are consumed in enormous quantities at Shavuoth.

Cheese Kreplach
(CHEESE-FILLED NOODLE TRIANGLES)

noodle dough (recipe page 19)
cheese filling as for Knishes (recipe page 174)

1 cup bread crumbs
2 tablespoons butter, melted
sour cream

Prepare the noodle dough; cut into 3-inch squares. Place a spoonful of filling on one half of each square; then fold over to make triangles. Press the edges together with a fork. Cook tightly covered in boiling salted water for 18 minutes. Drain. Sprinkle with buttered crumbs. (To butter the crumbs, shake in a frying pan with melted butter until they are coated.) Serve with sour cream. If preferred, dot with butter or shortening after boiling, then brown and crisp in the oven before serving. Makes about 2 dozen.

Cherry Varenikes
(CHERRY-FILLED NOODLE ROUNDS)

noodle dough (recipe p. 19)
3 cups tart red cherries
honey
butter

⅛ teaspoon mixed spices (ginger, cinnamon, and nutmeg), as desired
⅓ cup bread crumbs

Prepare the noodle dough; cut into 3-inch rounds. On half these rounds, place a spoonful of cherries, well drained. Drizzle the honey over the fruit; dot with butter. Mix spices with the crumbs and sprinkle each filling lightly. Thin slivers of crystallized ginger are sometimes added. Cover with the remaining rounds of dough; press edges together with a fork. Cook tightly covered in gently boiling salted water for 18 minutes. Drain. Bake for 10 minutes on a well-greased baking sheet in a hot oven (400° F.). Reduce heat to 300° F.; drizzle tops with honey and bake for an additional 10 minutes. Makes about 2 dozen.

Cheese Knishes
(CHEESE-FILLED CAKES)

2½ cups flour
2½ teaspoons baking powder
½ teaspoon salt
2 eggs
½ cup sour cream
3 tablespoons melted butter

½ cup milk
½ lb. pot cheese
1 to 2 tablespoons bread
    crumbs
1 tablespoon sugar
1 tablespoon raisins

To make the dough: Sift together the dry ingredients. Beat 1 egg well, and add ¼ cup sour cream. Stir this into the flour. Add the butter with part of the milk, stirring in more milk as needed to make a soft, but not sticky, dough. (Dry dough makes tough *knishes*.) Roll out ⅛-inch thick on a floured board. Cut into 3- to 4-inch rounds or squares. To make the filling: Mix together the remaining egg, ¼ cup sour cream, pot cheese, crumbs, sugar, raisins. Place a spoonful on half of each square or round; fold dough over to cover. Press edges together with a fork. Bake on a greased baking sheet in a moderate oven (350° F.) for 30 to 35 minutes—until brown. Makes 18.

Milchige Lukshen Kugel vies with *blintzes* as the outstanding favorite for Shavuoth. It may be served as a main dish or as a dessert.

Milchige Lukshen Kugel
(DAIRY-NOODLE PUDDING)

½ lb. broad noodles
½ to 1 cup pot cheese
2 eggs, separated
3 tablespoons melted butter

½ teaspoon salt
2 tablespoons sugar
½ cup sour cream
½ cup raisins

Cook noodles, in 2-inch pieces, in boiling salted water until tender. Drain, but not too dry. Stir the cheese into the noodles.

Beat the egg yolks with the butter, salt, and sugar. Fold into the noodles the egg yolk mixture, the sour cream, raisins, and the egg whites that have been beaten stiff but not dry. Turn into a buttered 2-qt. casserole or baking dish and bake in a moderate oven (350° F.) for about 45 minutes, or until the top is crispy brown. Serves 4 to 6.

In Roumania, one of the traditional dishes for Shavuoth is this famous Mamaliga, rich with butter as well as cheese.

Roumanian Mamaliga
(A CHEESE AND CORN MEAL DISH)

2 cups yellow corn meal
1 cup cold water
4 cups boiling water
1 teaspoon salt

⅓ cup butter
1 cup grated cheese, or 1 lb. pot cheese

There was a time when every housewife prided herself on the skill with which she could lightly sprinkle the corn meal into boiling salted water so that at the end of cooking there was never a lump. Modern cooks eliminate guesswork by mixing the meal with cold water, then stirring the paste into the boiling kettle. Use a large heavy pot and cook, stirring constantly, over low heat for at least 30 minutes—until the mush is thoroughly cooked. Add butter and cheese; serve at once in individual portions. Or mound corn meal mush high on a large platter; dot with butter and cover with cheese before bringing to the table. Each stirs in more butter as he eats, and some even spread the top with sugar or preserves. Serves about 6.

Two beautiful *challah* are to be found on the table for the family dinner. No holiday table would be complete without them, but they have special meaning at Shavuoth. This is in remembrance of the wheaten loaves baked in ancient days from the first wheat of the early spring harvest and laid on the altar in the Temple.

Wonderful coffee cakes are made for Shavuoth. They are rich with butter and bursting with cheese, honey, and every good thing.

Quick Coffee Cake
(NUT-FILLED OR STREUSEL-TOPPED CAKE)

⅓ cup butter   4 teaspoons baking powder
1 cup sugar   ¼ teaspoon salt
2 eggs   1 cup milk
2½ cups flour

For a nut filling:

1 cup broken nut meats   1 tablespoon sugar
1 tablespoon flour   1 teaspoon cinnamon

For a streusel top:

¼ cup confectioners' sugar   1 egg
¼ cup brown sugar   4 tablespoons butter

To mix the batter: Cream together the butter and sugar; then add the eggs one at a time and beat vigorously after each addition. Sift together the dry ingredients and add alternately with the milk, about ⅓ of each at a time.

For a nut-filled cake: Pour half the batter into a greased and paper-lined, 9-inch-square cake pan. Cover with 1 cup broken nut meats, mixed with the flour, sugar, and cinnamon. Cover with the remaining half of the batter. Bake in a moderate oven (350° F.) for 50 minutes. Sprinkle the top with brown sugar; return cake to oven until sugar melts and begins to brown. Remove from pan to cool.

For a streusel-topped cake: Pour the batter into a greased and paper-lined oblong baking pan about 6″ by 10″ in size, smoothing well into corners. Mix together the confectioners' sugar, brown sugar, egg, and butter, mixing to crumbs. Sprinkle this over the top of the cake. Bake in a moderate oven (350° F.) for 45 to 50 minutes. If the cake browns too rapidly, cover it with a sheet of brown paper. Remove from pan to cool.

Schnecken are all the heart could wish for. Make them rich with fruit and nuts; spread them thick with butter.

Schnecken
(LITTLE FRUIT AND NUT ROLLS)

1 envelope dry yeast	4 cups flour
¼ cup lukewarm water	½ teaspoon salt
4 tablespoons sugar	2 eggs
½ cup scalded milk	brown sugar
1 cup butter (or vegetable fat), melted	cinnamon, if desired
	1 cup raisins, chopped
1 cup sour cream	1 cup nut meats, chopped

Soften the yeast in the lukewarm, never hot, water; and dissolve the sugar in the scalded milk. Cool the hot milk to lukewarm. Add the softened yeast, sour cream, and melted butter. Add salt to flour; stir half the flour into the liquid. Then add the eggs one by one, beating vigorously after each addition. Add remaining flour sufficient to make a tender dough that can be transferred to a well-floured bread board. Knead dough for about a dozen turns. Place in a well-greased mixing bowl, turning the ball of dough about so that the surface will be well oiled from the butter in the bowl. Cover with a clean cloth; set in the refrigerator overnight (or, if preferred, double the amount of yeast and make the *schnecken* the same day). On the next day divide the dough into several pieces. Roll out each piece to about ¼-inch thickness. Spread with additional melted (or softened) butter, if desired. Sprinkle with brown sugar; cinnamon, if desired; nuts and raisins. Roll like a jelly roll. Cut into ½-inch slices. Place cut side down on a well-greased baking pan. Let rise in a warm, never hot, place, to double in bulk (will take about 2 hours). Bake in a moderate oven (375° F.) for about 20 minutes. Makes 5 dozen.

Bagels, cream cheese, and *lox* (smoked salmon)—this most delicious combination is fast becoming traditional for Shavuoth. There was a time when every Jewish housewife cherished her recipe for *bagels.* But today such excellent ones are made in the bakeries that they are rarely baked at home.

Bagels
(A DOUGHNUT-SHAPED ROLL)

1 envelope dry yeast
¼ cup lukewarm water
¼ cup butter (or vegetable fat)
1 tablespoon sugar

1 teaspoon salt
1 cup scalded milk
4 cups flour, about
1 egg, separated

Soften the yeast in lukewarm, never hot, water. Dissolve the butter, sugar, and salt in the scalded milk. Cool to lukewarm. Add softened yeast and mix well. Place about half of the flour in a large mixing bowl; make a well in the center and pour in the liquid. Add the egg white. Stir together until well mixed; then begin to add more flour to make a soft dough that can be turned out on a floured board for kneading. Knead until the dough is smooth. Place in a large, well-greased mixing bowl. Grease top of the dough and cover bowl with cloth. Set in a warm, never hot, place to rise to double in bulk. Knead again on floured board. Divide dough into quarters. Roll each portion into long finger strips and cut into six-inch pieces. Shape into rings, pressing ends together. Let stand on a floured board for about 10 minutes, to *begin* to rise. Drop *bagels*, one at a time, into a pot of water that is just under boiling. Cook on one side; then turn and cook on the other. Remove carefully to a greased baking sheet. Beat egg yolk with a spoonful of water and brush top of each *bagel*. Sprinkle with coarse salt, if desired. Bake in a hot oven (400° F.) for about 15 minutes—until golden brown. Makes about 2 dozen.

Cheese cakes of every description are Shavuoth delights. It is amazing how many different types there are, and all are popular. Some are as light as a feather and almost resemble a Sabbath sponge cake; others are much closer to a custard than a cake. The cake given here strikes a happy medium.

Cheese Cake

1 lb. pot cheese	⅔ cup milk
½ cup sugar	½ pt. sour cream
2 tablespoons flour	2 tablespoons sugar
dash of salt	1 teaspoon vanilla
1 egg, slightly beaten	graham cracker or zweibach
juice of ½ lemon	pie crust (recipe follows)

Press cheese twice through a sieve for a creamy, smooth consistency. Mix together the sugar, flour, and salt and stir into the cheese. Add egg, lemon juice and milk and beat together until well blended. Pour into graham cracker or zweibach crust and bake in a moderate oven (350° F.) for 30 minutes. Remove from oven, cool for about 10 minutes, then top with the sour cream mixed well with the sugar and vanilla. Return to the oven and bake for 10 minutes—until richly glazed.

Graham Cracker or Zweibach Crust
(FOR CHEESE CAKES OR PIES)

1½ cups fine graham cracker or zweibach crumbs	½ cup soft or melted butter
	½ teaspoon cinnamon
⅓ cup sugar	

Mix together all the ingredients and press into a 10-inch pie pan or spring form. Make filling according to preceding recipe, and pour in carefully.

Cheese cake served with a cup of coffee knows no season for popularity; it is always welcome. Coffee itself deserves a special word of mention, as Jews have doted on their coffee for almost more years than can be counted. A fortifying cup started many to early morning synagogue on the Sabbath or a holiday. And it was the Jews who introduced coffee drinking into England.

Rich Cheese Pie

1 lb. cream cheese, or ½ lb.
    each of cream and pot
    cheese
2 eggs, beaten
⅔ cup sugar

2 teaspoons vanilla
⅛ teaspoon salt
baked 10-inch pie shell
1 pt. sour cream
dash of nutmeg, if desired

Mix together the cheese, eggs, ⅓ cup sugar, 1 teaspoon vanilla, and salt, using rotary beater; preferably an automatic beater for a superb blending. If necessary, press cheese through a strainer, for filling must be as smooth as satin. Pour into a baked pie shell. Bake in a moderate oven (350° F.) for about 35 minutes. Cool for 10 minutes. Then beat sour cream to lightness (add nutmeg if desired), gradually adding the remaining ⅓ cup sugar and the remaining vanilla. Spread over top of the cool pie. Return to oven; bake for an additional 10 minutes, to form a rich glaze over surface of pie.

Harvest Cookies

1 cup pitted dates
1 cup seeded raisins
½ cup nut meats
2 cups whole wheat flour
¼ teaspoon salt
2 teaspoons baking powder

½ cup butter (or vegetable
    fat)
⅔ cup brown sugar
1 egg
½ cup milk
1 teaspoon vanilla

Cut the dates and raisins into small pieces. Chop the nuts coarsely. Sift together the flour, salt, and baking powder; add prepared fruits and nuts. Beat butter until creamy; add the sugar gradually, beating continuously; beat in the egg; add milk and flavoring, and stir in the flour. Blend well. Drop from a teaspoon onto a greased cooky sheet. Bake in a moderate oven (350° F.) for 10 to 15 minutes. Makes about 3 dozen.

THE FAMILY

In a Kosher Kitchen

The kosher home is one of the cornerstones of the Hebrew faith. It has nourished and enriched the lives of countless generations. The selection and preparation of food according to the dietary laws, observed in kosher homes, have served to protect the health and welfare of the Jewish people since very early days.

For the individual Jew, obedience to the dietary laws has ever been a satisfying discipline and a great source of strength, as well as a rich bond of kinship between himself and his fellow Jews.

The dietary laws, as observed down to this very day, are rooted in those given to Moses and Aaron: "Speak unto the children of Israel, saying: These are the living things which ye may eat among all the beasts that are on the earth. Whatsoever parteth the hoof, and is wholly cloven footed, and cheweth the cud, among the beasts, that shall ye eat.... These may ye eat of all that are in the water: whatsoever hath fins and scales.... This is the law ... to make a difference between the unclean and the clean" (Lev. 11:1-47).

It was necessary to expand and interpret these early precepts so that all might be given directions practicable for everyday living. The dietary laws were in answer to that need. They provide guidance essential to the maintenance of a kosher (ritually correct) home. They cover every aspect in the preparation of kosher food from the point when it is selected until it is served on the table, and include the manner of handling cooking utensils and dishes, as well as materials used in cleaning them. These rituals, as prescribed under the laws, are known as kashruth (kosher, to make ritually correct). Implicit in these laws, too, is a high cleanliness of person, as well as home.

All animals and poultry prepared for the kosher home are slaughtered according to ritual by a highly trained man known as a *schochet*. He is thoroughly instructed in the laws of kashruth and is also equipped with a knowledge of animal anatomy. In every Jewish neighborhood he enjoys great prestige.

Animals to be used must be quadrupeds that chew the cud and have cloven hoof. This includes sheep, goats, deer, and cattle. These must be slaughtered according to prescribed ritual. They cannot be used if torn by wild beasts or otherwise mutilated. Only forequarters may be used (except that other parts may be used when cleansed according to prescribed ritual). Only those animals may be used that have been properly examined and show no signs of disease or lesions. After slaughter by the *schochet* there must be further kashering at home in order to remove all blood.

Poultry must be slaughtered according to ritual by a trained *schochet* and may not include scavengers or birds of prey.

Fish is restricted to those with scales and fins. No shellfish may be used. The ritual of slaughtering by the *schochet* does not apply to fish.

Kashering of meat within the home:

(1) Soak the meat in cold water in a special vessel set aside for this purpose. Soak for ½ hour. Drain and rinse.

(2) Sprinkle with coarse salt; place on a perforated board and let stand for one hour, the board slanted to allow the blood to flow away.

(3) Wash the meat. It is now ready for cooking.

(4) Meat intended for broiling need not be soaked or salted. Kasher as for liver.

To kasher special organ meats:

(1) Liver is never kashered with meat. It is scored in two directions, washed, salted, and broiled over an open fire. During the broiling additional salt is sprinkled over the surface to assist in drawing out the blood. Wash after broiling to further remove blood and to remove the salt. It may now be served or used in the preparation of other dishes. All varieties of liver, including that of poultry, are prepared in this way.

(2) Heart must be cut open lengthwise, and veins and tips removed to allow the blood to drain off freely. It is then soaked and salted in the same way as other meat.

(3) Lungs are treated in the same way as heart.

(4) *Miltz* (spleen) must have veins removed and is then treated in the same way as other meat.

(5) Fat for clarifying must be skinned and is then treated in the same way as meat.

(6) Cut deep gashes in the length and width of udder. Squeeze out milk. Wash and then broil on a wire folding grill. Sprinkle with salt as it is broiled. Rinse.

(7) Bones with no meat or fat adhering to them must be soaked separately, and during the salting process may not be placed near the meat.

To kasher poultry after slaughter by the schochet:

The bird is drawn and all organs are removed from the center cavity before it is soaked and salted. The head, veins, and tendons of the neck must be removed. If the feet are to be used, claws and skin must be removed. Eggs (with or without shell) found in poultry must be treated in the same way as meat, but they must not touch the meat while in the process of soaking and salting. Also, such eggs may not be used with *milchige* foods.

Fish is not kashered in its preparation:

Fish does not require soaking and salting. It is a *pareve* food, which means that it may be eaten with *milchige* (dairy) foods or with *fleischige* (meat) foods.

Eggs are a pareve food:

This means that they may be cooked and served with meat or with milk. There is one prohibition with regard to eggs. An egg yolk that is found to have a speck of blood may not be used. It must be discarded.

"Thou shalt not seethe a kid in its mother's milk" (Deu. 14:21). This ancient prohibition is the basis of the laws against cooking meat and milk or milk products together, and serving them at the same meal.

Milchige (milk and milk-product) foods are not kashered:

Although no special kashering rules apply to the handling and preparation of these foods—cheese, butter, milk, sour cream, and sweet cream—extreme cleanliness is required at the source of their preparation, as well as in their preparation at home. Further, no animal fat or meat may be allowed to come into contact with these foods, or with utensils or dishes used in preparing or serving them.

Cooking with fats:

At one time the Jewish housewife was limited to the use of those fats (such as chicken and other poultry fat, as well as beef fat) that she could render in the kitchen.

> For cooking *fleischigs:*
>
> > chicken and other poultry fats
> > beef and other kosher meat fats
> > vegetable fat or oil

For cooking *milchigs:*

butter
kosher margarine
vegetable fat or oil

Vegetable fats and oils, liquid or solid, are *pareve* fats, so they can be used for cooking *milchige* and *fleischige* dishes.

Utensils and dishes in a kosher home:

Since *milchige* foods may not be prepared or served in utensils and dishes used for meats, there must be several sets of dishes for everyday use in the kosher home. One set of dishes, silver, and cooking utensils is reserved for *milchige* foods and another for *fleischigs.* The homemaker will usually have dishes of a different color or design so that they are easily distinguishable. These must be stored in separate cupboards and washed in separate pans, and separate dish towels must be reserved for each. There are also extra *pareve* glass dishes for cooking and serving. These are nonabsorbent and therefore interchangeable; they may be used for *milchigs* and *fleischigs.*

In addition to this, because no *chometz* (leaven) may come into contact with serving or cooking utensils used for the Passover season, there must also be a second two sets of dishes, silver, and cooking utensils reserved for Passover use. It follows then that a kosher home is supplied with four sets of this equipment, as well as glass for *pareve* use. As an exception to this, there are a few serving or cooking utensils in everyday use that are especially kashered for use during Passover (*see* page 127).

Planning and preparing meals:

In planning and preparing meals, the Jewish housewife must observe the distinction between *fleischige* and *milchige* foods. These must be cooked, prepared, and served in separate utensils and dishes, and may not be served at the same meal. There is a third group of foods that are *pareve* and may be served at either a *fleischige* or *milchige* meal. Fish and eggs are *pareve* foods. Meat and fish may be served at the same meal if the fish is served as a separate course, on a separate plate, preceding any meat dish, either soup or main dish. Meat and fish are not cooked together.

Cooking for the Sabbath:

No food may be cooked on the Sabbath. All cooking must be completed before sunset on Friday afternoon of each week. This has led to the development of such famous and delectable dishes as *cholent, petcha,* the Sabbath *kugel, tzimmes,* and other favorites.

Restrictions for Passover:

During the entire eight days of Passover no leavened bread or its products may be eaten; they may not even be found in any place within the home. (For other Passover restrictions, *see* pages 125 to 128.)

Kosher foods prepared outside the home:

There is a growing list of kosher foods prepared outside the home. Accredited rabbis are engaged by many modern food manufacturers to supervise the departments they have established for the preparation of kosher foods. Those prepared in strict accordance with the dietary laws include meats and dairy products; packaged, canned, and frozen foods; shortenings, fats, and oils—practically all food products not prohibited from use. In addition there is a wide range of cleaning materials available.

The Jewish cuisine is international in scope and includes

some of the finest dishes from the many lands where Jews have made their homes. Skillfully they have modified many of these dishes to conform to the dietary laws. Over and over again we find that the Jewish housewife has met this challenge, and from it have come some of the favorite specialties of the Jewish kitchen.

In ascribing the origin of certain famous Jewish dishes to definite countries it must be remembered that even though a dish may be popular in many places, it was generally some one country that brought it to its culmination. The following is a list of countries with some of their chief contributions to Jewish cooking:

Spain and Portugal: salmon dishes; a fondness for frying fish in oil; highly spiced dishes; olives; sharp peppers.

Germany: sweet-sour meat dishes; marinated fish, especially marinated herring; coffee breads.

Holland: pickled herring; cucumber pickles; butter cakes; *bolas* (jam rolls); *gefillte* fish.

Russia: kasha (buckwheat groats); *blintzes;* fermented beets; borscht of cabbage and beets; cheese; tea; black bread; pickled red cabbage, pickled melons, potato puddings, dill pickles, rich compotes, smoked salmon and other smoked fish.

Hungary: paprika veal and chicken (and many other paprika dishes), goulash, *strudel.*

Roumania: mamaliga (a corn meal dish), sweet pastries, jellies, salt fish.

Poland: egg noodles, fresh water fish dishes, herring dishes, sour cream dishes.

Italy: pastes (noodlelike dishes); *kreplach* (believed to be patterned after raviolas, noodle, and spaghetti dishes).

Middle East: honey dishes and pastries, especially *baclava;* cabbage-stuffed meat, sesame seed cakes and candies, fruit and nut dishes, vegetables, vegetable salads, *schav* (sorrel grass soup); some cereals.

Baltic area: smoked meats, cabbage, scallions, tomatoes.

France: soups; use of spices and herbs.

England: fruit fritters, puddings, boiled and stewed fish.

Family Celebrations

Every Jewish family shares its *simchoth* (celebrations) with the community, bringing its joys and sorrows to the synagogue where the entire congregation may share in them.

When a baby is born, there is great rejoicing. The father is called up to the *bimah* (the platform) for the reading of the Torah. A special prayer is offered for the welfare of both mother and child. If the child is a girl, it is named in the synagogue at this time.

Ben Zochar is the special celebration of the birth of a son. On the Friday evening after its birth, there is a ceremony at the synagogue, followed by feasting around the family table. On this night congratulations pour in from far and near.

Brith Milah (circumcision) is one of the most important of all ceremonies, adhered to tenaciously through the centuries. It is agreed by scholars and leaders that the ceremony of circumcision, together with observance of the Sabbath, has helped to preserve the Jews as a people. When a boy is circumcised, on the eighth day after its birth, it is believed that the Prophet Elijah is present to witness this renewed covenant of loyalty given by the Israelites to the Lord.

After the ceremony of circumcision, friends and relatives are entertained at home, and traditional foods are served. There will be *leckach* and *bronfen* (honey cake with whiskey or brandy); and there will be wine. This may be followed by chopped herring and *kichel*, served with wine; or by the most

189

elaborate of dinners with traditional dishes from Sabbath meals.

Pidyon-ha-ben is a special ceremony for the first-born male of the family. It is the occasion for great rejoicing, and recalls that fateful night of the Passover when the angel of the Lord passed over the homes of the captive Israelites, sparing their first-born males. This ceremony takes place on the thirty-first day after the child is born, except when this day falls on the Sabbath. In that case it must be postponed to a day within the next week. Feasting at home follows the ceremony in the synagogue. Tall glasses of hot tea are served with wine and brandy, with honey cakes, sponge cakes, and many other similar delicacies.

Bar Mitzvah is the ceremony of Confirmation for boys. It is a most impressive occasion, one of the most important in the life of a Jewish boy. Up to this time his father has been responsible for his acts. Now he is thirteen years old; he has become a man, accountable to himself and to God for his actions. His *Bar Mitzvah* takes place on the Sabbath following his birthday. He is called to the *bimah*, and in the presence of family and friends and all the congregation, he reads a prescribed portion of the Torah. He may even make a little speech that he would have rehearsed well beforehand. The parents frequently serve refreshments at the synagogue to all present, and then the happy occasion is celebrated with friends and family at home. The *Bar Mitzvah* boy receives many gifts and among the most treasured is always a man-sized *tallith*, a handsome prayer shawl with tasseled fringes at its four corners; and new *tephillin*, two long straps of black leather, each with a small box in which there is a parchment inscribed with verses from the Bible.

Today Reform, and some of the Conservative, synagogues hold a group ceremony of Confirmation on Shavuoth for the children trained in their schools. Both boys and girls who have reached the age of religious maturity are confirmed at this time in a ceremony that is solemn and joyous. Parties are given for the whole group and many families entertain at home for their *Bar Mitzvah* son or daughter.

T'naim, the betrothal ceremony, takes place when the marriage contract is signed in the presence of a happy company of family and friends. Following the signing, there will be refreshments—tall glasses of hot tea with lemon, brandy, wine, sponge cake and a great variety of delicacies.

Chassana, the wedding, is a very great ceremonial occasion. Late spring, after Shavuoth, is the favorite season for weddings, since they are prohibited between Pesach and Shavuoth, except for the day of Lag B'Omer. Weddings must never be solemnized during the three weeks of sorrow beginning on the 17th of *Tammuz* and ending with *Tisha B'Ab*.

The marriage ceremony is performed under a *chuppah* (a canopy) that has changed in appearance over the years. In early days, the *tallith* (prayer shawl) was the first canopy; greens and flowers were substituted for this later. Today there is often a silken canopy supported by four posts. During the ceremony a glass is broken. This is a reminder of the sorrow and sufferings endured by the Jewish people, and its roundness is symbolic of the cycle of life. The marriage table is rich with all the good things a family can provide. There are sweets of every kind, cakes and confections; and a *challah* of immense proportions over which *Kiddush* will be said.

There is great sorrow when death comes to the family of one of the members of a congregation. A memorial candle is kept burning in the synagogue for a week. There is reading from the Torah. At home there is also a memorial candle. When the mourners return from the burial, their first meal (generally prepared by friends in their absence) consists of hard-cooked eggs and *bagel*. These are symbolic in their roundness of the world with its ever-recurring changes from light to darkness, from joy to sorrow. Eggs also have another significance in that they are symbols of the seeds of life. *Shiva,* a week of mourning, is observed at home by the family of the deceased. During this period all relatives and friends are sure to come and offer their deep sympathy.

Glossary

An attempt has been made to transliterate Hebrew words and expressions to the phonetic pattern of Sephardic usage, since this is the form of the living tongue spoken in Israel today. However, where certain expressions are more easily recognizable in their Ashkenazic or Yiddish versions, these are given.

Adar. The twelfth month of the Hebrew year, usually corresponding to late February and early March.

Addir Hu. A song sung during the Seder.

Adloyada. Purim carnival in Tel Aviv.

afikoman. Literally, dessert. A piece of matza put aside at the beginning of the Seder and eaten at the end of the meal.

Akiba, Rabbi Joseph ben. Scholar and leader of the last rebellion against Rome.

Amoraim. Sages of the Talmud, third to sixth centuries.

bagel. A bread roll made of yeast dough and shaped like a doughnut.

balabuste. An efficient housewife.

Bar Kochba. Literally, son of a star. Leader of the last struggle against the Romans for independence in Palestine.

Bar Mitzvah. The ceremony for a boy reaching the age of religious maturity.

B.C.E. Before Common Era.

Ben Zochar. The celebration on the Friday night following the birth of a boy.

beryah. A perfect homemaker in every respect.

bessamim. Spices used in the *Havdalah* ceremony.

Bialik, Chayyim Nahman. Modern Jewish poet.

193

bikkurim. The first fruits of the early harvest that are gathered for the festival of Shavuoth.

bimah. The reading dais in the center of the synagogue.

blintzes. Very thin rolled pancakes, filled with cheese, fruit, or meat.

bob. Fava beans that are served as a special treat on Purim and Chamisha Asar B'Shevat.

bokser. The fruit of the carob tree, popularly known as St. John's bread.

Bread of Affliction. Matza, the unleavened bread of the Passover.

Brith Milah. The ceremony of circumcision.

calendar of Jewish holidays. Jewish holidays do not fall on the same days each year on the calendar of the Common Era. In the early days the Sanhedrin fixed the dates of the holidays and sent the news out from Jerusalem by messengers. Later dates were fixed by astronomical calculation. It was during the early periods, because of uncertainty about exact dates, that two days were observed for each holiday. Yom Kippur was an exception, since it is a fast day.

carnatzlach. A highly seasoned meat dish rich with garlic, Roumanian in origin.

Chad Gadya. (An Only Kid.) A song sung at the Seder.

challah. Sabbath twists of white bread. It is also made in a variety of forms for the various holidays of the year.

Chamishah Asar B'Shevat. Literally, the fifteenth day of the month of *Shevat.* The New Year of the Trees.

Chanukah. Literally, dedication. The Festival of Lights.

Chanukah gelt. Money given as a gift at Chanukah time.

charoseth. A mixture of chopped apples and nuts, seasoned with cinnamon and wine—a Seder symbol.

chassana. The wedding ceremony and celebration.

chazan. Cantor.

cheder. Elementary Hebrew school.

cholent. A Sabbath oven dish prepared on Friday and cooked overnight in a very slow oven.

chometz. Usually refers to bread and leaven forbidden during Passover. It also refers to utensils that have not been ritually prepared for Passover.

chremslach. A Passover delicacy—glorified pancakes.

chuppah. The wedding canopy.

Confirmation. The ceremony held by Reform and some Conservative synagogues for boys and girls reaching the age of religious maturity.

Daiainu. (Alone 'twould have sufficed us.) A song chanted at the Seder.

Days of Awe. The High Holy Days, beginning with Rosh Hashanah and ending with Yom Kippur.

dolma. An oriental dish in which grape or cabbage leaves are stuffed with meat, rice, and spices.

dreidel. Symbolic, four-winged top, spun by the children during the festival of Chanukah. Also called *trendel.*

einbren. Browned flour, used as thickening for gravy and sauces in stews, *tzimmes,* and other dishes.

eingemachts. Preserves.

Elijah's Cup. A cup for wine placed on the Seder table for Elijah, the prophet of hope and faith.

Elul. The sixth month of the Hebrew year, usually corresponding to late August and early September.

ethrog. The fruit of the citron, used with the festive bouquet on Sukkoth.

farfel. Noodle dough, grated or chopped into barley-sized grains.

fleischigs. Meat or meat products, or dishes containing meats.

galuptze. The Russian name for stuffed cabbage or grape leaves.

gefillte fish. Stuffed fish.

"G'mar chatima tova." "May the final inscription be good." Traditional greeting at the close of the High Holy Days.

greggers. Rasping noise-makers used especially at Purim.

gribenes. Cracklings resulting from the rendering out of fats, especially poultry fats.

"Gut yohr." A greeting meaning "good year."

"Gut yom tov." A greeting meaning "good holiday."

Haggadah. The book of the Seder, giving the story, meaning and the written order of the Passover ceremony.

halke. A large dumpling.

hamantaschen. Three-cornered cakes filled with poppy seed, traditional for Purim.

hamotzi lechem min harretz. The blessing over bread.

Havdalah. The benediction recited or chanted at the conclusion of the Sabbath.

helzel. Poultry neck filled with stuffing.

High Holy Days. The Ten Days of Awe, from Rosh Hashanah through Yom Kippur.

hoshanah. A branch of willow used on Hoshanah Rabbah.

Hoshanah Rabbah. Literally, the great hosanna. The seventh day of the Festival of Sukkoth.

ingberlach. Ginger honey candy.

Iyar. The second month of the Hebrew year, usually corresponding to late April and early May.

kasha. Literally, a mush from any cereal; today the usually accepted meaning is buckwheat groats.

kasher. To follow a ritual in the preparation of foods, especially the soaking and salting of meats and poultry before cooking, according to the Jewish dietary laws.

Kasher L'Pesaach. Fit for Passover. Food that is made ritually correct for Passover.

kashruth. The Jewish dietary laws.

katowes. A numeral game played during Chanukah.

keylitch. Very large challah twist.

kichlach. Cookies or wafers.

Kiddush. The prayer of sanctification of the Sabbath or of a holiday, recited over wine.

kishke. Beef casings, stuffed with seasoned filling and roasted; also known as *derma.*

Kislev. The ninth month of the Hebrew year, usually corresponding to late November and early December.

knaidlach. Dumplings.

knishes. Stuffed patties or dumplings.

Kol Nidre. A special prayer chanted on Yom Kippur.

kreplach. Noodle dough cut round or square and filled with cheese or meat—traditional for Purim, Hoshanah Rabbah, and Yom Kippur.

kuchen. Assorted coffee cakes.

kugel. Pudding.

Lag B'Omer. Thirty-third day of the period of mourning; scholars' holiday associated with Bar Kochba and Rabbi Akiba and disciples of the latter.

latkes. Pancakes of all varieties.

leaven. Bread and bread stuffs raised with yeast, baking powder, or baking soda.

leckach. A honey cake.

lox. Smoked salmon.

"L'shana tova tikatevu." "May you be inscribed for a good year." Traditional greeting during the season of the High Holy Days.

lukshen. Noodles.

lulov. The ceremonial bouquet of willow, myrtle, and palm branches used during Sukkoth. It also means palm branches.

Maccabees. Name given the Hasmonean family headed by Mattathias, a priest, whose famous son Judas led the successful revolt against the Syrians.

"Mah nishtanah." "Why is this different?" The opening words of the Four Questions recited during the Seder.

mamaliga. Traditional Roumanian dish of corn meal and cheese.

Ma'oz Tzur. (Rock of Ages.) Ancient hymn sung during Chanukah.

matza (pl. *matzoth*). Unleavened bread eaten during Passover.

matza cake meal. Extra-finely ground matza meal.

matza meal. Finely ground matzoth.

matza shel mitsvah. The matzoth of precept, specially prepared.

med. Mead; a fermented drink made of honey, hops, water, and ginger.

Megillah. Literally, a scroll, but generally used as referring to the Book of Esther.

mehren. Carrots.

menorah. Candelabra.

milchigs. Milk and milk products, or dishes made from them.

mitsvah. Religious precept; religious act; deed of religious merit.

M'lavah Malkah. The ceremony that celebrates the departure of Queen Sabbath on Saturday night.

mohn. Poppy seed.

mondelbrot. Special variety of almond-flavored pastry.

mondlen. Soup garnish; soup nuts.

moror. Bitter herb, generally horse-radish, symbolic food of the Seder.

nahit. Chick peas.

Nisan. The first month of the Hebrew year, usually corresponding to late March and early April.

Oneg Shabbath. Literally, delight in the Sabbath. A modern revival of the Shalosh Seudot. Sabbath afternoon meetings.

pareve. Applies to foods such as fish, eggs, fruit, and vegetables; foods that are neither *milchig* nor *fleischig.*

Paschal lamb. Symbolic food of the Seder.

Passover (Hebrew, *Pesach*). Commemorating the Exodus of
the Israelites from Egypt.

petcha. Calf's foot jelly. Sometimes called *Sulze.*

Pidyon-ha-ben. Redemption of the first-born.

pirogen. Pockets of yeast dough or pastry, stuffed with filling.

Purim. A historical festival, known also as the Feast of Lots.
Celebrates the story of Esther.

rabbi. Literally, my master. An ordained teacher of Jewish
law, authorized to decide questions of law and ritual; the
spiritual head of a congregation.

Rosh Hashanah. "Head" of the year; new year; first of the
High Holy Days, Day of Judgment.

Rosh Hashanah L'ailanoth. The New Year of the Trees.

rusell. Fermented beet juice used as vinegar during Passover.

schav. Sorrel grass soup.

schmaltz. Literally, fat. Rendered fats of meat and poultry.

schnecken. Little fruit and nut coffee rolls.

schochet. A man trained and authorized to slaughter animals
and fowl, in accordance with Jewish dietary laws.

Scholars' Day. See Lag B'Omer.

Seder. Order of Pesach service; traditional home ceremony
of the Passover.

seudah. Literally, feast. Generally refers to Purim parties.

Shabbath. The Sabbath.

shalach monas. Gift-giving at the time of the Purim festival.
Refers particularly to plates of cakes and confections.

Shalom aleichem. "Peace be unto you," traditional greeting.

Shalosh Seudot. The third meal of the Sabbath, eaten between afternoon and evening services.

shamas. Sexton of the synagogue; also the lighter taper used
to light other candles on a menorah.

Shavuoth. The Festival of the Torah; known also as the Feast of Weeks, and the Feast of Pentecost.

Shemini Atzereth. The eighth day of Sukkoth; the day of Solemn Assembly of the holiday week.

Shevat. The eleventh month of the Hebrew year, usually corresponding to late January and early February.

Shew-bread. Show-bread for the altar of the ancient Temple in Jerusalem.

shofar. Trumpet made from the horn of a ram; it is blown during the month of Elul and during the High Holy Days.

Simchath Torah. The last festival day of Sukkoth, the day of rejoicing in the Torah.

simchoth. Joyful occasions.

Simeon ben Yohai. Noted scholar, mystic.

Sivan. The third month of the Hebrew year, usually corresponding to late May and early June.

strudel. Paper-thin pastry, rolled and filled with sweet fillings.

sukkah. Literally, a booth. A booth or tabernacle (a temporary structure) erected for Sukkoth, Festival of the Booths.

Sukkoth. The Festival of the Booths; known also as the Feast of the Tabernacles.

tallith. Prayer shawl.

Talmud. Collection of writings, containing Jewish civil and religious laws.

Tashlich. Literally, casting away. A ceremony symbolizing the casting away of sins, into a stream of water.

teiglach. Small balls of dough cooked in honey.

Ten Days of Penitence. The ten holy days beginning with Rosh Hashanah and ending with Yom Kippur.

tephillin. A small square box containing a thin strip of parchment with inscription of text from Jewish law; worn on the left hand and forehead by Jewish males during the morning prayer on weekdays.

Tishri. The seventh month of the Hebrew year, usually corresponding to late September and early October.

T'naim. The betrothal ceremony.

Torah. Literally, the law. The Pentateuch, or "law of Moses."

tzimmes. A pudding made with vegetables, sometimes fruit and vegetables, and often with meat.

unleavened bread. Known as matza, baked for Passover, the only bread permitted during the Passover festival.

varenikes. Pastry made of rounds of noodle dough filled with fruit or meat.

varnishkas. Kasha with noodles.

varenyah. Preserves.

Yom Kippur. The Day of Atonement; tenth and last of the High Holy Days.

zemiroth. Religious table songs.

Index

202

Index of Recipes

A CATALOG OF SELECTED
DOVER BOOKS
IN ALL FIELDS OF INTEREST

A CATALOG OF SELECTED DOVER
BOOKS IN ALL FIELDS OF INTEREST

DRAWINGS OF REMBRANDT, edited by Seymour Slive. Updated Lippmann, Hofstede de Groot edition, with definitive scholarly apparatus. All portraits, biblical sketches, landscapes, nudes. Oriental figures, classical studies, together with selection of work by followers. 550 illustrations. Total of 630pp. 9⅛ × 12¼.
21485-0, 21486-9 Pa., Two-vol. set $25.00

GHOST AND HORROR STORIES OF AMBROSE BIERCE, Ambrose Bierce. 24 tales vividly imagined, strangely prophetic, and decades ahead of their time in technical skill: "The Damned Thing," "An Inhabitant of Carcosa," "The Eyes of the Panther," "Moxon's Master," and 20 more. 199pp. 5⅜ × 8½. 20767-6 Pa. $3.95

ETHICAL WRITINGS OF MAIMONIDES, Maimonides. Most significant ethical works of great medieval sage, newly translated for utmost precision, readability. Laws Concerning Character Traits, Eight Chapters, more. 192pp. 5⅜ × 8½.
24522-5 Pa. $4.50

THE EXPLORATION OF THE COLORADO RIVER AND ITS CANYONS, J. W. Powell. Full text of Powell's 1,000-mile expedition down the fabled Colorado in 1869. Superb account of terrain, geology, vegetation, Indians, famine, mutiny, treacherous rapids, mighty canyons, during exploration of last unknown part of continental U.S. 400pp. 5⅜ × 8½. 20094-9 Pa. $6.95

HISTORY OF PHILOSOPHY, Julián Marías. Clearest one-volume history on the market. Every major philosopher and dozens of others, to Existentialism and later. 505pp. 5⅜ × 8½. 21739-6 Pa. $8.50

ALL ABOUT LIGHTNING, Martin A. Uman. Highly readable non-technical survey of nature and causes of lightning, thunderstorms, ball lightning, St. Elmo's Fire, much more. Illustrated. 192pp. 5⅜ × 8½. 25237-X Pa. $5.95

SAILING ALONE AROUND THE WORLD, Captain Joshua Slocum. First man to sail around the world, alone, in small boat. One of great feats of seamanship told in delightful manner. 67 illustrations. 294pp. 5⅜ × 8½. 20326-3 Pa. $4.95

LETTERS AND NOTES ON THE MANNERS, CUSTOMS AND CONDITIONS OF THE NORTH AMERICAN INDIANS, George Catlin. Classic account of life among Plains Indians: ceremonies, hunt, warfare, etc. 312 plates. 572pp. of text. 6⅛ × 9¼. 22118-0, 22119-9 Pa. Two-vol. set $15.90

ALASKA: The Harriman Expedition, 1899, John Burroughs, John Muir, et al. Informative, engrossing accounts of two-month, 9,000-mile expedition. Native peoples, wildlife, forests, geography, salmon industry, glaciers, more. Profusely illustrated. 240 black-and-white line drawings. 124 black-and-white photographs. 3 maps. Index. 576pp. 5⅜ × 8½. 25109-8 Pa. $11.95

THE BOOK OF BEASTS: Being a Translation from a Latin Bestiary of the Twelfth Century, T. H. White. Wonderful catalog real and fanciful beasts: manticore, griffin, phoenix, amphivius, jaculus, many more. White's witty erudite commentary on scientific, historical aspects. Fascinating glimpse of medieval mind. Illustrated. 296pp. 5⅜ × 8¼. (Available in U.S. only)　　　24609-4 Pa. $5.95

FRANK LLOYD WRIGHT: ARCHITECTURE AND NATURE With 160 Illustrations, Donald Hoffmann. Profusely illustrated study of influence of nature—especially prairie—on Wright's designs for Fallingwater, Robie House, Guggenheim Museum, other masterpieces. 96pp. 9¼ × 10¾.　　25098-9 Pa. $7.95

FRANK LLOYD WRIGHT'S FALLINGWATER, Donald Hoffmann. Wright's famous waterfall house: planning and construction of organic idea. History of site, owners, Wright's personal involvement. Photographs of various stages of building. Preface by Edgar Kaufmann, Jr. 100 illustrations. 112pp. 9¼ × 10.

23671-4 Pa. $7.95

YEARS WITH FRANK LLOYD WRIGHT: Apprentice to Genius, Edgar Tafel. Insightful memoir by a former apprentice presents a revealing portrait of Wright the man, the inspired teacher, the greatest American architect. 372 black-and-white illustrations. Preface. Index. vi + 228pp. 8¼ × 11.　　24801-1 Pa. $9.95

THE STORY OF KING ARTHUR AND HIS KNIGHTS, Howard Pyle. Enchanting version of King Arthur fable has delighted generations with imaginative narratives of exciting adventures and unforgettable illustrations by the author. 41 illustrations. xviii + 313pp. 6⅛ × 9¼.　　21445-1 Pa. $6.50

THE GODS OF THE EGYPTIANS, E. A. Wallis Budge. Thorough coverage of numerous gods of ancient Egypt by foremost Egyptologist. Information on evolution of cults, rites and gods; the cult of Osiris; the Book of the Dead and its rites; the sacred animals and birds; Heaven and Hell; and more. 956pp. 6⅛ × 9¼.

22055-9, 22056-7 Pa., Two-vol. set $20.00

A THEOLOGICO-POLITICAL TREATISE, Benedict Spinoza. Also contains unfinished *Political Treatise*. Great classic on religious liberty, theory of government on common consent. R. Elwes translation. Total of 421pp. 5⅜ × 8½.

20249-6 Pa. $6.95

INCIDENTS OF TRAVEL IN CENTRAL AMERICA, CHIAPAS, AND YU-CATAN, John L. Stephens. Almost single-handed discovery of Maya culture; exploration of ruined cities, monuments, temples; customs of Indians. 115 drawings. 892pp. 5⅜ × 8½.　　　22404-X, 22405-8 Pa., Two-vol. set $15.90

LOS CAPRICHOS, Francisco Goya. 80 plates of wild, grotesque monsters and caricatures. Prado manuscript included. 183pp. 6⅜ × 9⅜.　　22384-1 Pa. $4.95

AUTOBIOGRAPHY: The Story of My Experiments with Truth, Mohandas K. Gandhi. Not hagiography, but Gandhi in his own words. Boyhood, legal studies, purification, the growth of the Satyagraha (nonviolent protest) movement. Critical, inspiring work of the man who freed India. 480pp. 5⅜ × 8½. (Available in U.S. only)

24593-4 Pa. $6.95

ILLUSTRATED DICTIONARY OF HISTORIC ARCHITECTURE, edited by Cyril M. Harris. Extraordinary compendium of clear, concise definitions for over 5,000 important architectural terms complemented by over 2,000 line drawings. Covers full spectrum of architecture from ancient ruins to 20th-century Modernism. Preface. 592pp. 7½ × 9⅜. 24444-X Pa. $14.95

THE NIGHT BEFORE CHRISTMAS, Clement Moore. Full text, and woodcuts from original 1848 book. Also critical, historical material. 19 illustrations. 40pp. 4⅝ × 6. 22797-9 Pa. $2.25

THE LESSON OF JAPANESE ARCHITECTURE: 165 Photographs, Jiro Harada. Memorable gallery of 165 photographs taken in the 1930's of exquisite Japanese homes of the well-to-do and historic buildings. 13 line diagrams. 192pp. 8⅜ × 11¼. 24778-3 Pa. $8.95

THE AUTOBIOGRAPHY OF CHARLES DARWIN AND SELECTED LETTERS, edited by Francis Darwin. The fascinating life of eccentric genius composed of an intimate memoir by Darwin (intended for his children); commentary by his son, Francis; hundreds of fragments from notebooks, journals, papers; and letters to and from Lyell, Hooker, Huxley, Wallace and Henslow. xi + 365pp. 5⅜ × 8. 20479-0 Pa. $6.95

WONDERS OF THE SKY: Observing Rainbows, Comets, Eclipses, the Stars and Other Phenomena, Fred Schaaf. Charming, easy-to-read poetic guide to all manner of celestial events visible to the naked eye. Mock suns, glories, Belt of Venus, more. Illustrated. 299pp. 5¼ × 8¼. 24402-4 Pa. $7.95

BURNHAM'S CELESTIAL HANDBOOK, Robert Burnham, Jr. Thorough guide to the stars beyond our solar system. Exhaustive treatment. Alphabetical by constellation: Andromeda to Cetus in Vol. 1; Chamaeleon to Orion in Vol. 2; and Pavo to Vulpecula in Vol. 3. Hundreds of illustrations. Index in Vol. 3. 2,000pp. 6⅛ × 9¼. 23567-X, 23568-8, 23673-0 Pa., Three-vol. set $38.85

STAR NAMES: Their Lore and Meaning, Richard Hinckley Allen. Fascinating history of names various cultures have given to constellations and literary and folkloristic uses that have been made of stars. Indexes to subjects. Arabic and Greek names. Biblical references. Bibliography. 563pp. 5⅜ × 8½. 21079-0 Pa. $7.95

THIRTY YEARS THAT SHOOK PHYSICS: The Story of Quantum Theory, George Gamow. Lucid, accessible introduction to influential theory of energy and matter. Careful explanations of Dirac's anti-particles, Bohr's model of the atom, much more. 12 plates. Numerous drawings. 240pp. 5⅜ × 8½. 24895-X Pa. $4.95

CHINESE DOMESTIC FURNITURE IN PHOTOGRAPHS AND MEASURED DRAWINGS, Gustav Ecke. A rare volume, now affordably priced for antique collectors, furniture buffs and art historians. Detailed review of styles ranging from early Shang to late Ming. Unabridged republication. 161 black-and-white drawings, photos. Total of 224pp. 8⅜ × 11¼. (Available in U.S. only) 25171-3 Pa. $12.95

VINCENT VAN GOGH: A Biography, Julius Meier-Graefe. Dynamic, penetrating study of artist's life, relationship with brother, Theo, painting techniques, travels, more. Readable, engrossing. 160pp. 5⅜ × 8½. (Available in U.S. only) 25253-1 Pa. $3.95

HOW TO WRITE, Gertrude Stein. Gertrude Stein claimed anyone could understand her unconventional writing—here are clues to help. Fascinating improvisations, language experiments, explanations illuminate Stein's craft and the art of writing. Total of 414pp. 4⅝ × 6⅜. 23144-5 Pa. $5.95

ADVENTURES AT SEA IN THE GREAT AGE OF SAIL: Five Firsthand Narratives, edited by Elliot Snow. Rare true accounts of exploration, whaling, shipwreck, fierce natives, trade, shipboard life, more. 33 illustrations. Introduction. 353pp. 5⅜ × 8½. 25177-2 Pa. $7.95

THE HERBAL OR GENERAL HISTORY OF PLANTS, John Gerard. Classic descriptions of about 2,850 plants—with over 2,700 illustrations—includes Latin and English names, physical descriptions, varieties, time and place of growth, more. 2,706 illustrations. xlv + 1,678pp. 8½ × 12¼. 23147-X Cloth. $75.00

DOROTHY AND THE WIZARD IN OZ, L. Frank Baum. Dorothy and the Wizard visit the center of the Earth, where people are vegetables, glass houses grow and Oz characters reappear. Classic sequel to *Wizard of Oz*. 256pp. 5⅜ × 8. 24714-7 Pa. $4.95

SONGS OF EXPERIENCE: Facsimile Reproduction with 26 Plates in Full Color, William Blake. This facsimile of Blake's original "Illuminated Book" reproduces 26 full-color plates from a rare 1826 edition. Includes "The Tyger," "London," "Holy Thursday," and other immortal poems. 26 color plates. Printed text of poems. 48pp. 5¼ × 7. 24636-1 Pa. $3.50

SONGS OF INNOCENCE, William Blake. The first and most popular of Blake's famous "Illuminated Books," in a facsimile edition reproducing all 31 brightly colored plates. Additional printed text of each poem. 64pp. 5¼ × 7. 22764-2 Pa. $3.50

PRECIOUS STONES, Max Bauer. Classic, thorough study of diamonds, rubies, emeralds, garnets, etc.: physical character, occurrence, properties, use, similar topics. 20 plates, 8 in color. 94 figures. 659pp. 6⅛ × 9¼. 21910-0, 21911-9 Pa., Two-vol. set $15.90

ENCYCLOPEDIA OF VICTORIAN NEEDLEWORK, S. F. A. Caulfeild and Blanche Saward. Full, precise descriptions of stitches, techniques for dozens of needlecrafts—most exhaustive reference of its kind. Over 800 figures. Total of 679pp. 8⅜ × 11. Two volumes. Vol. 1 22800-2 Pa. $11.95 Vol. 2 22801-0 Pa. $11.95

THE MARVELOUS LAND OF OZ, L. Frank Baum. Second Oz book, the Scarecrow and Tin Woodman are back with hero named Tip, Oz magic. 136 illustrations. 287pp. 5⅜ × 8½. 20692-0 Pa. $5.95

WILD FOWL DECOYS, Joel Barber. Basic book on the subject, by foremost authority and collector. Reveals history of decoy making and rigging, place in American culture, different kinds of decoys, how to make them, and how to use them. 140 plates. 156pp. 7⅞ × 10¾. 20011-6 Pa. $8.95

HISTORY OF LACE, Mrs. Bury Palliser. Definitive, profusely illustrated chronicle of lace from earliest times to late 19th century. Laces of Italy, Greece, England, France, Belgium, etc. Landmark of needlework scholarship. 266 illustrations. 672pp. 6⅛ × 9¼. 24742-2 Pa. $14.95

ILLUSTRATED GUIDE TO SHAKER FURNITURE, Robert Meader. All furniture and appurtenances, with much on unknown local styles. 235 photos. 146pp. 9 × 12. 22819-3 Pa. $7.95

WHALE SHIPS AND WHALING: A Pictorial Survey, George Francis Dow. Over 200 vintage engravings, drawings, photographs of barks, brigs, cutters, other vessels. Also harpoons, lances, whaling guns, many other artifacts. Comprehensive text by foremost authority. 207 black-and-white illustrations. 288pp. 6 × 9. 24808-9 Pa. $8.95

THE BERTRAMS, Anthony Trollope. Powerful portrayal of blind self-will and thwarted ambition includes one of Trollope's most heartrending love stories. 497pp. 5⅜ × 8½. 25119-5 Pa. $8.95

ADVENTURES WITH A HAND LENS, Richard Headstrom. Clearly written guide to observing and studying flowers and grasses, fish scales, moth and insect wings, egg cases, buds, feathers, seeds, leaf scars, moss, molds, ferns, common crystals, etc.—all with an ordinary, inexpensive magnifying glass. 209 exact line drawings aid in your discoveries. 220pp. 5⅜ × 8½. 23330-8 Pa. $3.95

RODIN ON ART AND ARTISTS, Auguste Rodin. Great sculptor's candid, wide-ranging comments on meaning of art; great artists; relation of sculpture to poetry, painting, music; philosophy of life, more. 76 superb black-and-white illustrations of Rodin's sculpture, drawings and prints. 119pp. 8⅝ × 11¼. 24487-3 Pa. $6.95

FIFTY CLASSIC FRENCH FILMS, 1912–1982: A Pictorial Record, Anthony Slide. Memorable stills from Grand Illusion, Beauty and the Beast, Hiroshima, Mon Amour, many more. Credits, plot synopses, reviews, etc. 160pp. 8¼ × 11. 25256-6 Pa. $11.95

THE PRINCIPLES OF PSYCHOLOGY, William James. Famous long course complete, unabridged. Stream of thought, time perception, memory, experimental methods; great work decades ahead of its time. 94 figures. 1,391pp. 5⅜ × 8½. 20381-6, 20382-4 Pa., Two-vol. set $19.90

BODIES IN A BOOKSHOP, R. T. Campbell. Challenging mystery of blackmail and murder with ingenious plot and superbly drawn characters. In the best tradition of British suspense fiction. 192pp. 5⅜ × 8½. 24720-1 Pa. $3.95

CALLAS: PORTRAIT OF A PRIMA DONNA, George Jellinek. Renowned commentator on the musical scene chronicles incredible career and life of the most controversial, fascinating, influential operatic personality of our time. 64 black-and-white photographs. 416pp. 5⅜ × 8¼. 25047-4 Pa. $7.95

GEOMETRY, RELATIVITY AND THE FOURTH DIMENSION, Rudolph Rucker. Exposition of fourth dimension, concepts of relativity as Flatland characters continue adventures. Popular, easily followed yet accurate, profound. 141 illustrations. 133pp. 5⅜ × 8½. 23400-2 Pa. $3.95

HOUSEHOLD STORIES BY THE BROTHERS GRIMM, with pictures by Walter Crane. 53 classic stories—Rumpelstiltskin, Rapunzel, Hansel and Gretel, the Fisherman and his Wife, Snow White, Tom Thumb, Sleeping Beauty, Cinderella, and so much more—lavishly illustrated with original 19th century drawings. 114 illustrations. x + 269pp. 5⅜ × 8½. 21080-4 Pa. $4.50

SUNDIALS, Albert Waugh. Far and away the best, most thorough coverage of ideas, mathematics concerned, types, construction, adjusting anywhere. Over 100 illustrations. 230pp. 5⅜ × 8½. 22947-5 Pa. $4.50

PICTURE HISTORY OF THE NORMANDIE: With 190 Illustrations, Frank O. Braynard. Full story of legendary French ocean liner: Art Deco interiors, design innovations, furnishings, celebrities, maiden voyage, tragic fire, much more. Extensive text. 144pp. 8⅞ × 11¾. 25257-4 Pa. $9.95

THE FIRST AMERICAN COOKBOOK: A Facsimile of "American Cookery," 1796, Amelia Simmons. Facsimile of the first American-written cookbook published in the United States contains authentic recipes for colonial favorites—pumpkin pudding, winter squash pudding, spruce beer, Indian slapjacks, and more. Introductory Essay and Glossary of colonial cooking terms. 80pp. 5⅜ × 8½. 24710-4 Pa. $3.50

101 PUZZLES IN THOUGHT AND LOGIC, C. R. Wylie, Jr. Solve murders and robberies, find out which fishermen are liars, how a blind man could possibly identify a color—purely by your own reasoning! 107pp. 5⅜ × 8½. 20367-0 Pa. $2.50

THE BOOK OF WORLD-FAMOUS MUSIC—CLASSICAL, POPULAR AND FOLK, James J. Fuld. Revised and enlarged republication of landmark work in musico-bibliography. Full information about nearly 1,000 songs and compositions including first lines of music and lyrics. New supplement. Index. 800pp. 5⅜ × 8¼. 24857-7 Pa. $14.95

ANTHROPOLOGY AND MODERN LIFE, Franz Boas. Great anthropologist's classic treatise on race and culture. Introduction by Ruth Bunzel. Only inexpensive paperback edition. 255pp. 5⅜ × 8½. 25245-0 Pa. $5.95

THE TALE OF PETER RABBIT, Beatrix Potter. The inimitable Peter's terrifying adventure in Mr. McGregor's garden, with all 27 wonderful, full-color Potter illustrations. 55pp. 4¼ × 5½. (Available in U.S. only) 22827-4 Pa. $1.75

THREE PROPHETIC SCIENCE FICTION NOVELS, H. G. Wells. *When the Sleeper Wakes, A Story of the Days to Come* and *The Time Machine* (full version). 335pp. 5⅜ × 8½. (Available in U.S. only) 20605-X Pa. $5.95

APICIUS COOKERY AND DINING IN IMPERIAL ROME, edited and translated by Joseph Dommers Vehling. Oldest known cookbook in existence offers readers a clear picture of what foods Romans ate, how they prepared them, etc. 49 illustrations. 301pp. 6⅛ × 9¼. 23563-7 Pa. $6.50

SHAKESPEARE LEXICON AND QUOTATION DICTIONARY, Alexander Schmidt. Full definitions, locations, shades of meaning of every word in plays and poems. More than 50,000 exact quotations. 1,485pp. 6½ × 9¼. 22726-X, 22727-8 Pa., Two-vol. set $27.90

THE WORLD'S GREAT SPEECHES, edited by Lewis Copeland and Lawrence W. Lamm. Vast collection of 278 speeches from Greeks to 1970. Powerful and effective models; unique look at history. 842pp. 5⅜ × 8½. 20468-5 Pa. $11.95

THE BLUE FAIRY BOOK, Andrew Lang. The first, most famous collection, with many familiar tales: Little Red Riding Hood, Aladdin and the Wonderful Lamp, Puss in Boots, Sleeping Beauty, Hansel and Gretel, Rumpelstiltskin; 37 in all. 138 illustrations. 390pp. 5⅜ × 8½. 21437-0 Pa. $5.95

THE STORY OF THE CHAMPIONS OF THE ROUND TABLE, Howard Pyle. Sir Launcelot, Sir Tristram and Sir Percival in spirited adventures of love and triumph retold in Pyle's inimitable style. 50 drawings, 31 full-page. xviii + 329pp. 6½ × 9¼. 21883-X Pa. $6.95

AUDUBON AND HIS JOURNALS, Maria Audubon. Unmatched two-volume portrait of the great artist, naturalist and author contains his journals, an excellent biography by his granddaughter, expert annotations by the noted ornithologist, Dr. Elliott Coues, and 37 superb illustrations. Total of 1,200pp. 5⅜ × 8.
Vol. I 25143-8 Pa. $8.95
Vol. II 25144-6 Pa. $8.95

GREAT DINOSAUR HUNTERS AND THEIR DISCOVERIES, Edwin H. Colbert. Fascinating, lavishly illustrated chronicle of dinosaur research, 1820's to 1960. Achievements of Cope, Marsh, Brown, Buckland, Mantell, Huxley, many others. 384pp. 5¼ × 8¼. 24701-5 Pa. $6.95

THE TASTEMAKERS, Russell Lynes. Informal, illustrated social history of American taste 1850's–1950's. First popularized categories Highbrow, Lowbrow, Middlebrow. 129 illustrations. New (1979) afterword. 384pp. 6 × 9.
23993-4 Pa. $6.95

DOUBLE CROSS PURPOSES, Ronald A. Knox. A treasure hunt in the Scottish Highlands, an old map, unidentified corpse, surprise discoveries keep reader guessing in this cleverly intricate tale of financial skullduggery. 2 black-and-white maps. 320pp. 5⅜ × 8½. (Available in U.S. only) 25032-6 Pa. $5.95

AUTHENTIC VICTORIAN DECORATION AND ORNAMENTATION IN FULL COLOR: 46 Plates from "Studies in Design," Christopher Dresser. Superb full-color lithographs reproduced from rare original portfolio of a major Victorian designer. 48pp. 9¼ × 12¼. 25083-0 Pa. $7.95

PRIMITIVE ART, Franz Boas. Remains the best text ever prepared on subject, thoroughly discussing Indian, African, Asian, Australian, and, especially, Northern American primitive art. Over 950 illustrations show ceramics, masks, totem poles, weapons, textiles, paintings, much more. 376pp. 5⅜ × 8. 20025-6 Pa. $6.95

SIDELIGHTS ON RELATIVITY, Albert Einstein. Unabridged republication of two lectures delivered by the great physicist in 1920–21. *Ether and Relativity* and *Geometry and Experience*. Elegant ideas in non-mathematical form, accessible to intelligent layman. vi + 56pp. 5⅜ × 8½. 24511-X Pa. $2.95

THE WIT AND HUMOR OF OSCAR WILDE, edited by Alvin Redman. More than 1,000 ripostes, paradoxes, wisecracks: Work is the curse of the drinking classes, I can resist everything except temptation, etc. 258pp. 5⅜ × 8½. 20602-5 Pa. $4.50

ADVENTURES WITH A MICROSCOPE, Richard Headstrom. 59 adventures with clothing fibers, protozoa, ferns and lichens, roots and leaves, much more. 142 illustrations. 232pp. 5⅜ × 8½. 23471-1 Pa. $3.95

PLANTS OF THE BIBLE, Harold N. Moldenke and Alma L. Moldenke. Standard reference to all 230 plants mentioned in Scriptures. Latin name, biblical reference, uses, modern identity, much more. Unsurpassed encyclopedic resource for scholars, botanists, nature lovers, students of Bible. Bibliography. Indexes. 123 black-and-white illustrations. 301pp. 6 × 9. 25069-5 Pa. $8.95

FAMOUS AMERICAN WOMEN: A Biographical Dictionary from Colonial Times to the Present, Robert McHenry, ed. From Pocahontas to Rosa Parks, 1,035 distinguished American women documented in separate biographical entries. Accurate, up-to-date data, numerous categories, spans 400 years. Indices. 493pp. 6½ × 9¼. 24523-3 Pa. $9.95

THE FABULOUS INTERIORS OF THE GREAT OCEAN LINERS IN HISTORIC PHOTOGRAPHS, William H. Miller, Jr. Some 200 superb photographs capture exquisite interiors of world's great "floating palaces"—1890's to 1980's: *Titanic, Ile de France, Queen Elizabeth, United States, Europa,* more. Approx. 200 black-and-white photographs. Captions. Text. Introduction. 160pp. 8⅞ × 11¾. 24756-2 Pa. $9.95

THE GREAT LUXURY LINERS, 1927-1954: A Photographic Record, William H. Miller, Jr. Nostalgic tribute to heyday of ocean liners. 186 photos of Ile de France, Normandie, Leviathan, Queen Elizabeth, United States, many others. Interior and exterior views. Introduction. Captions. 160pp. 9 × 12. 24056-8 Pa. $9.95

A NATURAL HISTORY OF THE DUCKS, John Charles Phillips. Great landmark of ornithology offers complete detailed coverage of nearly 200 species and subspecies of ducks: gadwall, sheldrake, merganser, pintail, many more. 74 full-color plates, 102 black-and-white. Bibliography. Total of 1,920pp. 8⅝ × 11¼. 25141-1, 25142-X Cloth. Two-vol. set $100.00

THE SEAWEED HANDBOOK: An Illustrated Guide to Seaweeds from North Carolina to Canada, Thomas F. Lee. Concise reference covers 78 species. Scientific and common names, habitat, distribution, more. Finding keys for easy identification. 224pp. 5⅜ × 8½. 25215-9 Pa. $5.95

THE TEN BOOKS OF ARCHITECTURE: The 1755 Leoni Edition, Leon Battista Alberti. Rare classic helped introduce the glories of ancient architecture to the Renaissance. 68 black-and-white plates. 336pp. 8⅜ × 11¼. 25239-6 Pa. $14.95

MISS MACKENZIE, Anthony Trollope. Minor masterpieces by Victorian master unmasks many truths about life in 19th-century England. First inexpensive edition in years. 392pp. 5⅜ × 8½. 25201-9 Pa. $7.95

THE RIME OF THE ANCIENT MARINER, Gustave Doré, Samuel Taylor Coleridge. Dramatic engravings considered by many to be his greatest work. The terrifying space of the open sea, the storms and whirlpools of an unknown ocean, the ice of Antarctica, more—all rendered in a powerful, chilling manner. Full text. 38 plates. 77pp. 9¼ × 12. 22305-1 Pa. $4.95

THE EXPEDITIONS OF ZEBULON MONTGOMERY PIKE, Zebulon Montgomery Pike. Fascinating first-hand accounts (1805-6) of exploration of Mississippi River, Indian wars, capture by Spanish dragoons, much more. 1,088pp. 5⅜ × 8½. 25254-X, 25255-8 Pa. Two-vol. set $23.90

A CONCISE HISTORY OF PHOTOGRAPHY: Third Revised Edition, Helmut Gernsheim. Best one-volume history—camera obscura, photochemistry, daguerreotypes, evolution of cameras, film, more. Also artistic aspects—landscape, portraits, fine art, etc. 281 black-and-white photographs. 26 in color. 176pp. 8⅜ × 11¼. 25128-4 Pa. $12.95

THE DORÉ BIBLE ILLUSTRATIONS, Gustave Doré. 241 detailed plates from the Bible: the Creation scenes, Adam and Eve, Flood, Babylon, battle sequences, life of Jesus, etc. Each plate is accompanied by the verses from the King James version of the Bible. 241pp. 9 × 12. 23004-X Pa. $8.95

HUGGER-MUGGER IN THE LOUVRE, Elliot Paul. Second Homer Evans mystery-comedy. Theft at the Louvre involves sleuth in hilarious, madcap caper. "A knockout."—Books. 336pp. 5⅜ × 8½. 25185-3 Pa. $5.95

FLATLAND, E. A. Abbott. Intriguing and enormously popular science-fiction classic explores the complexities of trying to survive as a two-dimensional being in a three-dimensional world. Amusingly illustrated by the author. 16 illustrations. 103pp. 5⅜ × 8½. 20001-9 Pa. $2.25

THE HISTORY OF THE LEWIS AND CLARK EXPEDITION, Meriwether Lewis and William Clark, edited by Elliott Coues. Classic edition of Lewis and Clark's day-by-day journals that later became the basis for U.S. claims to Oregon and the West. Accurate and invaluable geographical, botanical, biological, meteorological and anthropological material. Total of 1,508pp. 5⅜ × 8½.
21268-8, 21269-6, 21270-X Pa. Three-vol. set $25.50

LANGUAGE, TRUTH AND LOGIC, Alfred J. Ayer. Famous, clear introduction to Vienna, Cambridge schools of Logical Positivism. Role of philosophy, elimination of metaphysics, nature of analysis, etc. 160pp. 5⅜ × 8½. (Available in U.S. and Canada only) 20010-8 Pa. $2.95

MATHEMATICS FOR THE NONMATHEMATICIAN, Morris Kline. Detailed, college-level treatment of mathematics in cultural and historical context, with numerous exercises. For liberal arts students. Preface. Recommended Reading Lists. Tables. Index. Numerous black-and-white figures. xvi + 641pp. 5⅜ × 8½.
24823-2 Pa. $11.95

28 SCIENCE FICTION STORIES, H. G. Wells. Novels, *Star Begotten* and *Men Like Gods,* plus 26 short stories: "Empire of the Ants," "A Story of the Stone Age," "The Stolen Bacillus," "In the Abyss," etc. 915pp. 5⅜ × 8½. (Available in U.S. only)
20265-8 Cloth. $10.95

HANDBOOK OF PICTORIAL SYMBOLS, Rudolph Modley. 3,250 signs and symbols, many systems in full; official or heavy commercial use. Arranged by subject. Most in Pictorial Archive series. 143pp. 8⅛ × 11. 23357-X Pa. $5.95

INCIDENTS OF TRAVEL IN YUCATAN, John L. Stephens. Classic (1843) exploration of jungles of Yucatan, looking for evidences of Maya civilization. Travel adventures, Mexican and Indian culture, etc. Total of 669pp. 5⅜ × 8½.
20926-1, 20927-X Pa., Two-vol. set $9.90

DEGAS: An Intimate Portrait, Ambroise Vollard. Charming, anecdotal memoir by famous art dealer of one of the greatest 19th-century French painters. 14 black-and-white illustrations. Introduction by Harold L. Van Doren. 96pp. 5⅜ × 8½.
25131-4 Pa. $3.95

PERSONAL NARRATIVE OF A PILGRIMAGE TO ALMANDINAH AND MECCAH, Richard Burton. Great travel classic by remarkably colorful personality. Burton, disguised as a Moroccan, visited sacred shrines of Islam, narrowly escaping death. 47 illustrations. 959pp. 5⅜ × 8½. 21217-3, 21218-1 Pa., Two-vol. set $19.90

PHRASE AND WORD ORIGINS, A. H. Holt. Entertaining, reliable, modern study of more than 1,200 colorful words, phrases, origins and histories. Much unexpected information. 254pp. 5⅜ × 8½. 20758-7 Pa. $4.95

THE RED THUMB MARK, R. Austin Freeman. In this first Dr. Thorndyke case, the great scientific detective draws fascinating conclusions from the nature of a single fingerprint. Exciting story, authentic science. 320pp. 5⅜ × 8½. (Available in U.S. only) 25210-8 Pa. $5.95

AN EGYPTIAN HIEROGLYPHIC DICTIONARY, E. A. Wallis Budge. Monumental work containing about 25,000 words or terms that occur in texts ranging from 3000 B.C. to 600 A.D. Each entry consists of a transliteration of the word, the word in hieroglyphs, and the meaning in English. 1,314pp. 6⅜ × 10.
23615-3, 23616-1 Pa., Two-vol. set $27.90

THE COMPLEAT STRATEGYST: Being a Primer on the Theory of Games of Strategy, J. D. Williams. Highly entertaining classic describes, with many illustrated examples, how to select best strategies in conflict situations. Prefaces. Appendices. xvi + 268pp. 5⅜ × 8½. 25101-2 Pa. $5.95

THE ROAD TO OZ, L. Frank Baum. Dorothy meets the Shaggy Man, little Button-Bright and the Rainbow's beautiful daughter in this delightful trip to the magical Land of Oz. 272pp. 5⅜ × 8. 25208-6 Pa. $4.95

POINT AND LINE TO PLANE, Wassily Kandinsky. Seminal exposition of role of point, line, other elements in non-objective painting. Essential to understanding 20th-century art. 127 illustrations. 192pp. 6½ × 9¼. 23808-3 Pa. $4.50

LADY ANNA, Anthony Trollope. Moving chronicle of Countess Lovel's bitter struggle to win for herself and daughter Anna their rightful rank and fortune—perhaps at cost of sanity itself. 384pp. 5⅜ × 8½. 24669-8 Pa. $6.95

EGYPTIAN MAGIC, E. A. Wallis Budge. Sums up all that is known about magic in Ancient Egypt: the role of magic in controlling the gods, powerful amulets that warded off evil spirits, scarabs of immortality, use of wax images, formulas and spells, the secret name, much more. 253pp. 5⅜ × 8½. 22681-6 Pa. $4.00

THE DANCE OF SIVA, Ananda Coomaraswamy. Preeminent authority unfolds the vast metaphysic of India: the revelation of her art, conception of the universe, social organization, etc. 27 reproductions of art masterpieces. 192pp. 5⅜ × 8½.
24817-8 Pa. $5.95

CHRISTMAS CUSTOMS AND TRADITIONS, Clement A. Miles. Origin, evolution, significance of religious, secular practices. Caroling, gifts, yule logs, much more. Full, scholarly yet fascinating; non-sectarian. 400pp. 5⅜ × 8½.
23354-5 Pa. $6.50

THE HUMAN FIGURE IN MOTION, Eadweard Muybridge. More than 4,500 stopped-action photos, in action series, showing undraped men, women, children jumping, lying down, throwing, sitting, wrestling, carrying, etc. 390pp. 7⅞ × 10⅝.
20204-6 Cloth. $21.95

THE MAN WHO WAS THURSDAY, Gilbert Keith Chesterton. Witty, fast-paced novel about a club of anarchists in turn-of-the-century London. Brilliant social, religious, philosophical speculations. 128pp. 5⅜ × 8½. 25121-7 Pa. $3.95

A CEZANNE SKETCHBOOK: Figures, Portraits, Landscapes and Still Lifes, Paul Cezanne. Great artist experiments with tonal effects, light, mass, other qualities in over 100 drawings. A revealing view of developing master painter, precursor of Cubism. 102 black-and-white illustrations. 144pp. 8¾ × 6⅜. 24790-2 Pa. $5.95

AN ENCYCLOPEDIA OF BATTLES: Accounts of Over 1,560 Battles from 1479 B.C. to the Present, David Eggenberger. Presents essential details of every major battle in recorded history, from the first battle of Megiddo in 1479 B.C. to Grenada in 1984. List of Battle Maps. New Appendix covering the years 1967–1984. Index. 99 illustrations. 544pp. 6½ × 9¼. 24913-1 Pa. $14.95

AN ETYMOLOGICAL DICTIONARY OF MODERN ENGLISH, Ernest Weekley. Richest, fullest work, by foremost British lexicographer. Detailed word histories. Inexhaustible. Total of 856pp. 6½ × 9¼.
21873-2, 21874-0 Pa., Two-vol. set $17.00

WEBSTER'S AMERICAN MILITARY BIOGRAPHIES, edited by Robert McHenry. Over 1,000 figures who shaped 3 centuries of American military history. Detailed biographies of Nathan Hale, Douglas MacArthur, Mary Hallaren, others. Chronologies of engagements, more. Introduction. Addenda. 1,033 entries in alphabetical order. xi + 548pp. 6½ × 9¼. (Available in U.S. only)
24758-9 Pa. $11.95

LIFE IN ANCIENT EGYPT, Adolf Erman. Detailed older account, with much not in more recent books: domestic life, religion, magic, medicine, commerce, and whatever else needed for complete picture. Many illustrations. 597pp. 5⅜ × 8½.
22632-8 Pa. $8.50

HISTORIC COSTUME IN PICTURES, Braun & Schneider. Over 1,450 costumed figures shown, covering a wide variety of peoples: kings, emperors, nobles, priests, servants, soldiers, scholars, townsfolk, peasants, merchants, courtiers, cavaliers, and more. 256pp. 8⅜ × 11¼. 23150-X Pa. $7.95

THE NOTEBOOKS OF LEONARDO DA VINCI, edited by J. P. Richter. Extracts from manuscripts reveal great genius; on painting, sculpture, anatomy, sciences, geography, etc. Both Italian and English. 186 ms. pages reproduced, plus 500 additional drawings, including studies for *Last Supper, Sforza* monument, etc. 860pp. 7⅞ × 10¾. (Available in U.S. only) 22572-0, 22573-9 Pa., Two-vol. set $25.90

THE ART NOUVEAU STYLE BOOK OF ALPHONSE MUCHA: All 72 Plates from "Documents Decoratifs" in Original Color, Alphonse Mucha. Rare copyright-free design portfolio by high priest of Art Nouveau. Jewelry, wallpaper, stained glass, furniture, figure studies, plant and animal motifs, etc. Only complete one-volume edition. 80pp. 9⅜ × 12¼.   24044-1 Pa. $8.95

ANIMALS: 1,419 COPYRIGHT-FREE ILLUSTRATIONS OF MAMMALS, BIRDS, FISH, INSECTS, ETC., edited by Jim Harter. Clear wood engravings present, in extremely lifelike poses, over 1,000 species of animals. One of the most extensive pictorial sourcebooks of its kind. Captions. Index. 284pp. 9 × 12.
23766-4 Pa. $9.95

OBELISTS FLY HIGH, C. Daly King. Masterpiece of American detective fiction, long out of print, involves murder on a 1935 transcontinental flight—"a very thrilling story"—NY Times. Unabridged and unaltered republication of the edition published by William Collins Sons & Co. Ltd., London, 1935. 288pp. 5⅜ × 8½. (Available in U.S. only)   25036-9 Pa. $4.95

VICTORIAN AND EDWARDIAN FASHION: A Photographic Survey, Alison Gernsheim. First fashion history completely illustrated by contemporary photographs. Full text plus 235 photos, 1840–1914, in which many celebrities appear. 240pp. 6½ × 9¼.   24205-6 Pa. $6.00

THE ART OF THE FRENCH ILLUSTRATED BOOK, 1700–1914, Gordon N. Ray. Over 630 superb book illustrations by Fragonard, Delacroix, Daumier, Doré, Grandville, Manet, Mucha, Steinlen, Toulouse-Lautrec and many others. Preface. Introduction. 633 halftones. Indices of artists, authors & titles, binders and provenances. Appendices. Bibliography. 608pp. 8⅜ × 11¼.   25086-5 Pa. $24.95

THE WONDERFUL WIZARD OF OZ, L. Frank Baum. Facsimile in full color of America's finest children's classic. 143 illustrations by W. W. Denslow. 267pp. 5⅜ × 8½.   20691-2 Pa. $5.95

FRONTIERS OF MODERN PHYSICS: New Perspectives on Cosmology, Relativity, Black Holes and Extraterrestrial Intelligence, Tony Rothman, et al. For the intelligent layman. Subjects include: cosmological models of the universe; black holes; the neutrino; the search for extraterrestrial intelligence. Introduction. 46 black-and-white illustrations. 192pp. 5⅜ × 8½.   24587-X Pa. $6.95

THE FRIENDLY STARS, Martha Evans Martin & Donald Howard Menzel. Classic text marshalls the stars together in an engaging, non-technical survey, presenting them as sources of beauty in night sky. 23 illustrations. Foreword. 2 star charts. Index. 147pp. 5⅜ × 8½.   21099-5 Pa. $3.50

FADS AND FALLACIES IN THE NAME OF SCIENCE, Martin Gardner. Fair, witty appraisal of cranks, quacks, and quackeries of science and pseudoscience: hollow earth, Velikovsky, orgone energy, Dianetics, flying saucers, Bridey Murphy, food and medical fads, etc. Revised, expanded In the Name of Science. "A very able and even-tempered presentation."—The New Yorker. 363pp. 5⅜ × 8.
20394-8 Pa. $6.50

ANCIENT EGYPT: ITS CULTURE AND HISTORY, J. E Manchip White. From pre-dynastics through Ptolemies: society, history, political structure, religion, daily life, literature, cultural heritage. 48 plates. 217pp. 5⅜ × 8½.   22548-8 Pa. $4.95

SIR HARRY HOTSPUR OF HUMBLETHWAITE, Anthony Trollope. Incisive, unconventional psychological study of a conflict between a wealthy baronet, his idealistic daughter, and their scapegrace cousin. The 1870 novel in its first inexpensive edition in years. 250pp. 5⅜ × 8½. 24953-0 Pa. $5.95

LASERS AND HOLOGRAPHY, Winston E. Kock. Sound introduction to burgeoning field, expanded (1981) for second edition. Wave patterns, coherence, lasers, diffraction, zone plates, properties of holograms, recent advances. 84 illustrations. 160pp. 5⅜ × 8¼. (Except in United Kingdom) 24041-X Pa. $3.50

INTRODUCTION TO ARTIFICIAL INTELLIGENCE: SECOND, ENLARGED EDITION, Philip C. Jackson, Jr. Comprehensive survey of artificial intelligence—the study of how machines (computers) can be made to act intelligently. Includes introductory and advanced material. Extensive notes updating the main text. 132 black-and-white illustrations. 512pp. 5⅜ × 8½. 24864-X Pa. $8.95

HISTORY OF INDIAN AND INDONESIAN ART, Ananda K. Coomaraswamy. Over 400 illustrations illuminate classic study of Indian art from earliest Harappa finds to early 20th century. Provides philosophical, religious and social insights. 304pp. 6⅝ × 9⅜. 25005-9 Pa. $8.95

THE GOLEM, Gustav Meyrink. Most famous supernatural novel in modern European literature, set in Ghetto of Old Prague around 1890. Compelling story of mystical experiences, strange transformations, profound terror. 13 black-and-white illustrations. 224pp. 5⅜ × 8½. (Available in U.S. only) 25025-3 Pa. $5.95

ARMADALE, Wilkie Collins. Third great mystery novel by the author of *The Woman in White* and *The Moonstone*. Original magazine version with 40 illustrations. 597pp. 5⅜ × 8½. 23429-0 Pa. $9.95

PICTORIAL ENCYCLOPEDIA OF HISTORIC ARCHITECTURAL PLANS, DETAILS AND ELEMENTS: With 1,880 Line Drawings of Arches, Domes, Doorways, Facades, Gables, Windows, etc., John Theodore Haneman. Sourcebook of inspiration for architects, designers, others. Bibliography. Captions. 141pp. 9 × 12. 24605-1 Pa. $6.95

BENCHLEY LOST AND FOUND, Robert Benchley. Finest humor from early 30's, about pet peeves, child psychologists, post office and others. Mostly unavailable elsewhere. 73 illustrations by Peter Arno and others. 183pp. 5⅜ × 8½. 22410-4 Pa. $3.95

ERTÉ GRAPHICS, Erté. Collection of striking color graphics: *Seasons, Alphabet, Numerals, Aces* and *Precious Stones*. 50 plates, including 4 on covers. 48pp. 9⅜ × 12¼. 23580-7 Pa. $6.95

THE JOURNAL OF HENRY D. THOREAU, edited by Bradford Torrey, F. H. Allen. Complete reprinting of 14 volumes, 1837–61, over two million words; the sourcebooks for *Walden*, etc. Definitive. All original sketches, plus 75 photographs. 1,804pp. 8½ × 12¼. 20312-3, 20313-1 Cloth., Two-vol. set $80.00

CASTLES: THEIR CONSTRUCTION AND HISTORY, Sidney Toy. Traces castle development from ancient roots. Nearly 200 photographs and drawings illustrate moats, keeps, baileys, many other features. Caernarvon, Dover Castles, Hadrian's Wall, Tower of London, dozens more. 256pp. 5⅜ × 8¼. 24898-4 Pa. $5.95

AMERICAN CLIPPER SHIPS: 1833–1858, Octavius T. Howe & Frederick C. Matthews. Fully-illustrated, encyclopedic review of 352 clipper ships from the period of America's greatest maritime supremacy. Introduction. 109 halftones. 5 black-and-white line illustrations. Index. Total of 928pp. 5⅜ × 8½.
25115-2, 25116-0 Pa., Two-vol. set $17.90

TOWARDS A NEW ARCHITECTURE, Le Corbusier. Pioneering manifesto by great architect, near legendary founder of "International School." Technical and aesthetic theories, views on industry, economics, relation of form to function, "mass-production spirit," much more. Profusely illustrated. Unabridged translation of 13th French edition. Introduction by Frederick Etchells. 320pp. 6⅛ × 9¼. (Available in U.S. only) 25023-7 Pa. $8.95

THE BOOK OF KELLS, edited by Blanche Cirker. Inexpensive collection of 32 full-color, full-page plates from the greatest illuminated manuscript of the Middle Ages, painstakingly reproduced from rare facsimile edition. Publisher's Note. Captions. 32pp. 9⅜ × 12¼. 24345-1 Pa. $4.95

BEST SCIENCE FICTION STORIES OF H. G. WELLS, H. G. Wells. Full novel The Invisible Man, plus 17 short stories: "The Crystal Egg," "Aepyornis Island," "The Strange Orchid," etc. 303pp. 5⅜ × 8½. (Available in U.S. only)
21531-8 Pa. $4.95

AMERICAN SAILING SHIPS: Their Plans and History, Charles G. Davis. Photos, construction details of schooners, frigates, clippers, other sailcraft of 18th to early 20th centuries—plus entertaining discourse on design, rigging, nautical lore, much more. 137 black-and-white illustrations. 240pp. 6⅛ × 9¼.
24658-2 Pa. $5.95

ENTERTAINING MATHEMATICAL PUZZLES, Martin Gardner. Selection of author's favorite conundrums involving arithmetic, money, speed, etc., with lively commentary. Complete solutions. 112pp. 5⅜ × 8½. 25211-6 Pa. $2.95

THE WILL TO BELIEVE, HUMAN IMMORTALITY, William James. Two books bound together. Effect of irrational on logical, and arguments for human immortality. 402pp. 5⅜ × 8½. 20291-7 Pa. $7.50

THE HAUNTED MONASTERY and THE CHINESE MAZE MURDERS, Robert Van Gulik. 2 full novels by Van Gulik continue adventures of Judge Dee and his companions. An evil Taoist monastery, seemingly supernatural events; overgrown topiary maze that hides strange crimes. Set in 7th-century China. 27 illustrations. 328pp. 5⅜ × 8½. 23502-5 Pa. $5.95

CELEBRATED CASES OF JUDGE DEE (DEE GOONG AN), translated by Robert Van Gulik. Authentic 18th-century Chinese detective novel; Dee and associates solve three interlocked cases. Led to Van Gulik's own stories with same characters. Extensive introduction. 9 illustrations. 237pp. 5⅜ × 8½.
23337-5 Pa. $4.95

Prices subject to change without notice.
Available at your book dealer or write for free catalog to Dept. GI, Dover Publications, Inc., 31 East 2nd St., Mineola, N.Y. 11501. Dover publishes more than 175 books each year on science, elementary and advanced mathematics, biology, music, art, literary history, social sciences and other areas.